William Inge and the
Subversion of Gender

ALSO BY JEFF JOHNSON

Pervert in the Pulpit:
Morality in the Works of David Lynch
(McFarland, 2004)

William Inge and the Subversion of Gender

Rewriting Stereotypes in the Plays, Novels, and Screenplays

JEFF JOHNSON

foreword by Jackson R. Bryer

McFarland & Company, Inc., Publishers
Jefferson, North Carolina, and London

LIBRARY OF CONGRESS CATALOGUING-IN-PUBLICATION DATA

Johnson, Jeff, 1954–
    William Inge and the subversion of gender : rewriting stereotypes in the plays, novels, and screenplays / Jeff Johnson ; foreword by Jackson R. Bryer.
    p.   cm.
    Includes bibliographical references and index.

    ISBN 0-7864-2062-6 (softcover : 50# alkaline paper) ∞

    1. Inge, William—Criticism and interpretation. 2. Gender identity in literature. 3. Sex role in literature. I. Title.
PS3517.N265Z726   2005
812'.54—dc22   2004028967

British Library cataloguing data are available

©2005 Jeff Johnson. All rights reserved

No part of this book may be reproduced or transmitted in any form or by any means, electronic or mechanical, including photocopying or recording, or by any information storage and retrieval system, without permission in writing from the publisher.

On the cover: Ralph Meeker poses for Kim Stanley in *Picnic* (Theatre Guild, 1953)—*Photofest*

Manufactured in the United States of America

McFarland & Company, Inc., Publishers
  Box 611, Jefferson, North Carolina 28640
    www.mcfarlandpub.com

For Carla

Acknowledgments

Special thanks to Jackson R. Bryer; without his encouragement this book would not have been written.

Also thanks to Peter Ellenstein and the Inge Festival community for their gracious support.

Thanks finally to Howard Stein, director of my 1997 National Endowment for the Humanities award, whose guidance proved essential for my research.

Parts of this book have appeared as essays in *American Drama* (University of Cincinnati) and the *Journal of American Drama and Theatre* (City University of New York).

Table of Contents

Acknowledgments vi
Foreword by Jackson R. Bryer 1
Preface 7

1. Stereotypes, Gender Roles and Gendermandering 11
2. The Critics 26
3. Major Works: *Come Back, Little Sheba; Picnic; Bus Stop;*
   The Dark at the Top of the Stairs; Splendor in the Grass 49
4. Minor Works: *A Loss of Roses; Natural Affection;*
   Where's Daddy?; Good Luck, Miss Wyckoff 103
5. Short Plays 142

Bibliography 185
Index 189

Foreword
by Jackson R. Bryer

Early in the preface to his stimulating and revealing new study of the work of William Inge, Jeff Johnson describes how his interest in Inge began in 1994 when he answered a call for papers from the annual William Inge Theatre Festival in Independence, Kansas. At that point, Johnson confesses, "I had never heard of the festival, had never been to Kansas, much less the town of Independence, and had scant knowledge of Inge's work." As the person who accepted the paper Johnson wrote for the 1994 Inge Festival and thus in some small way launched him on the journey that led to this book, my own history with William Inge and with the Inge Festival is quite different from his.

For anyone who grew up, as I did, going to the theater in New York City in the 1950s, the name of William Inge conjures up some of my most memorable early playgoing experiences. I was too young to see *Come Back, Little Sheba* in 1950; but Janice Rule and Ralph Meeker in *Picnic* (1953), Kim Stanley in *Bus Stop* (1955), and Pat Hingle, Teresa Wright, and Eileen Heckart in *Dark at the Top of the Stairs* (1957) are performances I shall never forget. In the 1950s, Inge's four consecutive Broadway hits, which were rapidly made into equally successful films, made him the decade's star dramatist. His two rivals for that designation, Arthur Miller and Tennessee Williams, who had burst on the scene in the 1940s with Miller's *All My Sons* (1947) and *Death of a Salesman* (1949) and Williams's *The Glass Menagerie* (1945) and *A Streetcar Named Desire* (1947), did not in the 1950s have nearly the popular and critical success Inge enjoyed. While Williams did have one major hit, *Cat on a Hot Tin Roof* (1955), and one modest success, *The Rose Tattoo* (1951), none of his other three plays of the decade—*Camino Real* (1953), *Suddenly Last Summer* (1958), and *Sweet Bird of Youth* (1959)—approached the success Inge achieved; and neither of Miller's two plays of the '50s, *The Crucible* (1953) and *A*

View from the Bridge (1955), had initial runs of 200 performances (by contrast, *Picnic, Bus Stop,* and *Dark at the Top of the Stairs* each ran for over 450 performances).

Inge's four plays were not only successful and occasions for memorable performances by some of the great actors and actresses of the time; for a young man coming of age in New York in the staid and placid 1950s, they presented an immensely appealing romantic view of life in a part of the country that was unfamiliar and seemed vaguely exotic. I never forgot the impact those plays had upon my impressionable teenage mind.

In 1979 I was a panelist for the National Endowment for the Humanities, considering applications from libraries seeking funding to catalogue special collections. One application came from a junior college in Kansas that held the papers of someone whom the other panelists called William Ingee (with a hard g). When they dismissed him as a person they had never heard of, I protested. My fellow panelists pointed out that the application was poorly written. When I continued to insist that Inge was an important literary and dramatic figure, they replied, "If you think he's so important, we'll fund you to go to Kansas and tell them how to write a proposal!" William Inge had briefly attended Independence Junior College in 1931-32 and had donated some of his papers to the school in 1969. Following his suicide in 1973, his sister in 1976 had honored his wish to leave his personal library and more of his papers to the college.

I must admit that I eagerly accepted my fellow panelists' offer to send me to Independence, Kansas. As a city boy from the northeast, I had long known that my understanding of Inge's milieu was uninformed and largely vicarious. Upon my arrival at the Tulsa airport (the major airport closest to Independence), I was greeted by Tom Snyder—not only the assistant dean at the college but also its athletic director—who was picking up me and a prospective student athlete for the two-hour car ride from Tulsa to Independence. In Independence, I saw Inge's house with its large front porch that is so typical of houses in the town (the original title for *Picnic* was *Front Porch*) and the stairway that led to the frightening dark at its top; I saw Inge's grave; and I saw the town park where, every fall, Independence celebrates Neewollah (Halloween spelled backwards), the event immortalized in *Picnic* and made even more memorable by William Holden and Kim Novak dancing to *Moonglow*, the famous theme music for the film. I dutifully advised the library on improving their grant proposal (they ultimately received NEH funding), and I met Margaret Goheen, a speech and theater instructor at the college who had known Bill Inge. Margaret told me that she wanted to start an annual event at the college in honor of Inge and invited me to return for the first such occasion the next year—which I did.

The first William Inge Theatre Festival took place on May 3, 1982, on what would have been Inge's sixty-ninth birthday. It consisted of a showing of a brief multimedia presentation about Inge, featuring interviews with locals and Broadway luminaries who had known him, and a panel discussion in which I participated with two others, on "William Inge: A Perspective in 1982." In 1983, the festival was expanded to three days, and Goheen persuaded distinguished American playwright Jerome Lawrence, who had been a close friend of Inge, to accept the first William Inge Award for Lifetime Achievement. That award became the centerpiece of succeeding Inge festivals, which now number 23.

Thus it is that the William Inge Theatre Festival has become an annual rite of April at which theater practitioners and enthusiasts gather from all over the country and where, as one participant has put it, "the American theater becomes the most important topic of conversation for that one weekend of the year." The festival has expanded to four days, and Independence Junior College has become Independence Community College. Margaret Goheen, who planned and directed the first nine festivals, died in 1990 and was succeeded by Jill Warford, who presided for the next 10 years and was in turn succeeded by Peter Ellenstein, the current director. Every important member of Inge's generation of playwrights and many from the next generation have received the Inge Award, which, in 1992, was renamed the William Inge Award for Distinguished Achievement in the American Theatre—to reflect the fact that most of its recipients are still writing plays. Over the 23 years, many of this country's leading actors, actresses, directors, and critics have participated by giving workshops, participating on panels, and performing in the tribute to the honored playwright which has become the signature event of the festival on Saturday evening. About a decade ago, the festival realized another of Margaret Goheen's dreams by inaugurating the presentation of a "New Voices" Award to a young playwright, one of whose works also receives a staged reading.

Virtually from the beginning, another feature of the Inge Festival has been the William Inge Conference, an afternoon session in which scholars deliver short papers devoted either to the work of William Inge or to that of the year's honored playwright. It was as a participant in this conference segment in 1994 that I first met Jeff Johnson. His paper on that occasion and those that he delivered at subsequent Inge Festivals have led directly to this book. It is striking to realize how much of the recent scholarship on Inge that Johnson mentions began as a paper delivered at an Inge Festival or was stimulated by attendance at the festival. Ralph F. Voss, whose 1989 Inge biography remains the single most essential secondary source on the playwright, has attended almost every Inge Festival and derived valuable information, contacts, and encouragement from his presence there. Critics like Albert Wertheim, Susan Koprince, Arthur McClure, and Patricia McIlrath, whose work Johnson cites, all either began their Inge research by giving a paper at the festival or explored already-begun study further through their festival presentations. I am convinced that the existence for the past 23 years of the William Inge Theatre Festival has played a major role in creating the academic and popular "buzz" about Inge, a buzz that has led to an increased number of revivals of his plays in regional theaters, on Broadway, and on television, and has also led directly to this first full-scale critical reevaluation of Inge's writings.

Johnson's study brings a completely fresh perspective to bear on Inge's work, a perspective that we were certainly incapable of adopting in the 1950s and were probably not equipped to utilize until quite recently. Through the lenses of gender study, a greater understanding of and tolerance for sexual difference, and a heightened awareness of sexual stereotyping, Johnson offers us readings of Inge's plays that both complicate them and increase our understanding of them. Some of us have sensed for many years that there was more going on in Inge's plays than simple midwestern romantic rituals and tribulations; we were aware of their bittersweet tone and often tragic undercurrents. What Johnson has done is to give us a language in which to speak more clearly and precisely of just what those undertones and subtexts are. In doing so, he has made very clear that these are much more complex and probing works than their surfaces reveal and than their critics in the 1950s—and often in the half-century since—have given them credit for being.

Johnson's coinage of the catchy and useful term "gendermandering" totally explodes the popular and persistent myth that Inge is a sentimental lightweight not worthy of serious critical examination. He defines the term as "the intentional undermining of expected gender roles for the dramatic purpose of politically and socially destabilizing social norms" and sees its importance as exposing "the pernicious cultural habit of gender stereotyping" and "intensifying the stress inherent in the conflict between what is considered natural and unnatural, normal and abnormal, based on values by social contracts of expected gender behavior." Thus, Johnson contends convincingly, Inge prepared "the groundwork for the gender-bending so prevalent in contemporary aesthetics."

Ultimately, though, the value of Johnson's book is that even a reader skeptical of the specifics of his thesis will benefit from the ways in which he analyzes the characters and situations in Inge's works. One does not have to agree with his reliance on recent studies by Joanne Meyerowitz, Camille Paglia, Elaine Showalter, and Robert Vorlicky to find his readings stimulating and challenging. Johnson's work inaugurates serious critical study of William Inge. No reader will look at Doc in *Come Back, Little Sheba*, Rosemary in *Picnic*, Bo and Cherie in *Bus Stop*, Lottie in *Dark at the Top of the Stairs*, or many other Inge characters in the same way after absorbing Johnson's analyses of them. In the tradition of the best literary criticism, Johnson's book does not provide the final word or end the discussion; it expands and deepens that discussion. One can only hope that it convinces future critics that there is much more to say about William Inge.

Preface

This book is a culmination of my reading Inge through his use of an apparatus I identify as gendermandering, a technique that reveals patterns of gender-role reversals which Inge exploits not only for dramatic effect but also to subvert gender-role expectations in our collective cultural imagination. I begin with an account of stereotypes and established gender roles, especially as they were reinforced socially during the 1940s and 1950s, then locate in Inge's work specific instances of gendermandering that undercut the expected behavior of these culturally determined constructs. While I refer to nearly all of his work, I concentrate on material that, first, is strictly Inge's, not adaptations or collaborations, and, second, work that has been published and so is readily available for the general reading public. That list includes his major plays, a collection of his short plays, the screenplay of *Splendor in the Grass* (1961), and his novel *Good Luck, Miss Wyckoff* (1970). I also discuss some of his rather inaccessible material, including a few short plays that have been published miscellaneously, as well as some of the unpublished manuscripts held in the Inge Collection at Independence Community College, Independence, Kansas.

I intentionally disregard *My Son Is a Splendid Driver* (1971), Inge's debilitating *roman à clef* that Ralph Voss, Inge's biographer, describes as "a largely factual memoir thinly garbed as fiction" (6). *Driver* reads more like a sentimental autobiography than a serious novel, and though aesthetic flaws arguably plague it, *Driver* remains of interest to anyone researching how the biographical facts of Inge's life inform his work. Since I have made a point of ignoring biographical considerations, I refer those readers seeking factual information about Inge to Voss's *A Life of William Inge: The Strains of Triumph* (1989), a book that is vital to any study of Inge and one that I found invaluable. Other various titles associated with Inge—including well-known adaptations—have also been omitted if, in my judgment, they do not fit within the scope of this book, but that does not necessarily mean they cannot be read within the same context.

I also revisit much of the existing criticism about Inge's work, both historical and contemporary, not to resituate Inge within the modern American canon but to reconsider the context of some criticism, especially that which has direct bearing on the subject at hand: the subverting of stereotypical behavior that informs Inge's major work and elevates the impact of his plays from mere theater into the broader social arena of current sexual politics and contemporary expectations of gender.

My interest in Inge began in 1994 with a call for papers from the William Inge Theatre Festival in Independence, Kansas. I can't remember how I came across the flyer, but I had never heard of the festival, had never been to Kansas, much less the town of Independence, and had scant knowledge of Inge's work. I vaguely recalled the premise of the film version of *Bus Stop* (1955), and was familiar with *Picnic* (1956), if only by the title. But the flyer sparked my curiosity enough to send me delving into the stacks to learn more about this revered American playwright that somehow, in all my graduate classes in American theater filled with O'Neill, Miller, Williams and Albee, I missed.

Coming at Inge blind, as it were, may have been an advantage. With no expectations, I read intuitively. No critical context. No biographical frame. No visual spoilers. No sense of production values. Just raw text. The first thing I noticed was the strong undercurrent of sexuality in his plays, and the paper I submitted, entitled "Moral Balance and Sexual Symmetry in *Bus Stop*," accepted for the Inge Festival's 1994 program, explored Inge's use of sexual alignments to illustrate the disruption and reconciliation between symmetrically paired couples. This structural symmetry illustrates Inge's understanding of the significance in human affairs of an ordering principle, a logic that organizes the inchoate, alogical urges of human emotions; ultimately, it represents the artistic imposition of form on the chaotic elements of life.

By now intrigued with Inge, I used his work as the basis for further research in 1997 while participating in a National Endowment for the Humanities seminar conducted by Howard Stein at Columbia University on American playwrights from 1920 to 1950. I detected a pattern in Inge I defined as gendermandering—a term derived from the political practice of gerrymandering—which attempts to define what I read as Inge's subversive manipulation of stereotypes for the purpose of intentionally undermining expected gender roles and thereby destabilizing social norms. I noticed too how Inge plays with what I describe as switch-hitting archetypes: the dramatic tension in his plays often relies on gender-role reversals maintained through gendermandered characters—that is, those that pretend to essentialist characteristics yet essentially act against type. I applied the concept to Inge's four Broadway hits, and portions of the research appeared in *American Drama* and the *Journal of American Drama and Theatre*.

Having become fairly well acquainted with his work, I remain impressed with the fidelity Inge inspires. This lasting faith in his vision may be a result of his writing plays to "dramatiz[e] something of the dynamism ... in human motivations and behavior" (Foreword, *Four Plays*, vii). His remark underscores the playwright's concern with Aristotle's two primary elements of drama: action and character, or, in more modern terms, plot and psychology. And though Inge does manage successfully to create in his work strong dramatic tension through the dynamics of story and situation, a deeper current runs below the surface, that of characters suffering not only from their conflicts with others, and not only from plot-imposed barriers to their immediate material goals: it is a more existential drama, of people divorced from their mythical, cultural essence, of people forced into roles they are ill equipped to play.

1
Stereotypes, Gender Roles and Gendermandering

In her 1994 inaugural address as president of Barnard College, Judith Shapiro notes:

> discussions of gender difference turn into sweeping and ethnocentric generalizations about what men and women are basically like. Thus, women are said to be inherently nurturant, skilled at relationships, imbued with a deep, intuitive sense of when the garbage needs to be taken out. Men, on the other hand, are predisposed toward certain aggressive pursuits, ranging from laboratory science to rape, and also exhibit a possibly genetically-based inability to see when the garbage needs to be taken out.... [W]e have seen rather too much perpetuation of gender folklore in recent years, in both scholarly and popular writing. We need to bear in mind that gender stereotypes are a paradigm case of what Columbia sociologist Robert Merton long ago identified as "self-fulfilling prophecies." It is our belief in them that makes them true.

Shapiro echoes the views of many cultural commentators from across the political spectrum and academic community, and these concerns have produced some rather colorful gender criticism, with titles like *The Feminized Male Character in Twentieth Century Literature* (1995) by Nancy McCampbell Grace, or *Am I a Man or a Woman?* (1996) by Sandra Davis. And though many of these studies strain apoplectically for significance, not all of these gender-based approaches to literature are so easily dismissed, as they both provoke and explore legitimate questions regarding modern definitions of femininity, masculinity, and gender roles in social contexts. Elaine Showalter in her *Sexual Anarchy: Gender and Culture at the Fin de Siècle* (1990), argues that gender-typing often occurs as a

Hal (Ralph Meeker) poses for Millie (Kim Stanley) in the Theatre Guild production of *Picnic* (1953), directed by Joshua Logan at the Music Box Theatre. Millie's controlling gaze objectifies Hal, allowing him willingly to accept his role as narcissist and mask his innate femininity. Neatly illustrating the gendermandering at the core of Inge's work, Hal's masquerading as a macho ideal is exposed as mere homoerotic posturing. Like Inge's other pin-ups, he becomes an object of female desire, reversing the expected gender-play by relinquishing the role of voyeur traditionally reserved for men. (Photofest)

response to perceived social and historical crises: "In periods of cultural insecurity, when there are fears of regression and degeneration, the longing for strict border controls around the definition of gender ... becomes especially intense" (4). And although her study is concerned mainly with the portrayal of women in fin de siècle "literature, art and film" (3), she points out that "masculinity is not more natural, transparent, and unproblematic than 'femininity' [and] is a socially constructed role, defined within particular cultural and historical circumstances" (8). Further, she argues, because of the self-conscious need to choose and maintain a socially defined and acceptable identity, "many men found their part of the equation as difficult to sustain as women did theirs, and the source of much anxiety" (9).

One thing is certain: the distinctions between male and female gender roles are socially acknowledged, reinforced—often punitively—and so interwoven with the fabric of American culture that even as astute a chronicler of political trends as Maureen Dowd, no traditionalist neo-con by anyone's measure, cites how in a "delicious gender-bender, Condoleezza Rice triumphs as the macho infighter, driving Rummy into a diva-like meltdown" (Dowd A35).

Many critics of historic and contemporary cultures incorporate gender studies as an integral part of their analyses, and in doing so, whether reluctant or resigned, they validate—by recognizing them to criticize them—the very binary opposition between One and Other those same critics often hesitate to acknowledge and even rigidly deny. Shoshana Felman, in *What Does a Woman Want?* (1993), rhetorically questions "the enigmatic truth of sexual difference" (2), but admits that "[s]exual difference raises, thus, on the one hand, questions of desire, and on the other hand, questions of violence: the truth of difference is at once its power and its violence" (2). David West, in *An Introduction to Continental Philosophy* (1996), cites feminist deconstructionists like Gayatri Spivak questioning "even the characteristically postmodern opposition between excluding subject or identity and marginalized other" (West 215), while he represents Julia Kristeva and Luce Irigaray as cautioning their readers to "be suspicious of any 'politics of identity' which seeks to contain the 'flux' or 'flight' or resistance within a fixed and almost certainly compromised identity" (215). Elisabeth Badinter, in *The Unopposite Sex: The End of the Gender Battle* (1986), argues that while "men and women are profoundly modifying the image they have of themselves and of the Other" (xi), it is still a fact that "the distinction between the sexual roles is the root cause of inequality" (xii), and in a not too subtle feminist call-to-arms she pledges to dismantle the gender distinctions that she considers anathema in "those democratic societies currently generating a completely new model: the resemblance between the sexes" (xiv).

But it is exactly that "anxiety" Showalter isolates, describing men and women sustaining socially defined sexual roles and the politics of gender identity, that provides the dramatic tension in Inge's work, and yet it is the gender subversions that many of his critics ignore, misread, or dismiss. Clearly, sexual stereotypes defining femininity, masculinity, and gender roles in social contexts were well established during the '50s, the heyday of Inge's career. In fact, after the disruption of the war years, fixed gender typing was not only desirable, it was required in order to seed the idealism associated with the postwar recovery in America, and the illusion of the well-made family was perpetuated as a necessary condition of social stability at every level of society. The codifying image of Mom, Dad, Buddy and Sis as the "all–American family" relied as much on religious, political and business interests as it did on members of the family understanding and sticking to their expected familial roles. Dana Heller argues that the contemporary clichéd image of the '50s' domesticity represents today a "nostalgia for a lost aesthetics" (2) but concedes the fact that archetypes—what Heller calls, borrowing Freudian parlance, the "family romance" (3)—are "very much alive in post–World War II American culture" (3). The "hubby" was a breadwinner; the "little lady" was a nest-maker; their language was euphemistic, "Mary Tyler Moore's sentimental sitcom speak" (2); the "kids" were heterosexual spitting images of their parents—after all, the mythical middle-class America in the '50s did not expect the acorn to fall very far from the tree: such was the media staple in everything from advertising and popular culture through systems of belief to professional careers.

Many feminists argue that the images projected in the prevailing stereotypes of the '50s are radically different from the facts. Joanne Meyerowitz, for instance, writes in *Not June Cleaver: Women and Gender in Postwar America, 1945–1960* (1994) that contemporary versions of the '50s good life are "steeped in nostalgic longing for an allegedly simpler, happier, and more prosperous time" (1) and the truth is that for many Americans the '50s created "an ironic story of declension" (1). She points out what the stereotypes attempt to conceal: obviously, in the postwar years many people "were not white, middle-class, and suburban ... neither wholly domestic nor quiescent" (2). Barbara J. Coleman, in "Maidenform(ed): Images of American Women in the 1950s," derides the notion of "'the stay-at-home' mom image so popular on television shows like *Leave It to Beaver*" (18). Aside from tinkering with more exotic conspiracy theories linking postwar U.S. military propaganda with Maidenform bras (e.g., "the underwear industry was inextricably connected to the military establishment" [13]), she forcefully argues that in the '50s "[c]ontrol and vigilance were the watchwords" (17), especially "[c]ontrol of sexuality ... essential to safeguarding freedom" (17). Also, citing employment figures from the era, she proves that contrary to the stereotype of the sitcom mom, "more women than ever before were working outside the home" (18). Meyerowitz concludes, "this tenacious stereotype [that] conjures mythic images of cultural icons—June Cleaver, Donna Reed, Harriet Nelson ... flattens ... history ... reducing the multidimensional complexity of the past to a snapshot" (2).

Both Heller and Meyerowitz trace the exposure of this family romance as a construct that "cuts across all genres ... reinventing itself in all forms of cultural production and consumption" (Heller, 7) to Betty Friedan's *The Feminist Mystique* (1963). Meyerowitz writes that it was Friedan who "homogenized ... and simplified postwar ideology ... reinforced the stereotype that portrayed [the] middle-class [as] domestic, and suburban" (3). Meyerowitz rightly points out that not all Americans in the '50s were "quintessential white middle-class housewives" (3) happily ensconced in their homogenized suburban utopias, but when she discusses the themes, characters and families of mainstream realistic drama in the '50s, she concedes that the archetypes invariably reflect the dominant patriarchal ideology, and that the set of social codes endemic to upwardly mobile, affluent white America provides an idealized vision of home and family that domesticated and subordinated women (3). By its nature, the mirror of popular culture both creates and sustains these stabilizing codes of the cultural imaginary by confirming rather than criticizing the world it reflects. And, with the advent of television, nowhere was the cultural imaginary more stringently imposed and sustained than in television programming—especially as it became the dominant force in shaping middle-class values (along with advertising)—until, by the mid-'50s, whether truly representative or not, the model families from television became entrenched archetypes in our collective national consciousness. Certainly prior to 1960, and especially during Inge's period, gender roles were strictly enforced, even if they were merely a veneer covering the complexity of gender relations many experienced but few publicly acknowledged.

Stereotypes have existed since one set of cultural identity codes encountered an opposite (the One, in popular vernacular, recognizing, often fearing and finally clashing with its infamous Other). Such conflict, of course, renders the nature of beauty as diffuse and difficult to determine as any sublimated Ideal. And the battle of the sexes, resulting in the supposed dominance of a patriarchal cosmology, is as ancient as the first taboo—behavioral codes that, as Reay Tannahill notes in *Sex in History* (1980), "once established, were deliberately transformed into a weapon against women's self-assertion" (45). Camille Paglia agrees, arguing in *Sexual Personae* (1990) that these gender stereotypes are not necessarily merely transient qualities conjured up by the dominant patriarchal ideology to fit the times but are a product of "another crucial strategy of the Apollonian west in the long struggle with Dionysus" (18). Her invocation of Apollo and Dionysus may be a simplification of Nietzsche's more subtle distinction in his discussion of Greek tragedy, but her point that stereotypes based on mythical cultural archetypes transcend epochs and shifting political or social codification is nevertheless secure. In contrast to Felman, Spivak and others who challenge the bifurcation of sexual identification, Paglia traces the assignment of separate, fixed gender roles to men and women back to the ancient conflict between earth-cult and sky-cult religions. For her, men cleverly managed a "switch of the creative locus from earth to sky ... from belly-magic to head-magic" (9) and in doing so have become "sexually compartmentalized ... condemned to a perpetual patter of linearity, focus, aim, directedness" (21) which leads to a pathological "dissociation of sex and emotion, to temptation, promiscuity and disease" (21). Whereas Paglia associates men with math, logic, and "spiritual castration" (13), women, on the other hand, represent nature in all its terrible gore and beauty. Women are metaphorically aligned with "liquid nature, a miasmic swamp whose prototype is the still pond of the womb" (12). Women are "chthonian" (15), associated with blood, cycles, the mysteries of childbearing; fluid, shapeless, "ever-elusive" (32); raw Dionysian Nature in opposition to Apollonian Art, filled with "daemonic vitality" (25) and "waxing and waning in lunar phases" (10).

Corollary to these cultural lines of sexual definitions throughout history, the superficial image of the "normal" man, circa 1950, is one of strength and resolution. He is the head of the household, a tough decision-maker, emotionally distant, whether in the boardroom, the bedroom, or the local bar, but he always wears the pants and provides for the family. In Paglia's paradigm, he is metaphorically rooted in the archetype of Apollo, god of substance, logic, sobriety, reason, precision and order. His light emanates from the sun; his geometry favors the straight line; he represents certainty, linearity and closure. On the other hand, the superficial image of a "normal" female of the same period tends to be one of deference, a passive partner in domestic bliss, June Cleaver baking cookies in pumps and pearls, more interested in the conveniences of modern suburbia, laundry detergent and pot roasts than world affairs, payroll parity, a career, politics or the hard knocks of the world outside her social life. Her cultural archetype is Dionysus, god of wine, passion, emotion, depth, mystery, disorder: his sheen is the cool reflected light of the moon; his geometry favors circles; he revels in openness, dissolution.

But just as stereotypes, throughout history, have been created, acknowledged and politically engineered, as early as Aristophanes they have been a rich source for the satirical savagery of manners, as mocked as they were ingrained. Even during the supposedly stodgy so-called American "Victorian" era, gender-based rituals were fair game for satire, as evidenced by Mrs. Herbert B. Linscott's "Suffragette Evening," from her classic primer for theme parties, *Bright Ideas for Entertaining* (1905), which encourages women to dress in a "mannish way" (quoted in *Harper's*, 30), as the men are required to "keep quiet while the women talked politics" (30) and "the occupations of the sterner sex ... become those formerly handled by women" (29). Even today, consumer advertising is filled with examples of stereotyping and gender exploitation: one telephone company spot depicts two design graphic artists arguing over an illustration—the male wants to use a bar graph, the woman a pie chart.

As these sexual stereotypes are reinforced socially, politically and culturally, and so become self-fulfilling, what is evident is that beneath every stereotype lies a truth, and without question, during the '50s, gender distinctions were strictly codified to demarcate "normalcy" in relations between the sexes, from the condescending attitude of legislation to the Ozzie and Harriet role-model marriage, from the ingrained social stigmas by which the relationships between men and women were judged normal or aberrant to considering certain behavior either acceptable or unacceptable, healthy or sick. But an examination of the stereotypes stemming from the '50s, of both men and women, is particularly significant for understanding the women's liberation movement in the '60s, the rise of feminist studies in the '70s, and the proliferation of men's identity groups in the '80s like Robert Bly's male affirmation movement and the phenomenon of so-called "Promise Keepers." And given the politically charged context of contemporary gender studies, stereotypes have become more than weapons in the battle for cultural identification: they have become prescriptive tools for regulating—and, at times, legislating—personal behavior. As the demarcations between the dangerously deviant (thus outlawed) and the merely eccentric (and therefore tolerated) become murky, stereotyping offers the artificial but comfortable chimera of clarity.

In their illustrated collection of essays *Constructing Masculinity* (1995), the editors argue for "reconfiguring traditional political, social, and aesthetic definitions of gender" (Govan, viii). Citing the work of

Judith Butler, Anne Fausto-Sterling, Carole Vance, et al., they suggest that "gender, rather than merely constructed, is performative ... operations that render complex meanings about the normative standards that we cannot escape" (Berger, 3), often producing a "rigid and fictive construction of reality ... condemned to conform to binary sexual differences that appear to be inevitable, even natural" (4).

The idea that an existential construct can become politically and culturally subversive, can challenge the notion of a national cultural assimilation of archetypes, acknowledged, maintained, and referred to as fact, and can expose "gender discontinuities ... [as] a coercive ideal that exists principally to protect the norm" (4) is also effectively argued in Jackie Byars' *All That Hollywood Allows: Re-Reading Gender in 1950s Melodrama* (1991). Echoing the work of Molly Haskell and Tessa Perkins, Byars writes that stereotypes "are ideology made tangible" (73), and challenges the "validity" (73) of forming stereotypes that "involves selecting ideological significant personality traits ... and making those attributes seem innate" (73). The point is that stereotypes, while lacking any intrinsic truth, once ingrained begin to influence, inform and determine social codification and behavioral patterns that transcend mass media.

One immediately thinks of the Dan Quayle/*Murphy Brown* flap during the 1992 presidential election, a strange confluence of reality and fiction wherein Quayle criticized what he considered the show's glorification of a single working-woman's decision to have a child without the benefit of a "traditional" patriarchal family structure, "lambast[ing] the character Murphy Brown for choosing to have a child out of wedlock" (Handy, 81). (One could hardly distinguish the reality—Quayle as vice president—from the fiction—the character played on television by Candice Bergen.) The political and social fallout from this sort of social disruption is recorded in the April 14, 1997, issue of *Time* (that archetypal prime arbiter of contemporary middle-class values) that reports on the eponymous sitcom star Ellen DeGeneres announcing her homosexuality during an episode broadcast on network television. The headline reads, "Roll Over, Ward Cleaver, And tell Ozzie Nelson the news" (Handy, 79). Aside from the intertextual allusion to a black rock 'n' roll anthem by Chuck Berry (covered for white baby boomers by the Beatles), the headline at least proves the existence of a cultural hegemony expressly favoring a '50s style nostalgic version of a typical middle-class American family in which the male is privileged, the female subordinate, and the children spitting images of Mom and Dad—the whole white bread family mere clones of the "people next door." Even the titles of the early archetypal shows belie the underlying cultural paradigm: *Life with Father* (1953–1955), *Father*

Knows Best (1954–1960), *My Three Sons* (1960–1972). The families are generic and interchangeable: *Leave It to Beaver* (1957–1963), *Dennis the Menace* (1959–1963), *The Dick Van Dyke Show* (1961–1966). With few exceptions, the model for each family is based on the stereotypes stemming from acceptable male and female gender roles established in the postwar years and reinforced through popular cultural media, television in particular. The *Time* article, while marking exceptions in the continuum, acknowledges the "type" from the '50s paradigm of *I Love Lucy* (1951–1961) through that of *The Cosby Show* (1984–1992), pointing out that the first "double marital bed" (81) did not occur until 1965 in *Bewitched* (1964–1972).

Ironically, during the '50s, the major plays of Inge tend, at first glance, to affirm the commonly accepted gender distinctions of the '50s. While acknowledging the theoretical gender-based feminist approaches critics such as Christine Gledhill, Laura Mulvey and Linda Williams bring to film criticism, Byars justifiably cites Columbia Pictures' adaptation of Inge's play *Picnic* as exemplifying "female-oriented film melodramas of the 1950s [that] call attention to gendered identity construction during a period when precisely what it means to be a woman—and, as a result, what it means to be a man—were becoming controversial issues" (147). The success of the film version of *Picnic*, for Byars, is a result of its ability to allow the female protagonists "integration in the (heterosexual) social order [by] acquir[ing] a mate and participat[ing] in a heterosexual dyad" (147). Citing Michael Wood, she argues that another Inge film, *Come Back, Little Sheba* (1953), follows a similar "rigid narrative structure" (115) which, like *Picnic*, reaffirms socially conditioned behavior, casting the woman as the corrective nexus of the family, her success determined by her ability to overcome "deviance" (118) and maintain or recreate "a domestic order, a family" (118).

Extending this media-enforced social codification into theater, and to the types of plays that Inge was writing in the '50s, Robert Vorlicky, in his *Act Like a Man: Challenging Masculinities in American Drama* (1995), defines realism as the "dramatic mode that makes the strongest claim to forging links between a play's theatrical system and its cultural context" (1). The focus of his book is restricted to "the canon of realist male-cast drama" (1), but in his opening chapter Vorlicky offers a wide-ranging review of recent feminist criticism, exploring the male "'hegemony of realism'" (2), suggesting that realism in drama offers an "account of reality ... thoroughly determined by patriarchal ideology" (1). While Byars establishes the realist model for women in films during the '50s, and Vorlicky that of the male in more recent theater, both recognize "a realist model of rigid gender polarization" and "the asymmetries of gender [that] affect the construction of ... subjectivity" (Vorlicky, 3).

While it is true that in his plays Inge utilizes for dramatic effect the gender-determined roles expected of women in the dramatic realism of the '50s, he also manages at the same time to subvert the very stereotypes and archetypes the public used to reassure itself of its normalcy. This subversion is a technique that might best be defined as "gendermandering"—that is, the intentional undermining of expected gender roles for the dramatic purpose of politically and socially destabilizing social norms. It becomes a method used by playwrights and supported by play directors as a means to "gender-culture realignment" (Heller, 17), allowing for "a radical de-centering of master narratives" (4) so that gender "boundaries that might have previously served to fix and divide ... prove to be fluid and dissolvable" (5). In the same way Nietzsche used analysis to destabilize analysis, and Kant used logic to set the limits of logic, Inge uses gendermandering to counterbalance "modernity's overinvestment in the gender specificity of separate spheres" (10), exploding "the postwar domestic stereotype and its meanings, how and where it was produced" (Meyerowitz, 2).

The concept of gendermandering is a derivation from the practice of gerrymandering, in which voting districts are manipulated or falsified unfairly to gain a voting advantage for one particular party over another. And like gerrymandering, gendermandering can also be culturally subversive, acknowledging and employing stereotypes for dramatic effect while seeming simultaneously to condemn them. Traditionally, gerrymandering suggests dirty politics, a tool remnant of New York's Tammany Hall or the Chicago "machine" or Jim Crow laws in the South, employed to "fix" an election by securing a safe seat created for a politician who is able to cull the predictably favorable voters into his or her designated district. In the '90s, though, gerrymandering was prescribed by preeminent political theorists like Lani Guanier to "correct"—that is, literally to "fix"—voting blocks, many of which were originally rigged by the entrenched incumbent but redrawn to include representatives for minority voters. In gerrymandering, you acknowledge a voting pattern, then manipulate it to guarantee a desired result.

The same is true of gendermandering, in which a stereotype is designated to a character but is then manipulated by the writer to expose the stereotype for what it is. The writer starts with an artificial set of social codes imposed on a character (similar to a voting block) then works to subvert the type by reversing the expected patterns of behavior (as in voting patterns). Just as many people believe that voting districts are not in the least arbitrary but are somehow culturally inherent, "natural" or established by tradition, so too are the characters who populate fiction often thought of as neither arbitrary nor free but determined, fixed, their behavior codified by nature and tradition. They can never escape the pigeonholes in which they are so conveniently parked. Therefore, like gerrymandering, which attempts to redraw political patterns of expected voting behavior, the purpose of gendermandering is to redraw the boundaries of fixed social patterns of behavior, giving the lie to "nature" and "tradition" as factors in determining a person's choice of self.

Gendermandering is not, however, necessarily a tool that might somehow enhance a legitimate examination of "women's issues." For instance, in a play like Rachel Crothers' *He and She* (1930), the focus is on women struggling for equal professional and political rights, but in Crothers' drama the issue is forefronted; the women want to maintain their "nature" while pursuing careers outside the traditional roles of housewife and mother, maintaining their distinctions while working to eradicate the injustices, inequities and prejudices imposed on them by the typical reactionary societal definitions of what a woman was supposed to be in the early 1900s. By actually forefronting the issue, it is, as it were, "declawed": the women did not want to become masculine or act against their biological nature; they wanted realignment toward equity and harmony in their lives.

The use of gendermandering is different. It exposes the pernicious cultural habit of gender stereotyping while confirming it by exploiting the expected sexual behavior of characters for dramatic effect, intensifying the stress inherent in the conflict between what is considered natural and unnatural, normal and abnormal, based on values governed by social contracts of expected gender behavior. Inge's plays, then, while exposing the stereotypical sexual patterns of the '50s, were also culturally transitional, preparing the groundwork for the gender-bending so prevalent in contemporary aesthetics.

Inge, of course, is not without precedence in his exploitation of cultural gender typing for dramatic effect. The technique is as old as Aristophanes. *Lysistrata* certainly could not have enhanced the standing of that particular class of women, even though they were portrayed with a power base capable of inspiring envy in the most reluctant contemporary feminist. A better model for Inge is Shakespeare's *Macbeth*, in which Lady Macbeth acknowledges sexual differences and yet exploits them through her machinations to taunt her husband into realizing their ambitions. Her famous "unsex me here" (1.5.41) is but one of her many taunting tropes by which she tries to overcome her nature, will herself out of her maternal, caring, "womanly" self and assume the role of a man in order to carry out her and her husband's murderous plans.

Of the plays that may have influenced Inge during the period immediately before his professional debut, O'Neill's *Beyond the Horizon* (1920) is perhaps the best example of a work which exposes the pernicious cultural habit of gender stereotyping while, willfully or not, confirming it. The crux of the play involves the choices the two brothers make regarding the girl they both think they love. Robert is an effeminate male reveling in dreams of exotic travel who trades in his plans to run off with his uncle on a sailing adventure for a naive moonstruck romantic gesture at marriage to the girl with whom his brother Andrew is in love. Andrew is an earnest, hardworking, practical man about the farm, his brother's opposite, but desperate and embarrassed after he learns of Robert's plan to marry Ruth, Andrew steps in to take his brother's place on his uncle's ship, leaving Robert behind to run the farm. Robert, however, is painfully mismatched. Ruth is a tough playmaker in the realpolitik of emotional warfare, and soon Robert's decision to stay and try to manage the farm—a job for which he is at best hopelessly ill suited—leads to the ruin of both the farm and the marriage. His decision also leads to the death of his father, his mother, and finally his daughter Mary. Meanwhile, Andrew has made a fortune farming land in Argentina, but he ends up losing it all gambling in commodities—a profession he is no better at than his brother is farming. In the end, he returns too late to save his brother's life, or Ruth's soul, and they are left with only their loss, guilt and suffering between them.

O'Neill's gendermandering is most evident in the relationship between Robert and Ruth. Atypically, Robert is the sensitive, nurturing, maternal element in the marriage, while Mary is resentful: she ignores their child or scolds her. She is neither a caring nor a loving supportive wife. As Robert wastes away from a debilitating disease, Mary only hardens, becoming more coarse, less sympathetic, and soon begins to resemble not her sniveling mother so much as her vindictive father-in-law Mayo. At one point she accuses Robert of having "never been man enough to work" (O'Neill, 127) and thinks she was a fool to believe in his "cheap, silly, poetry talk" (127). But Andrew is also displaced from his nature. He is, on one hand, a man among men, the misplaced agent of Mary's salvation. On the other hand, exiled from the land he loves, he never marries—never has any relationships with women as far as we know. In fact, a not too subtle allusion to homosexual male bonding occurs in the scene where Robert tells his uncle Scott he is not going with him, and before Andrew decides to take his brother's place, the venerable captain first complains that he has renovated the cabin —"it's all painted white, an' a bran' new mattress on the bunk, 'n' new sheets 'n' blankets 'n' things" (103)—then he wonders about his crew—"what will they think?" (103)—and when the captain accepts Andrew in his brother's stead, he does so almost as he would a wife: "They're liable as not to think it was a woman I'd planned to ship along" (103).

As in classical drama, the people in O'Neill's play are victims of their choices, because the choices they make go against their nature. In a sense, the decisions they make are "unnatural," and this is the basis for their individual tragedies. Andrew was best suited to stay and work the farm as his father intended, and his natural pairing would have been with Ruth; his nature was to be the anchor of the family. Robert's truths lay "beyond the horizon," where he could have satisfied his wanderlust, his sensitive nature, free to experience and to express the awesome poetry of life. (True to his nature, Andrew cannot even write about his experiences; his letters are scant on details and matter-of-fact to a fault.) In O'Neill's vision, the people pay for their existential mistakes: choosing against their nature, they are left to blame only fate or luck.

Another play that certainly complements Inge's use of gendermandering as a tool in his work is Williams' *Cat on a Hot Tin Roof* (1955). Williams' Brick and Maggie, like O'Neill's Robert and Ruth, are also gendermandered cross-dressers. Again, the conflict is between the natural and the unnatural—or better, between what is expected, what is normal, and what is unexpected or abnormal. Maggie "loves to run with dogs" (Williams, 896) and takes on all comers, while Brick hides in the bathroom from his mother—who is, by the way, also uneasy with her son's behavior, tending, however predictably, to blame Maggie, telling her bluntly, "when a marriage goes on the rocks, the rocks" (903) are in the bed. Big Daddy too, aware that Brick is "crippled" (919), can only hope Brick might restore his manhood in typical male fashion, by "cuttin' ... a piece of poon-tang" (921). After all, Big Daddy's idea of success in old age is to find a "choice" (935) woman and "hump her from hell to breakfast" (935). So, aside from all the business with Skipper, Brick is feminized, weak and passive, a broken dreamer (literally) who has traded in his trousers for a pair of silk pajamas. Maggie, on the other hand, exhibits the mannerisms stereotypically associated with a man: she is strong, sensible, logical, a fighter who calls Brick, in her locker-room style, "an ass-aching Puritan" (887). She even admits that she has become "hard" (890) just as Brick confesses that he is getting "softer" (891)—evidence of his impotence. Clearly, Maggie has displaced Brick as the male in the relationship.

Gendermandering in Inge is best illustrated by his talent for creating potent female characters that exhibit patently male qualities and seemingly dominant male characters that display archetypal feminine traits. In *Bus Stop*, for instance, several peripheral characters behave in a reassuringly stereotypical manner, and yet they also act to contrast expected patterns of behavior with the atypical patterns of the other main characters. Will, the sheriff, is a bit prudish but an okay guy, a typical right-thinking midwestern pragmatist. Elma is a stereotypical inquisitive young girl, and Carl, the bus driver, comes off as a particularly stereotypical rutting-stag. Even Lyman, for all his nastiness, is predictably vulgar and pedophilic. More curious, however, are the examples of the switch-hitting gendermandered types: Bo and Cherie, Virgil and Grace. The two women are sexually experienced and confident. Cherie feigns innocence, though she readily admits that she has "led a wicked life" (*Four Plays*, 209) and had "other boyfriends" (209). She is a tough, street-smart, resourceful runaway who quit school at 12 and never looked back. While infused with the Dionysian—or feminine—qualities of emotional depth, intuition, and passion, she also exhibits unusually strong Apollonian—or masculine—qualities of contrivance, masking, superficiality, and reason. She is resilient, surviving by her wits as much as her looks, capable, chameleon-like, of playing any role that fits her immediate needs: the helpless victim, the aggressive vamp, the diffident struggling talent naively in search of the career-making gig. Conversely, Bo is plagued by the very qualities he finds most abject in others—qualities he, of course, cannot recognize in himself, those feminine Dionysian "flaws" of emotional excess, disorder, inebriation. Claiming he never drinks, he's intoxicated with himself. Prey to inexplicable destructive urges, he gives off more heat than light. Bo lacks the one primary quality that most defines the Apollonian male: the ability to play, to recognize theater, to adapt to a role. Bo must be; he is the thing itself, not a replica; he lacks the luxury of distance from himself that Cherie enjoys. By the end of the play, he learns to act the role of gentleman, is thereby tamed and so fit to assume the role of a normal househusband.

Grace and Virgil likewise reverse the stereotypical personae of male and female role-playing. Grace is the one who is sexually confident, who likes a man with "big hands" (204), who is savvy enough to keep even hornier-than-thou Carl in line. In contrast, Virgil prefers a sort of solipsistic, Platonic bunkhouse camaraderie to any active sexual engagement, homo- or heterosexual. In fact, Grace could well be played as a man, given the predominant masculine (or Apollonian) characteristics she displays. She is a strong individual, single, divorced, practical and orderly. But most of all, she is able to adapt, to control. She is also capable of a cool distance from her emotions—another primary Apollonian trait. When Carl slips into sentimentality, romancing Grace, weakened by his need for her, she rebuffs him with biting irony, undercutting his fumbling attempts at seduction with a cool, logical bottom line. He quips that his friend "Dobson speaks very highly of you" (164). She responds, "Well ... he better. Now what you gonna have?" (164). Grace maintains her world—and the diner—on her terms, delegating, advising, taking what she wants, giving what she needs. She is the Apollonian essence of stability and good judgment. Virgil, on the other hand, is the epitome of Dionysian subjectivity: he relies strictly on intuition, having no worldly experience to back himself up. At first glance, he seems like a good diplomat: cautious, circumspect, and levelheaded. But in essence he is moderate in the extreme. He is a loner because he cannot escape his own subjectivity, cannot role-play successfully enough to integrate with society. He cannot project, his individuality collapses into itself, and he is left isolated in his solipsism.

Like political gerrymandering, gendermandering is not necessarily always a pernicious practice. Indeed, in *Bus Stop* the technique often leads to a rather neat parallelism of sexual symmetry and moral balance. From the opening scene, the play version of *Bus Stop* is crackling with sexual tension. Even before everyone is out of the bus, the pairing begins. Elma, the innocent, goes for the cynical old drunk Lyman (the lying man). By the end of the play she's impressed that "he wanted to make love to me" (218). The sexually mature Grace hooks up with Carl, the driver (pun intended). Later, as Bo and Cherie stumble through their mating charade, even Virgil and Will couple as diplomats, figures of stability and compromise (though Virgil cannot maintain his role). The symmetry of these sexual alignments is more than a mere device to drive the plot: it establishes the central theme of disruption and reconciliation.

But Inge's gendermandering is certainly culturally subversive: in fact, it may have signaled the beginning of a general tearing of the social fabric of the '50s later ripped away by the counterculture in the '60s. Unquestionably, a progression occurred in the twentieth century from the prejudice of expected stereotypical gender patterns of behavior in the early years, to the cross-dressing plays of midcentury, to the breakdown of gender distinctions in the '60s, to, finally, the androgyny so prevalent in contemporary culture, and Inge's gendermandering may be read as a key link in the chain connecting these gender-based dialectics.

2

The Critics

Is it true—what Shelley writes me that poor John Keats died at Rome of the Quarterly Review?
—Letter from Byron to John Murray, 26 April 1821

Are you aware that Shelley has written an elegy on Keats—and accuses the Quarterly of killing him? ...However—he who would die of an article in a review—would probably have died of something else equally trivial....
—Letter from Byron to John Murray, 31 July 1821

My death will not be related in any way to the vicious review you wrote of my book.
—Byron to a critic in Inge's unpublished play *The Love Death*

Inge is often misread as a sentimentalist. Arthur F. McClure, for instance, in a rather harmless book eulogizing a Kansan favorite son—a study he himself admits is a cursory review of "William Inge and his world" (13)—nevertheless suggests that Inge's work "stressed what he thought was the essential goodness of the human heart" (69), an appraisal that may testify more to McClure's admiration for Inge than for the playwright's unflinching view of the compromises, cruelties and frustrations at the heart of the human endeavor. But McClure's point of view—his attitude toward his subject—neatly illustrates a prevailing and arguably misplaced perception of Inge as an intellectual lightweight, a purveyor of homespun wisdom and down-home truisms about "a pastoral America" (57) whose "works explored the relationships and the challenges of romantic love" (4). Like many critics that focus celebrating Inge's work rather than elucidating the dark edge of his sensibility, McClure presents a defensive sympathy with the playwright's life and career, relying on euphemisms and evasions to camouflage, simplify and restrict the scope and penetration that makes Inge so much more than a regional playwright.

McClure stresses Inge's midwestern roots, and he is every bit as possessive as other commentators who claim Inge as their own—Patricia McIlrath, for instance, who spent 30 years as artistic director of Missouri Repertory Theatre in Kansas City. In her "William Inge, Great Voice of the Heart of America," she recalls how she was "drawn to Inge somewhat because of my Middle West roots" (46). For McIlrath, Inge "knew small-town life perfectly, its agonies and its ecstasies; he knew, possibly personally, the agony of assuming moral responsibility for one's own acts, a strong trait and virtue in the Middle West" (49). Inadvertently, while espousing his virtues as a playwright of "universal" (51) themes, McIlrath perpetuates the impression of Inge as a limited regional anomaly. This fickleness is a common phenomenon expressed by many self-appointed Inge apologists. They tend to agree with critics who dismiss Inge as a minor playwright of limited scope and talent while constantly reiterating Inge's stature as "the first playwright to examine the Midwest with real insight" (52). McIlrath admits, "Inge's plays may not be all that our sophisticated or even pseudo-sophisticated contemporary world wants to see" (49), yet in his defense she stresses the virtue of his "understanding and love for the Midwest and its people" (49).

Underscoring the paradox of finding a panoramic scope in Inge's alleged limited regional vision, McClure, like McIlrath, suggests that Inge's midwestern roots afford him a unique perspective on "the fabric of American life which reminds audiences of the surprising resilience born of traditional values in the family" (McClure, 7). He bases Inge's moral veracity on a rather bizarre theory that people from the Midwest, if not morally superior to the decadent denizens populating the extremities of the contiguous 48 states, "have a tendency to see themselves as the champions of American virtue, and to look askance at the forces they feel are corrupting other sections of the nation" (7). Such virtuous insight, according to McClure, stems from an equally odd notion that "[h]istorically, Americans place far more emphasis on a good family life than on having a high income, material possessions, or social recognition" (7). These fantasies would be news to many of Inge's protagonists who suffer, fail and settle old debts more out of desperation than any sense of transcendental, unqualified love.

Equally puzzling (if not oxymoronic), McClure complains repeatedly about what he sees as attacks from the critics who complain about Inge's sentimentalism while he rejoices in the very sentimentality he claims the critics object to. McClure insists that "[a] search for meaning in Inge's works is intimately related ... with nostalgia" (3), but he fails to account for how Inge's depiction of a superficial, wistfully idealized pastoral Heartland serves mainly as a pretext for his devastating deconstruction of it.

McClure simultaneously ascribes Inge's professional failures in the '60s to a shift in public attitudes toward art and politics, yet celebrates what he considers Inge's heartfelt hokeyness. He writes: "At first, the sentimental nature of his work was praised, but late in his career it was criticized for being out of date" (3). He derides the fact that Inge's work "had once drawn critical praise, [but] fell from favor and was criticized for being out-of-date and sentimental ... was castigated for what was seen as an overabundance of sentimentality" (68), and he chastises critics that describe Inge's "work as 'sentimental' and 'overrated' and 'mediocre'" (61). But McClure, inadvertently (one hopes), is intent on putting out fire with gasoline. For him, *Summer Brave* (1962) is "a love story of two lonely and unhappy persons, both trying to prove that there was something more to them than physical beauty" (65). In *A Loss of Roses* (1959) Helen "has an open capacity for love and a steadfastness which never has been fully allowed to develop in a relationship" (61). *Splendor in the Grass* describes a young couple coming to realize "that while they have lost the chance of experiencing a complete love, they both have at last found in the past a new strength to face the future" (59). He reads their irrepressible sex drive as nothing but an attempt "to consummate their deep love for each other" (58). At the end of *The Dark at the Top of the Stairs* (1957), "there is the feeling that there is nothing to fear in the dark at the top of the stairs, if somebody is climbing them with you [and] if somebody can offer love or understanding to you, then the endless stairway of life is an easier climb" (53). The resolution of *Come Back, Little Sheba* (1950) illustrates how "Doc and Lola, left alone, realize that they have only one another and resolve to make what they can of their future life together" (25). McClure's enthusiasm for what he considers Inge's sentimentality is summed up with his plaintive plea: "can there ever be too much sentiment in a world such as ours?" (68)

Apparently not for McClure. For others, the issue of Inge's sentimentalism is trickier. This critical discrepancy may be attributed to the difficulty of reading Inge's endings: he opens the conclusions not with irony but ambiguity, and what seems wholesome, romantic and complete at first glance, on closer inspection belies the easy sound-bite truisms many commentators rely on either to praise or dismiss Inge's peculiar take on the human condition. One critic, Steven R. Centola, notes how Inge's plays end with characters fatally compromised, reconciling not in good faith but in what Sartre calls *mauvais foi*, or bad faith. Inge's characters, Centola writes, suffer "the corrosive effect of compromise ... and show why compromise alone, especially when it amounts to little more than sexual repression, cannot serve as the foundation of a happy marriage or as the basis for a civilized society" (101). Specifically, he cites *Come Back, Little Sheba* as an example, not of Doc and Lola experiencing "a new realization of their need for each other" (McClure, 25), but of "a reconciliation that is based on nothing else than the promise of more lies and debilitating compromises" (Centola, 103). This reading of Inge, in which "guilt, loneliness, and despair, are the price ... characters pay for living in bad faith" (113) may come closer to the truth of Inge's dramatic vision than the facile critics that, like McClure, defend Inge for his alleged sentimentality, or those, like Robert Brustein, who condemn him for it, or still others, like Stanley Kauffmann, who blame Inge's perverse contrariety on his closeted homosexuality.

To suggest that Inge's homosexuality affords him some special sensibility both to limn and erase the expected gender demarcations of his characters might seem reductive and facile, but to ignore the psychological crisis his sexuality caused in his life seems equally fatuous. Some critics like Albert Wertheim, intent on "reading it gay" (207), force the issue, accusing other critics of imposing agendas that ignore or downplay the homosexuality inherent in Inge's work while promoting their own readings as gospel. Wertheim, in "Dorothy's Friend in Kansas: the Gay Inflections of William Inge," recognizes a gendermandered reading of Inge's work, conceding that "Inge is subverting conventional assumptions and stereotypes of male and female behavior" (194–195) while insisting that "[t]hese characterizations ... overlook, perhaps deny, the sexuality and significant homoeroticism from which Inge's plays spring" (195). In what might otherwise, in a less passionate mode, be considered a mere overstatement, Wertheim writes that "a gay sensibility informs his major plays, is refracted in them, and most importantly permits him special insights, insights derived from his personal experience of gay alterity" (198). Reading within a context he calls the "semiotics of desire" (204), Wertheim claims special insights too, but often Wertheim's creative critical confabulations reduce Inge's dramatic action to a phallicistic sexual dynamic that restricts instead of opens the play of meanings in Inge's work.

It seems self-evident that a critic who addresses Inge's subversion of expected gender roles must explain Inge's conflicted sexuality, and this conflict is accounted for as a causal component of the process that results in gendermandered characters, but Wertheim insists that only a gay reading of Inge's plays will "open up" (194) his work to reveal the truth "that gay men knew what these plays were about" (195). Not only does Wertheim stake out a privileged position for his preferred audience, but he also claims that without a gay sensibility one may somehow miss the truth of Inge's dramaturgical intent: "To read Inge's plays without acknowledging their gay inflections is to see them as less than they are" (198). This is the sort of complaint that can be turned back on the complainer with equal validity.

However, his complaint that "critics have been profoundly silent about the homoerotic tones in Inge's work" (198) is empirically accurate but surely not a mystery. One can safely assume that, especially during the '50s, homosexual coding between insiders, including hostile critics, was mutual. Outing of popular and commercially successful playwrights as a McCarthyite tactic might have proven fatal even for the accuser and may well have threatened the entire industry. Otherwise, beginning with Kauffmann's 1966 article in the *New York Times*, writers have at least obliquely addressed Inge's "gay inflections," usually as a complementary element to a more comprehensive exegesis, even though the few critics writing seriously about Inge did shy away from underscoring the "homosexual tones" prevalent in Inge's work.

The problem with Wertheim's position is that while claiming his gay reading offers a complete—even absolute—correction of other critical considerations concerning Inge's major plays, his view actually illustrates only a facet of Inge's talent as a playwright. (It is unhelpful that as evidence of the "homoeroticism from which Inge's plays springs" Wertheim provides two photographs of Inge in drag [196, 197]). More appropriate and engaging are his specific explications of Inge's work in the context of queer theory, but these observations too, when overly narrow and polemical, obfuscate more than they enlighten. He encourages, for instance, a specifically gay critical context regarding male-male identification with Inge's cross-dressed hunks like Turk and Hal while acknowledging the male-female attraction of the women to those hunks too, but he ignores the female-female infatuation generated by some of Inge's women, especially for Marie, Madge and Cherie, so his queer reading seems particularly skewed toward gay men.

For Wertheim, *Picnic* (1953) epitomizes the "the ways in which Inge's gay sensibility inform his dramatic works" (198). In an elaborate explication that paradoxically reinforces a negative gay stereotype—that of promiscuous sexual predators lusting after buff, super-masculine males—Wertheim hangs the text like a gay *Sports Illustrated* cheesecake calendar, filled with strutting studs who appeal to a catholic audience of licentious gawkers:

> Indeed, what Inge manages to craft by writing a play that is on one level about the sexual awakenings of underdeveloped or

repressed females and on another level about homoeroticism is no mean feat, for *Picnic* ultimately provides a representation of sexuality that transcends gender and orientation. As they come to understand both these aspects of *Picnic*, straight playgoers will find themselves unintentionally, but nevertheless ineluctably, forced to speak and understand the language of gay desire [204].

Likewise, in *Come Back, Little Sheba* Wertheim's critical gaze focuses on the contrast between Turk, with his "prizewinning phallus" (205) and "the dependable, conventional, sexually colorless" (205) Bruce, peripheral characters who, between them, frame Doc as "a character drawn by a dramatist who brings his knowledge of gay lives, gay neuroses, and alcoholism to bear" (206). In *Bus Stop*, Wertheim employs an elaborate cryptanalysis to discover not only a coded anagram transposing "Elma" into "male" and marking Lyman's name as indicating "the sex with which he prefers to lie" (208) but also "Inge brilliantly inscribing a gay text within the margins of a straight one [that] no gay-alert audience member would nowadays fail to perceive" (208). Applying the same sort of gay cryptology in *The Dark at the Top of the Stairs*, Wertheim finds beneath the "(parody of?) conventional heterosexuality, and often overwhelming it ... the play's far more powerful, dangerous, homoerotically subversive plot" (211). Wertheim summarizes Inge's technique, specifically in reference to his dramatic strategy in *The Dark at the Top of the Stairs*, but operative (according to Wertheim) in all his major plays, as "overlaying a gay plot onto a straight one" (214). He concludes that Inge's major plays "derive their power through their *in petto* gaiety" (215). Using a perverse translation of the Italian phrase "in the breast" signifies—stresses—Wertheim's cabalistic reading of Inge which, like gendermandering, is finally subversive. For Wertheim, this subversion enables Inge's audience "to overcome its innate homophobia" (215), and this is fine and true, but the constrictions of Wertheim's vision also limit Inge's importance, as the gay issues Inge addresses are contained within a larger context that, through his radical gendermandering, explodes the discourse beyond the narrow application of "gay inflections," exposing a more universal questioning of stereotypes that challenges even Wertheim's reading.

Ralph Voss, in his exhaustive biography *A Life of William Inge: The Strains of Triumph*, is more tempered than Wertheim. Wertheim argues that Voss avoids the homosexual "connection except in regard to those works in which an overtly gay man appears" (195). To be fair, even while acknowledging Inge's homosexuality and citing many reputable sources that testify to the influence of his sexual dilemma in his work, Voss does hesitate to draw the obvious conclusion that Inge's understanding of sexually conflicted characters and his uncanny ability to portray dramatically the slippage in practice of fixed gender roles are essentially connected to his own crisis as a closeted homosexual living through one of the most virulently anti-gay decades in American history. Voss documents in detail how Inge was forced to conceal his sexuality, describing him as always "peeking out of the closet" (Voss 256). Voss even cites a passage from *Driver*—that "largely factual memoir thinly garbed as fiction" (6)—in which Joey, Inge's stand-in, first sleeps with his girlfriend. He confesses: "It's almost as if I were the boy making love to the shy girl" (quoted in Voss, 47). Exactly. But the closest Voss comes to asserting that Inge's androgyny is the key to his insight into sexually confused characters is when he writes that Inge, as a gay man in a repressive society, "via analysis understood himself and his upbringing perfectly, and that understanding often informed his art" (274). Nevertheless, Voss's conclusion that Inge's homosexuality and the psychoanalysis he employed to deal with it "informed" his work reiterates what is evident in the text: Inge carves close to the bone while shaping universal themes out of "small-town dramas" (275).

The facts of Inge's life, as Voss provides them, clearly imply that no matter how much Inge suffered privately from being "a homosexual during the Eisenhower era" (274), in his best work he profited artistically from this alienation, gaining significant insight from his own forced sexual duplicity. Of course, the blatantly homosexual characters—like Pinky in *Where's Daddy?* (1966) or Spencer Scranton in *The Boy in the Basement* (1962)—are less complex than the gendermandered, psychologically conflicted characters befogged by sexual ambiguity that populate his major plays. The characters from his later plays, mainly unpublished one-acts developed after his mother's death (Voss, 200), tend to be sketches, confessional mouthpieces for Inge's frustration; their conflict is explicit, and, worse, typical. Voss, to his credit, makes a point of not oversimplifying Inge's epicene insight. He does, however, document Inge's struggle with a society so puritanically convinced of its moral superiority that it feels compelled to condemn people based on their sexuality. This socially imposed stigma naturally led to Inge's overwhelming sense of guilt, betrayal and anger in a world that acknowledged him as an artist while condemning him as a homosexual (were he to be publically exposed).

In contrast, R. Baird Shuman, in his otherwise comprehensive exegesis *William Inge* (1965), never mentions Inge's homosexuality. In fact, homosexuality—even in reference to characters in Inge's plays that are explicitly homosexual—is not listed as a category in the index. Such an omission may say more about the marketing strategy of the publishers than of Shuman's hesitancy to draw attention to, at that time, such a taboo subject. Whatever the case, Shuman's allusions to homosexuality are essentially pejorative and categorical. While ignoring the clever—if obvious—homosexual implications in the relationship between Bo and Virgil, and the equally central but perhaps more subtle attraction between Sammy and Sonny and Hal and Alan, Shuman describes Ronnie in *A Loss of Roses* as "a somewhat prototypical homosexual ... whose libido is on occasion put down by Madame Olga's stern authority" (95), and, self-reflexively, Shuman merely insinuates that Inge "hints at the homosexual theme by introducing Ronnie into the play" (98). Donnie, in *Natural Affection* (1963), "has had problems with a homosexual guard" (111), and Vince in the same play "has homosexual leanings ... directed toward Bernie" (112). Shuman addresses homosexuality in Inge's plays only when the characters' sexuality is so blatant, overt and rude (but not necessarily central to the fabric of the drama) that Shuman simply cannot, in good faith, as it were, continue to ignore the elephant on stage. For him, *The Boy in the Basement* "is concerned with homosexuality" (125). Likewise, *The Rainy Afternoon* (1962) "is concerned, as well, with sadism" (125), and *The Tiny Closet* (1962) "deals with repressed homosexuality, manifested in transvestism" (125). Shuman's squeamishness with Inge's more subtle and crafted characterizations—the gendermandering at the crux of his work challenging stereotypical gender roles—is evident in his masking of male-male bonding as "paternal" (125, 157) or idealized. He correlates "the Virgil-Bo relationship" (125) in *Bus Stop* with that of Barney and Dell in *The Mall*, (1962): "the platonic relationship between the mentally unbalanced man and his friend who takes a purely paternal interest in his welfare" (125). Dell, for Shuman, "represents the love of a close friend, the outgoing love which is selfless and which is motivated by the genuine concern and interest of one human being for another" (157), but Mr. Newbold in *The Tiny Closet* is "living with a problem to which he has adjusted relatively well" (142). Discussing one of Inge's boldest plays, *The Boy in the Basement*, in which Inge's guilt and self-loathing are expressed through images of death, sadism and necrophilia, Shuman manages a condemnatory tone, implying that Spencer cannot realize his desire for Joker because "he is far too honorable to introduce Joker to the homosexual experience" (138). Referencing Inge's other overtly homosexual play, *The Tiny Closet*, Shuman notes that Inge has "complicated the basic condition by superimposing upon it the additional element of fetishism with a base of transvestism" (142).

Given the moral filter through which Shuman reads Inge, evident in his inability to address the homosexual underpinnings that created such complexity in Inge's characters and, through gendermandering, liberate them from the "standardized gallery of characters" (125) that Shuman finds so comfortably predictable, one can only question the range of understanding Shuman musters regarding the destabilizing gender dynamics central to Inge's work. When Shuman likens the "love triangle" (160) involving Ben, Tom and Ann in *The Strains of Triumph* (1962) to that of the "love triangle broadly suggestive of the Marie-Turk-Bruce one" (125) in *Come Back, Little Sheba* or "the Hal-Alan-Madge triangle" (161) in *Picnic*, it is clear that Shuman can only visualize the heterosexual coupling of the boy and girl with the third boy being the odd man out, when in fact a more interesting and in some cases more plausible dramatic truth explores the male-bonding—especially of Hal and Alan and Turk and Bruce—in which the girl becomes the antidote for the emotional confusion the men suffer in a society that condemns certain desires the boys themselves may not fully comprehend.

For whatever reason—marketing, decorum, protocol, moral bias—Shuman shies away from a frank discussion of Inge's homosexuality and the impact it had on his work—especially in his use of gendermandering. He tends to focus on Inge's preoccupation with what he identifies as "strong Oedipal overtones" (76) and a "strong Oedipal undertone" (112), as if references to Freud's theory of the Oedipus complex were coded expressions for homosexuality. Voss agrees that Inge's interest in the dramatic possibilities of the Oedipal conflict probably stemmed from the psychoanalysis Inge was undergoing during this period. Voss writes, "Working out the Oedipal conflict is bound to have been a principal part of Inge's analysis process during these years. It can hardly be purely coincidental that such a conflict also found its way into his writing" (142). He finds in *The Dark at the Top of the Stairs*, *A Loss of Roses*, *Natural Affection*, and *Splendor in the Grass* the influence of "Freudian psychology and the need to understand—and forgive—one's parents" (142).

Freud's theory of infantile sexuality expressed in the Oedipus complex is debatable and problematic—often considered in contemporary psychology as more myth than science—but Inge was certainly well-versed in Freudian psychology, and clearly both the motives of his characters as well as the structural scheme in many of his later plays—especially *A Loss of Roses* and *Natural Affection*—are drawn from the triangular relationship inherent in the complex.

Simplifying such a complicated (and familiar) theory like the Oedipus complex certainly does it injustice, but in short Freud believed that during the first five or six years of life a male child is confronted with certain stages of development. Failure to pass successfully through these stages or experiencing a trauma during one of these stages supposedly results in psychic damage. The key stage is the Oedipus complex. (The counterpart for the female child, the Electra complex involving "penis-envy," while equally rich, imaginative and bizarre, is beside the point in this discussion, though Shuman does refer to this theory (89) in reference to Reenie Flood's relationship with her parents in *The Dark at the Top of the Stairs* and Jackie Loomis' involvement with the two men in her life, her father and Bus Riley, in *Bus Riley's Back in Town* [1962]). The two fundamental features of the Oedipus complex, the triangular structure between the child and the parents and the constitutional bisexuality of all human beings, at first allows the child to identify with both parents, regardless of the biological sex of the child. But soon the boy develops a libidinal bond with the mother, his source of nourishment and plenitude, and begins to resent the father as a rival for the mother's attention. The boy, however, according to Freud, unconsciously fears that his father will castrate him as punishment for his sexual desire for his mother. This fear of castration successfully brings the boy through the complex by causing him to give up or retreat from his unconscious desire and to identify with his father as his biological model. As the complex is resolved, the child balances his attraction and hostility to achieve a harmonious relationship with both parents.

In "normal" development, the Oedipus complex is dissolved or destroyed when the son identifies with the father and no longer views him as a rival. The boy's hostility toward the father culminates in a desire to kill him and take his place. But as the boy continues to identify biologically with the father, he tempers his hostility and, according to Freud, develops his masculinity. The son then develops a nonsexual ("aim-inhibited") love for the mother and is then free to find a female sexual partner other than the mother. But the implications of the Oedipal complex can intensify and ultimately become so powerful that the boy cannot resolve the anger toward his father, the love-object of the mother. If the boy fails to identify with the father, and instead assumes an affectionate, feminine attitude toward the father, he may develop jealousy toward the mother, viewing her as a rival for the attention of the father.

Within this context, Freud traces the roots of male homosexuality back to this infantile inability to assume masculinity when a son fails to master the Oedipus complex. He treats homosexuality as an abnormality caused by the inability of the boy to identify with a detached or absent father. The boy instead forms an unusually intense bond with a doting, overbearing or overaffectionate mother. Coupled with his castration fear at the hands of an angry father-rival, the penis-adoring child in the Freudian homosexual model develops disgust for the woman because she lacks the coveted phallus, and thus the boy seeks other men as love objects.

Shuman seems to have adopted Freud's opprobrious attitude toward homosexuality. He cites Freud's theory only once as a "complex" (89), labels it a "theme" (94), an "issue" (90), a "situation" (73, 74, 90), but most often Shuman refers to the complex as a "problem" (28, 44, 73, 74, 75, 89, 91, 123, 125). He seems to rely on the negative aspects of the Oedipus theme as a psychological catch-all to understand, for instance, Doc's "feelings for Marie" (44) in *The Dark at the Top of the Stairs*, the "formidable Oedipus situation" (73) between Cora and Sonny overshadowing her relationship with Doc, the "Oedipus problems ... suggested again by Sammy" (74) in the same play, and "the oversimplified resolution of the Oedipus problem in *A Loss of Roses*" (75). In fact, Shuman claims, "[a]ll of Inge's major plays have strong Oedipus overtones" (76) and suggests that "*A Loss of Roses* is not without possibilities, but its success depends upon ... making Lila the center of the action. This change would enable him to make the Oedipus problem less important, and much would be gained if this problem were stated less directly" (123).

Here, Shuman's critical assessment, with the caveat that Inge place less dramatic necessity on the Oedipal relationships governing the dramatic possibilities within Inge's family portraits, is ironical. The key to the best of Inge's work lies in his use of gender role reversals that resonate beyond the clinical terminology many critics and commentators apply to keep any disturbing work of art safely categorical. In theater, the impulse of critics like Shuman is to objectify, label or codify the action — basically to explicate it and by doing so to render it safe, using a clever praxeological cunning to convert the concrete action of a play into theory—as if containing the action in a convenient psychological box were an existential prerogative. Shuman, citing Eric Bentley's complaint about what he calls Inge's "priapism" (Bentley, 22), concedes that for Inge's characters "contact is more often achieved through sex than through real understanding" (Shuman 169), but this comment makes it sound as if the two—sexual contact and real understanding—were somehow mutually exclusive. Shuman does note that "Inge is strongest in depicting female characters" (169), but he never pursues a technical explanation as to why Inge is so successful creating cross-gendered characters or why the sexuality of the characters interferes with their emotional maturity.

Of course, the mystery as to how writers bring life to their characters has tantalized and frustrated critics from Aristotle to Harold Bloom, and has admittedly produced more smoke than fire. (See, for example,

Keats' letter of November 22, 1817, regarding "negative capability.") Still, the issue with Inge is not necessarily what it is in his biography that accounts for his success as an artist capable of creating such convincing female characters—a talent, according to Shuman, that has been "generally recognized" (169) by critical consensus. The issue instead is about what dramatic techniques Inge employs to achieve the plausibility that makes his best work so engaging and how this craft might be accounted for critically. A first step in understanding Inge's art is to avoid shying away from the psychosexual tension driving Inge's characters and the sexual ambivalence his characters must confront during the course of what otherwise would be an ordinary day.

And yet it is exactly the sexuality in Inge's work that became the *causa bellum* for the most fervent of his contemporary critics hyperventilating about Inge's alleged prurience—Bentley's "priapism." In fact, Shuman seems unable to divorce himself from Inge's sexually charged themes. He applauds the "redemption through sex theme which pervaded the earlier plays" (168) but laments that in Inge's later work "sex becomes a most destructive force" (168) and concludes that Inge's one-act plays "are overtly concerned with sex" (168), a kind that offers no "form of redemption" (168). Many critics like Shuman, in a sort of knee-jerk backlash against Freud, either reject Inge's foregrounding of the sexual psychology of his characters or deride him for being "a dramatist of considerable limitations" (Brustein, 53) who "has been accused of giving a sexual construction to every action" (56). Even Ethan Mordden, in his deliberately cursory and (less deliberately prejudiced) *The Fireside Companion to the Theatre* (1988), writes that Inge's talent "is the most questionable" (155) because, Mordden implies, his plays deal with nothing more than "the sexual psychology of Midwestern life" (155).

Inge's big four—hits all of them—come in for plenty of puritanical derision, although the opprobrium is often couched in bogus polemics, as if the discomfort the reviewers felt about Inge's subject matter could be objectified by dismissive remarks concerning issues of aesthetics. *Newsweek* called *Sheba* a "drab play" ("New Play," 74) and euphemistically described the *mise en scene* as "an untidy Midwestern household" (74) wrenched apart "with the discovery that the dewy-eyed Marie is just a bit of a slut" (74). *Time* also zeroes in on "the awful internal bleeding of mismated lives" ("New Play in Manhattan," 81) that disintegrate on Doc's "discovering that their college-girl boarder is turning, like Lola, into a slut" (81). (It is worth noting that the reviewer in *Time* seems to identify with Doc's self-pitying mischaracterizing of Lola, who is certainly a flirt but hardly a "slut.") Harold Clurman, a sensitive Inge ally and director of *Bus Stop*, went out of his way to explain why *Sheba* is "a good play" ("A Good Play," 23)—which Clurman defines as "one that embodies a true experience of life" (23)—while he highlights what seemed to disturb the other critics: "repressed people living, with all their inhibitions, moral confusion, awry ideals and profound isolation, in a kind of Middletown heartbreak house ... a form of suicide literature were it not for an element of tenderness that sweetens it" (23). Brooks Atkinson basically takes the same tack writing about *Picnic*. While lavishing praise on the production, he tempers his approbation with a wink and a nod to those hungry for the sensational grit of acceptably naughty theater. He claims that Inge, with *Picnic*, reached "full maturity" (1), and that the play exhibits "a certain hard-headed devotion to the truth" (1). But Atkinson cannot help framing his enthusiasm for the "engrossing story" (1) and Inge's "easy versatility" (1) by describing the characters as "commonplace people living in a frowzy part of a small Kansas town" (1). But to Atkinson the play is in essence never more than "a barnyard fable—chanticleer and the scurrying hens" (1). Likewise, in his *Commonweal* review of *Picnic*, Richard Hayes first lauds Inge as a playwright "with more energy and vitality than that of any American dramatist of his generation" (603). But even for him, as for Atkinson, *Picnic* is a play about "a sexual situation, common and gross" (603). He calls the play "a graph of emotion most skillfully described" (603), but at the end of the day the play for Hayes "is a kind of ritual dance, involving the boy and girl only as sexual objects" (603). The reviewer in *Newsweek* also claims that *Picnic* is "an honest, absorbing, and finally a remarkable play" ("Reviews," 84) but stresses the steamy bits, especially concerning Hal, "a well-muscled exhibitionist, sure of his attraction for women ... a guttersnipe Pan in the backyard" (84). Brustein (whom Voss cites too) sums up *Bus Stop* as "a vulgar folk vaudeville with night-club acts and dirty jokes" (53), and Patrick Dennis, in a piece perhaps prophetically entitled "A Literate Soap Opera," insists Pat Hingle's Doc "is wonderfully convincing as [Lola's] unlettered, sexy husband" (21). Tom Driver in the *Christian Century* warns of "a pervasive quality in all the plays best described as subliminal sex. There is plenty of overt sex too" (18).

Etcetera.

By the time *Natural Affection* opened, the critics were livid, and smelling blood after the failure of *A Loss of Roses*, emboldened. Shuman quotes Howard Taubman's review of *Natural Affection* in the *New York Times*, in which the critic implies that Inge's characters are psychologically sick (118–119). He also quotes Norman Nadel of the *New York World-Telegram* saying that Inge and his director were determined "to produce the dirtiest play of the year" (120) and Richard Watts in the New York *Post* writing that all *Natural Affection* proved was that "the sensationally lurid is not Mr. Inge's field" (120). Comments about *Splendor in the Grass* are also typical of the turn in the critical tide regarding Inge's later work. Voss quotes Brendan Gill calling the film "as phony a picture as I can remember seeing" (Voss, 196). Stanley Kauffmann complained about the "simplistic, mechanical view of sex and life and its protracted sententiousness" (196).

Obviously critical barbs at Inge abound—especially after he was awarded the Pulitzer Prize (1963), an event derided by Theophilus Lewis as "exceeding 'all recent efforts to achieve absurdity'" (quoted in Shuman, 166). But in a canny essay Voss characterizes as a "calculated ambush" (180) and a "critical mugging" (182), Robert Brustein had as early as 1958 addressed Inge's sexual sensationalism in a prescient piece entitled "The Men-taming Women of William Inge." The blurb from the *Harper's* article suggests that Brustein will discuss Inge's "formula for turning domestic romance into gold at the box office" (52), but Brustein actually develops a much more sharply honed and potentially devastating critical point: "beneath the naturalistic dirt and cobwebs lies a view of man as blandly nervous as that held by Rodgers and Hammerstein—and more sinister since it robs the individual of his aspiration, his heroism, and even his manhood" (52). The essay cuts a fine critical slice into Inge's dramatic skein, but the article may not be as far askew as many of Inge's apologists past and present like to think.

Brustein opens his essay wondering, in a city that considers "the Midwest as a large mass of unidentified land west of Sardi's" (52), what "accounts for Inge's present-day popularity" (52). He suggests one reason is because Broadway can claim Inge as its "first authentic Midwestern playwright" (52) who corrected the "homogenized" version of the Midwest presented to New York audiences by *Oklahoma!* (1943) and *The Music Man* (1957), thereby "restoring to Midwesterners their privilege to be as traumatized by life as any other Americans" (52). The tenor of his piece, however, quickly turns irreverent. He writes, for instance, that *The Dark at the Top of the Stairs*, "drones on like a Midwestern cricket" (53) and describes Inge's genre as "domestic romance" (53). Contrasting Inge and Williams, considering what he calls their "she-dramas" (53), Brustein notes how for Williams, in the "struggle between a man and a woman, the woman's victory does not necessarily mean the man's defeat" (53). He accuses Inge (as Voss notes) of toeing the formulaic line so that "Inge's plays end—like most romances—in marriage or reconciliation" (53) and he complains that Inge's plays suffer a kind of aesthetic myopia because his plotlines somehow endorse conventional mores, celebrating family, hearth and home—especially heterosexual marriage—as the preferred if flawed solution guaranteeing an uneasy détente in the war between the sexes.

Why many of Inge's defenders—including Voss—view this observation as heretical and negative is odd, given that it seems so axiomatic. Even Harold Clurman, Inge's erstwhile compeer, nearly waxes poetic in his praise of Inge's simplicity:

> Inge was the dramatist of the ordinary. He plumbed no great depths, but this limitation does not negate the honesty or genuineness of his endeavor. Inge really knew and felt his people; he was kin to them. His plays provide insights into their childlike bewilderment, their profound if largely unconscious loneliness…. The narrowness of their scope, their American "provincialism," is in his case an asset rather than a liability ["Theatre," 92].

Despite his admitting that Inge's work displayed "too heavy a dependence on the therapeutic aspects of Freudian psychology" (92), and that "serious critics thought the early plays too sweet, sentimental, facile" (92), Clurman was convinced that "Inge was underestimated" (92).

Janet Juhnke agrees. Confronting Brustein directly in an article entitled "Inge's Women: Robert Brustein and the Feminine Mystique," Juhnke admits that the late '50s marked a significant change in aesthetic and political sensibility, "from social-psychological theatre to radical 'absurdist' drama" (103). She objects mainly to Brustein's privileging the female as an archetypal dominatrix, suggesting that a "closer look at Inge's plays makes clear that they neither depict nor favor matriarchy and that their female characters are more tamed than taming" (104). Juhnke agrees with many of Inge's other critics "that female characters are the most interesting and important characters in Inge's plays" (104), but she rejects the equally well-bandied opinion that Inge's "men are weak and tamed, the women possessive and castrating" (104), citing both "Brustein's and Shuman's specious attacks on 'castrating' women in Inge" (107). She concludes that "the male-female relationships in his plays are far too subtle and complex to be subsumed under a single label: men-taming women" (107).

Nevertheless, Brustein may not be as far off-target as critics like Juhnke and Voss suggest. *Come Back, Little Sheba*; *Picnic*; *Bus Stop* and *The Dark at the Top of the Stairs* do, without apology, end in reconciliation tied inextricably to men acknowledging that they cannot maintain their veneer of masculinity, and as if reborn through their confessions, they are rehabilitated and accepted back into the family as decent companions to their females. Lola wears Doc down through her dogged perseverance. Madge persuades Hal to quit dreaming and drifting and to set up house in Tulsa where he will "get a job hoppin' bells at the Hotel Mayo" (Inge, 141). Cherie tames Bo like a horse trainer busting a bronco. Cora reclaims Rubin from his straying and treats him like a wayward but penitent child.

Such facile plot strategies provoked Gerald Weales, for his entry in *American Drama Since World War II* (1962), to claim that Inge's reputation hinged on a popular capitalistic value system, and within that "strange belief in the corollary relationship between income and reputation, Inge also came to be accepted as one of America's leading dramatists" (41). Weales believes in the mythical Inge, the gay midwesterner prescribing hominess and a "love-panacea ... sex-salvation" (46). In a bitter rebuke to Inge's success, Weales criticizes him for his "articulate self-awareness" (42)—another dig at the *de rigueur* pop-psychology of U.S. drama, circa late '50s and early '60s—and his "phallic romanticism" (47), a concept that Weales, Brustein and others equate with Inge's alleged sentimentality, soap opera sensibility and "sex-as-salvation" (46) happy endings. He finally dismisses Inge with an insult: "I could throw a handful of paper clips out of the window ... and hit a half-dozen ordinary people who have more life, more vitality, more originality, and more serious problems than the lonely, longing people who infest Inge plays" (44).

Harsh, yes. And patently unfair. Explicable only in the context of Weales' misreading, evident is his conclusion that "the prevailing message of the plays is that love is a solution to all social, economic, and psychological problems" (46). Weales accuses Inge of having "transferred the romantic-comedy ending to all of his plays" (46). Except Weales never accounts for Inge's con job on the "romantic-comedy ending." To claim that so-called "romantic-comedy" resolutions were used by Inge to reinforce "Broadway's prevailing belief that love conquers all" (46), Weales ignores the gendermandered, subversive decentering of socially engineered, culturally determined patterns of sex role behavior.

On the other hand, Inge's superficial but convincing romantic-comedy endings are not necessarily detrimental to the aesthetic integrity of his plays. The draft of *Picnic* Inge preferred, for example, *Summer Brave*, with its downbeat final act, was unquestionably improved when Inge, thanks to Joshua Logan's insistence (Voss, 129), resorted to the formulaic ending required of generic romance. Even so, Voss argues that, first, Inge's four major plays do "all show 'tamed' men, if by 'tamed' one means a willingness to seek solace or comfort in the kind of heterosexual love relationship usually associated with marriage" (183) and, secondly, that "it is unreasonable to imply that all drama is necessarily mediocre or trite if it portrays the human need for love or reinforces the institutions of marriage and family" (183). Ironically, Voss ends up making the point he intends to repudiate. Inge's plays *are* narrow, parochial and formulaic, but that does not mean they are any less powerful than other plays with more scope, depth or vision. Brustein's charge that Inge "merely changes his forms rather than his content" (57) is neither unreasonable nor particularly astute, and Brustein's comments about Inge's "simplistic view of life ... without heroism, wit, intelligence, or even true energy" (57), while not totally unfounded, are exactly the sort of rabbit punches Voss objects to. Perversely, after the cheap shots stop and the smoke of battle clears, the fact is, Inge's plays prove how lives held together by clichés *can* be dramatically rendered without the plays themselves being wrecked by the very clichés they purport to explode.

Brustein's other explanation as to why Inge was, in his opinion, so undeservedly popular on Broadway in the '50s is more salient and difficult to refute: "Despite its flirtation with the 'dangerous' subjects of modern drama (sex and violence), Inge's drama is in the end ameliorative" (57). That his plays are "ameliorative" alone in no way condemns them to the remainder rack of American drama, but to argue that this need to ameliorate troubled families relies on the notion that "whatever is dark and evil can be expunged by the comfort of a woman" (57) requires nuance to finesse constructively. Brustein complains that, in the "limited boundaries of Inge's moral and social perspectives" (56), the men must give up these "masculine" verities and succumb to the woman whose "job is to convert these rebels into domestic animals" (56). And while Voss correctly questions why these men should not seek out the solace of a woman, suggesting "Inge may have depicted resilience in marital life and family values because, as a lonely homosexual, he would have liked to have been able to believe in them" (182), Brustein's oversimplification of Inge's simplicity begs a much more complex question: Brustein acknowledges the gender roles inherent in male and female relationships, listing, for example, the qualities demanded of a healthy American male, circa 1950—"his aggressiveness, his promiscuity, his bravado, his contempt for soft virtues, and his narcissistic pride in his body" (56)—but Brustein fails to appreciate how Inge exploits and subverts these stereotypical gender models of behavior for dramatic effect.

In essence, Brustein's observations may be right, for the most part, but he draws the wrong conclusions. The genius of Inge lies in his gendermandered characters, the role-reversals that bring into question the nature of gender and of society's discomfort when such distinctions are blurred.

To consider Brustein's essay even a left-handed compliment is charitable: he celebrates Inge's grubby realism while grousing about his sentimentalism and, of all things, the feminization of his male characters. But Brustein cannot be so easily dismissed, in Voss's words, as "shrewdly building upon a few insights that he stretched for maximum effect" (183) or whose essay deserves consideration only as an exercise in "the rhetorical force of plausibility linked with good writing style" (182). Actually Voss, in his summary of that critical skirmish of 1958 (the combat metaphors are Voss's) is as unfair to Brustein as he thinks Brustein is to Inge. Brustein claims Inge's work is modest, even mediocre. A reasoned assessment of Inge's work up to that point—regardless of the financial success of the Broadway hits—supports Brustein's opinion. But Voss, having accurately summarized Brustein's position, still feels compelled, somewhat untenably, to defend Inge's work, not for his radical reevaluation of the socially reinforced gender roles circa 1950, but as a wholesome example of solid American theater depicting heartland families living real lives.

Brustein's point, as Voss describes it, is that "Inge's four successful plays are 'preachy' endorsements of family life and love in which dominating females tame the freedom and spirit of the leading men though a kind of symbolic emasculation" (181). At the risk of sacrificing his own critical integrity, Voss cannot claim that Brustein is wrong, and he even agrees that "Inge's plays could be viewed as Brustein saw them" (182). But Voss's observation that Brustein's criticism could be applied to "the audiences and critics who liked the plays" (182), while irrelevant to Brustein's theme, is not totally beside the point. Brustein, aware that pandering to audiences is anathema to progressive art, is attacking the sentimentalism and melodramatic pap dominating the productions of the '50s as well as the sensibility of the theater-going public that supported the industry. In a theater business dominated by musicals, farces, and what now literally might be called "straight" plays in the style of Miller and Williams, many critics of the late '50s, including Brustein, were hungry for a new kind of drama, and Inge, a representative (or scapegoat) of the prevailing style, was, as Voss rightly points out, an easy target, "a vulnerable playwright who did not know how to bob and weave" (182). But Albee had yet to surface from the shadows off Broadway, "the nihilists" (Brustein, 57) Beckett and Ionesco were enigmatic antitheater renegades, and English upstarts Osborne and Pinter were still basically unknown, so in this context, Inge, as Brustein's "bullseye" (182), was more a victim of the times and the expectations of the critical elite than an easy mark, as Voss implies, off of whom Brustein hoped to score career points.

Voss tries to deflect what he considers Brustein's "punch" (182) by personalizing the attack, referring disdainfully to Brustein by repeating the *Harper's* blurb: "a fast-rising young drama critic" (180–81, 182, 183). Of course, Inge never made any pretense of being avant-garde, but by Voss's own assessment Inge did want to be taken seriously. The fact that "Brustein could not have known how important the widespread acceptance of his word was to Inge's fragile equilibrium" (182) should not detract from Brustein's critique. Voss's tetchiness seems to mirror the response from Inge's friends, who, instead of engaging in what could have been an enriching debate, circled the wagons. In a low moment of clashing personalities clouding critical discourse, Voss recalls how Inge's friend William Gibson wrote to *Harper's* to ask why the magazine was not "publishing his article, written in the last two minutes, on Brustein's life's work" (183). This kind of defensive banter and slinging insults, while understandable, does little to advance an otherwise important dialog. That a letter writer in the same issue wonders how she could "ever have enjoyed the four plays so much" (183) again hardly qualifies as a defense.

Voss soon, however, settles down "to assess these plays, as well as Brustein's judgments, anew" (183). What follows is a serious rebuttal of Brustein's complaints, but the more Voss argues the intrinsic qualities of Inge's four famous plays, the more he seems to verify Brustein's main point: that those plays do deal with family relationships in parochial settings that "constitute a kind of aesthetic isolationism" (Brustein, 57) limiting Inge's vision, and that the leading men all do succumb to the wiles, the will or the charms of the corresponding women characters. Voss concludes that in his plays Inge "dealt with universals of human experience, as all good dramatists do" (183). The problem is the aesthetic discrepancy between the desire to write about grand themes and the ability of the writer to execute his vision. Certainly all playwrights strive to portray the grimy grandeur of human experience, but some do so more successfully than others. The question, in the case of Inge, is not whether he wanted to confront universal values but how close his vision came to being realized through his chosen medium: drama.

It is this issue of Inge's aesthetic worth as an artist that concerns Stanley Kauffmann in his invidious 1966 essay in the *New York Times*, "Homosexual Drama and Its Disguises." In Kauffmann's opinion, Inge's homosexuality, instead of being considered a positive quality that informed his understanding of conflicted characters, is instead a negative trait that explains why critics like Brustein think Inge's depictions of family strife ring patently false. Kauffmann believes that "postwar American drama presents a badly distorted picture of American women, marriage, and society" (Kauffmann, 1). He ostensibly argues that society has forced

Doc (Wallace Ford) mothers Marie (Peggy Nelson) in the Theatre Guild production of *Come Back, Little Sheba* (1950) directed by Daniel Mann at the Booth Theatre. Like Inge's other gendermandered males, Doc denies his maternal essence by resisting his innate femininity, but his domesticity is clearly signaled by his apron and business in the kitchen. His overinvestment in Marie's purity to atone for his guilty conscience blinds him to the truth: his dysfunctional marriage and alcoholism result from his inability to accept his natural, subordinate, sterotypically submissive role in his relationship with Lola. (Photofest)

homosexual playwrights to "masquerade" (1), complains that he is "weary of disguised homosexual influence" (1), and petitions for the honest acceptance of homosexual writers so they might be allowed to render their particular experience into drama. The implication, of course, is that homosexuals are incapable of creating plausible straight characters, as if to write about murder one must be a murderer.

James Fisher, in a 1995 essay entitled "The Angels of Fructification: Tennessee Williams, Tony Kushner, and Images of Homosexuality on the American Stage," confronts Kauffmann's contention that homosexuals cannot escape their homosexuality and are thus, because of their sexuality, unable artistically to depict any experience outside their supposedly hermetic gay existence. Fisher writes: "Kauffmann implies that homosexual writers have no right to write about anything but gay characters— an attitude which would logically imply that men are unable to write about women and vice versa" (Fisher). To further counter Kauffmann's assertion, Fisher quotes Albee's response to this seemingly self-evident absurdity: "Albee firmly refutes the idea that he, or Williams, employs transference in his plays: 'Tennessee never did that, and I can't think of any self-respecting worthwhile writer who would do that sort of thing. It's beneath contempt to suggest it, and it's beneath contempt to do it'" (Fisher).

The key to Kauffmann's screed is the way he mischaracterizes, through a distorted lens of undiluted bigotry, "the materials of the three writers" (1)—obviously Williams, Inge and Albee—that happen, bizarrely, to include "the viciousness toward women, the lurid violence that seems a sublimation of social hatreds, the transvestite sexual exhibitionism" (1). Such prejudice might also explain Brustein's facetious description of Inge as "the first spokesman for a matriarchal America" (Brustein, 57). It is nevertheless hard to recognize Inge's work in much of Kauffmann's essay, as what he considers to be most "culturally risky" (Kauffmann, 1) about "these people" (1) suffering from "this one neurosis" (1) is the camp influence, the "adulation of sheer style" (1), which he considers "an instrument of revenge on the main body of society" (1), sacrificing "social relevance" (1) to promote a "vindictiveness toward the society that constricts and, theatrically, discriminates against them" (1). Surely, Kauffmann does not have in mind Inge's early plays, at least as far as they illustrate Kauffmann's complaint about plays that "exalt style, manner, surface" (1), but given his reactions to *Splendor in the Grass* and *Where's Daddy?*, Kauffmann definitely counts Inge as one in the triumvirate of unholy gay writers who transformed Kauffmann's critical exasperation into cultural paranoia. More pertinent, though, to Inge's aesthetics is Kauffmann's complaint that "the marital quarrels are usually homosexual quarrels with one of the pair in costume" (1). Though he is undoubtedly referring to Albee's *Who's Afraid of Virginia Woolf?* (1962), Kauffmann, had he not perhaps been so obstinately blinded by his prejudice, might have used his analysis to illustrate the gendermandering Inge applies to otherwise conventional characters, so that, in this fresh context, Kauffmann's comments, instead of serving as a pretext for his outlandish discrimination, might have illuminated Inge's incisive sympathy for characters who, although they appear "admirably 'normal'" (1), live uncomfortably within their prescribed gender distinctions.

Curiously, Voss defends Inge from both Brustein and Kauffmann by suggesting "[n]ot one of the Inge women ... has any more choice in the role she is expected to play than the man has" (253). Inadvertently, Voss here reaffirms the very noxious gender-typing Inge so dexterously tries in his plays to subvert. The implication is that fixed social, symbolic, ontological and semiotic hierarchies existentially determine Inge's men and women. In fact, Kauffmann seems to make the point that Voss dodges: Inge's secret life was germane to his forte: creating fluid characters at play, unfixed from their sexual differentiation, resisting the pigeonholes society attempts to assign them.

Voss is not alone in underestimating Inge's ironical treatment of women. Voss openly confesses his sympathy, as a fellow Kansan, for the people populating Inge's plays, and it may be his identifying so personally with Inge's characters that leads Voss to accept at face value the roles assumed by Inge's characters. As Linda Ben-Zvi points out in her review of his book, Voss considers Inge a playwright whose works are "critiques of America in the 30s and 40s: lost, troubled, seeking love and security that constantly elude them" (357). Taking on a stereotypical identity to fit comfortably within a social milieu is, of course, one way a person, displaced by circumstances—whether from economic hardship, geopolitical strife, a natural disaster or sheer bad luck—attains solace in a strange and complex, often foreign world. Susan Koprince, in her article "Childless Women in the Plays of William Inge," agrees:

> Inge's major plays are especially revealing of the 1950s in that they emphasize the traditional roles of mothers, as well as the power that mothers are capable of wielding within a family. Indeed, critics such as Ralph Voss and R. Baird Shuman have pointed to the central importance of mother figures in Inge's dramas. [Many of Inge's female] characters generally fit the negative stereotype of childless women that prevailed during the post-war era, a stereotype which, to some extent, still persists today [251].

Voss tends to reinforce Koprince's argument. He writes, "During the time of his greatest success, Inge's work seemed only to endorse heterosexual marriage and traditional families" (252). This, Voss claims, is the "crux" of Brustein's "disastrous criticism" (252). He goes on to defend Inge for promoting conventional families—exactly Brustein's complaint, and indirectly Kauffmann's, as the latter felt Inge's family portraits were distorted by his masquerading. Both critics were, in essence, objecting to Inge's faulty use of plausibility in his plays. And, in effect, Voss agrees with Brustein and Kauffmann while attempting to defend Inge for promoting conventional families, "endorsing them by a kind of default" (253) in an act of "covert capitulation" (252). Voss, rightly, never moralizes, neither condemning nor condoning Inge's homosexuality, but he does argue that Inge's sexuality shaped his perspective, providing him with a "unique vantage point" (253).

The problem with Voss's position vis-à-vis Inge's depiction of "traditional families" is that, from a slightly more skewed perspective, Inge's families are not so traditional after all. While they appear to take on the stereotypical roles the communities expect them to settle into, Inge's most dynamic characters actually refuse their cookie-cutter roles, resisting the two-dimensional patterns of sexual codification Brustein and Kauffmann complain about, and Voss justifies, and emerge as gendermandered, free-floating agents of subversion.

3
Major Works
Come Back, Little Sheba; Picnic; Bus Stop; The Dark at the Top of the Stairs; Splendor in the Grass

In his later plays, Inge's (mis)adventures in Freudian psychotherapy tend to weaken the dramatic effectiveness of the situations, especially when he allows the theories to dictate behavior, denying his characters the existential freedom necessary for dramatic truth to emerge from their actions. But in his early plays, Inge often uses Freudian paradigms as tools to organize the narrative structure and to sustain the dramatic drive toward the resolution of central conflicts within the text—a technique especially beneficial in a play as carefully designed around conflicting motives as *Come Back, Little Sheba*. And to accommodate these contrasting urges, Inge also borrows from Hegel the structural patterns contained in a typical Hegelian dialectic, which, in the case of *Come Back, Little Sheba*, help explain how Inge manages to drive the conflict between Lola and Doc forward through a diachronic narrative. Hegel's dialectic consists of two opposing forces—a thesis and an antithesis—held in opposition, each struggling for dominance: both eventually destroy the negative aspects of each other and recombine the remaining positive qualities into a resolution or synthesis. The synthesis then splits into opposing forces that posit a second dialectic that will again resolve in another synthesis and so on. This, concludes Hegel, explains historical progress toward an ultimate final absolute synthesis in which all struggle ceases at the point of perfection.

Freud, too, is concerned with motivational drives, the primary impetus in his assessment being desire, or undifferentiated will. Each individual manifests its "self" through a reification of the subconscious urge for satisfaction experienced at a primordial level existing beyond the reach of conscious intellectual understanding. The primary drive people strive to organize and express as self—or ego—Freud calls libido, the emotional craving prompting human activity. An individual in a civilized society, instead of acting spontaneously to satisfy these urges at primitive levels of sex and violence, learns to channel the will, seeking satisfaction in what Freud calls aim-inhibited love. This conditionally learned inhibition and the resulting sublimation allow a person to direct psychic energy into activity that is more socially acceptable, useful or regarded as higher on the cultural or moral scale. Thus, in *Come Back, Little Sheba*, Inge incorporates a sound philosophical Hegelian dialectic for his dramatic structure, while from Freud he borrows an equally grounded psychological impetus inducing his characters to act out their surface lives based on their unconscious primal desires.

But even with the Freudian and Hegelian overlays, the virtue of the play lies in the way Inge details the lives of people cast into stereotypical roles they cannot maintain. The present action is fairly static, compared to the background story. Doc Delaney had been a promising pre-med student forced to quit school when he and his then girlfriend Lola, "Beauty Queen of the senior class" (14), found out she was pregnant as a result of their first sexual tryst. Because they could not visit a real doctor, who might reveal the truth—that they were forced to marry because of the unplanned pregnancy—the baby died during childbirth and Lola was left infertile. Doc became a chiropractor instead of a medical doctor and a bad drunk prone to violent binges, while Lola turned from the prettiest and most popular girl in school into a slatternly, childless, overweight and sentimental housewife. Accentuating the misery in their lives, the boarder, Marie, plans to marry Bruce, her long-term boyfriend now living in Chicago, but meanwhile she satisfies her carnal cravings with Turk, a local high school hunk. The action on the day of the play centers on the receipt of a telegram from Bruce announcing his imminent visit, an event that will precipitate Marie's breaking off her relationship with Turk. When Doc finds out that Marie is sleeping with Turk, and realizes she is not the icon of purity he had always believed, the discovery sends him first to the bottle, then into a violent assault on Lola, landing him in City Hospital before he returns home to reconcile with his wife.

While their superficial life is built around a routine marriage, Lola and Doc find themselves at odds with both their social roles and their private expectations. This oppositional positing of conflicting desires is obvious in the contrasting motives of Doc and Lola. Both Doc and Lola display public lives that run counter to their natural inclinations. For instance, Doc appears pragmatic, but his cynicism is a product of his unreformed romanticism. Lola seems like a romanticist, but she is actually a hard-nosed realist bent on survival. It is within this ironic masking that the action of the drama unfolds.

The role reversal—or gendermandering—is evident in the first scene, developed through a series of ironical exchanges between Doc and Marie, then Doc and Lola, but the discrepancy linking Lola's and Doc's imaginative anemia to Marie's vitality begins visually even before the action begins. The stage is divided into two rooms, marking the thematic divide between the Delaney's expectations and the reality in which they live. The time of the play is *"late spring"* (Inge, *Four Plays*, 5), a time of renewal, rebirth and resurrection, but the description of the Delaney's house, where the living room is *"decorated with cheap pretense at niceness and respectability"* (5) and the woodwork in the kitchen is *"dark and grimy"* (5), echoes Eliot's notion of April in *The Wasteland* as "the cruelest month" (Eliot, *Wasteland*, 1,161), offering no regeneration, no new beginnings, no salvation. Even the fact that the house is situated in a *"semi-respectable neighborhood"* (Inge, *Four Plays*, 5) indicates Doc's fallen social status, from his potential position in the community as a medical doctor ripe with financial success and professional respect to a frustrated, dry-drunk chiropractor whose life is *"cluttered and even dirty"* (5).

The scene opens with Marie, wearing *"a sheer negligee and smart, feathery mules"* (6) meeting Doc in the kitchen. Doc, who *"tucks towel into vest for apron"* (5), is solicitously maternal, asking Marie if he can prepare her breakfast. Marie's seemingly innocuous observation actually makes the point: "Most husbands would never think of getting their own breakfast" (6). For Doc, their morning encounter takes on the character of a date, as he suggests, "sit here and I'll serve you your breakfast now, Marie, and we can eat it together, the two of us" (6–7), but Marie, the calculating coquette *"dancing away from him"* (7), spoils the moment by opting instead to bathe. As Doc contemplates his ideal—Marie as the virgin maiden embodiment of purity and innocent youth—Lola interrupts him. Dressed in a *"lumpy kimono [and] dirty comfies"* (7), she clearly intrudes on his reverie, replacing, as it were, Marie's *"cheerfulness"* (5) with *"a morning expression of disillusionment"* (7). Lola also acknowledges Doc's apparent appropriation of the feminine role in the household dynamic: "I oughta be getting your breakfast, Doc, instead of you gettin' mine" (7).

The role reversal indicates disorder in their lives. The implication is clear: their relationship is unnatural. Lola, almost regretfully, admits that as long as Doc stays sober she will "know how you're gonna be when you come home" (9), as if Doc's domestication has thrown the natural order of things off-balance. In this context, his struggle against alcoholism is a struggle against his savage self, his innate virility, often manifested in animal-like violence, his drunkenness merely defiance in the face of a world willing to crush his spirit for the sake of good behavior. Lola, sexually frustrated and spiritually disappointed with the predictability of their mundane existence, recognizes this too, and even though he threatens her with physical harm, she understands how Doc's climatic drunken rage unleashes the only honest passion in the play. The catharsis after Doc's collapse is clearly sexual, and for a brief moment drains them both of their pent-up energy. By the time Doc has "recovered," Lola has reassumed her proper role in the kitchen and, as if she has been restored to her proper stereotypically expected role as Doc's wife, offers to cook him breakfast, thus correcting in the final scene the disjunction that began in the opening sequence when Doc opened the play preparing breakfast for the two women.

Doc, a reformed sinner and dry drunk demanding purity in a world he sees as corrupted by venal excesses, suffers a paralytic guilt about his past. He is bitter that his first sexual episode with Lola led to her pregnancy, bitter because a midwife botched the delivery and the baby died in childbirth, and bitter that he lost his inheritance, had to give up medical school and instead became a chiropractor and an alcoholic. So his idealizing Marie—whose name signifying the Madonna takes on existential meaning for him—stems from this desire for expiation. When he sees her drawing, he wants her to "paint lots of pretty pictures" (6) and recalls a painting his mother kept over her mantelpiece that "[m]ade you feel religious just to look at it" (6). Marie's saying a bath makes her feel "fresh and clean" (7) has a spiritual significance for Doc, denoting his desire for a clear conscience. Inge's directing note describes Doc's reaction to Lola's telling him about Marie kissing Turk as "*[a]n angry denial*" (10), and Doc admits he wants to believe that she is "clean and decent" (11), as if making out with Turk would disqualify her morally from any position of virtue in his ethology. He views Marie's drawing Turk in the living room as unseemly, complaining, "It's not right" (25). Of course he approves of Bruce because Bruce is absent and Doc can assign him a virtuous character no matter how phantom those attributes might prove. His choice of music is Schubert's *Ave Maria*, which, according to Inge's note, gives him a sense of "ethereal beauty" (29), allowing him to transcend his corporeal corruption and aspire to a purity of spirit, what Inge describes as "*an ideal beauty*" (29). In a neatly deflating dramatic moment, drawing a sharp contrast between the ideal world Doc longs for and the loamy truth of his fleshy existence, the spell aroused by *Ave Maria* is broken by Lola, who interrupts him, saying she is "pooped" (29), a word which Doc objects to because it sounds scatological and "vulgar" (29).

Doc has set himself up for disappointment by overinvesting his faith in Marie, who, even if she were virginal and clean and decent, could never live up to his expectations of innocence. His final disillusionment comes when he hears Turk laughing in Marie's bedroom. Inge's note reads: "*It sounds like the laugh of sated Bacchus*" (44). Then he discovers Turk sneaking out of Marie's bedroom, and his spiritual and physical collapse is complete. He takes the whiskey and goes on a binge. Drunk and blinded by self-pity, he reverses his absolutist morality, calling Lola and Marie "a couple of sluts" (56) and bitterly claiming that Marie will probably have to marry Bruce, "the poor bastard" (56), the same way he was forced to marry Lola. His either-or, virgin-or-whore taxonomy mirrors the moral dialectic driving the key conflict in the play, and the resolution—the synthesis—can only occur once Doc realizes the truth about people, that they are neither all good nor all bad but are merely human. His "slip" (59) and the recognition of his own moral failings prompt him to ask Lola for forgiveness, a meliorative shift from years of blaming her. The "sad-looking old bird dog" (68) that he has become is still capable of love, and more importantly, of being loved.

Doc, a dysfunctional Dionysian, craves the Apollonian world of strength and order and reason that he expects, and to which he assumes he is culturally entitled. He desperately clings to images, to his Apollonian mask of decency, as he suffers the dark destructive urges of his Dionysian desire. He dotes on Marie's pretense of innocence, describing her as "clean and decent" (10), "clean and fresh" (11), one of the "nice girls" (11) who represent for him a simple hunky-dory world in which the sordid grit of existence is deferred, and appearance is the only necessary truth. His struggle is to maintain this chimera of convention, where people assume the roles he assigns them according to what he believes is the proper social codes of normality so that he can locate and define himself within this psychotheatrical *mise en scene*. To maintain an identity, to project clarity and reason and order—trademarks of the Apollonian male—he must, of course, stay sober, but his inclination is to drink, to destroy his carefully constructed ego-identity, to dissolve the established boundaries of personality in a Dionysian revelry of the senses, to lose himself in the unconscious, wiping out memory of the constantly reconstructed self. In a revealing allusion, Doc is entranced by Schubert, the syphilitic Classicist who mastered the Apollonian technique of structuring the inchoate nature of passion into the geometry of music. Doc envies the composer's ability to arrange and objectify his feelings, but to do so is a trick of the will well beyond Doc's experience; he is best at cheap card tricks, using the same sleight-of-hand by which he hoodwinks himself, half-believing in a world of his own projection.

Lola has also invested her desire in Marie, only for her Marie represents the sexual vitality and youthful opportunities that Lola was denied when she was a schoolgirl. Lola was, after all, "the 'it' girl" (31) who won the Charleston contest at the homecoming dance and had lots of boys calling her for dates. But she recalls how her strict, unforgiving father would punish her for "holding hands" (14) and confesses to Marie that she "never had any fun" (14) until she met Doc, having "saved all her dates" (31) for him. Whereas Doc wants to forget the past, Lola is steeped in it, living vicariously through Marie's exploits with Turk and Bruce and the wistful memories she conjures up in her attempts at intimacy with Doc. He, of course, dismisses her reminiscing, telling her, "you've got to forget those things" (32). His advice is, "If you can't forget the past, you stay in it forever and never get out" (33). But for her, their dating was "the happiest time of our lives" (32). This contrasting approach to events in their past illustrates the fissure in their marriage, Lola relishing the romance of "a nice spring" (32) and Doc regretting all he had to give up because of Lola's pregnancy. But as if to qualify her memories, she repeats the refrain "those years vanished—vanished into thin air" (32), using the same phrase to describe the disappearance of Little Sheba as well as the brief life of the blooms on the lilacs she places on the dinner table she sets for Bruce and Marie.

Her longing to recover her vanished years, however, waxes more pathetic than poetic. Her attempt to flirt with the postman deteriorates into a maudlin complaint laced with painfully personal details about Doc's alcoholism that only embarrasses the postman. Her yearning for romance and a return to that special spring of her youth is embodied in her dog, aptly called Little Sheba, whose name alone is meant to evoke the mysteries of the Middle East during the reign of King Solomon, but, like Lola's imagination, the diminutive "little" signifies the reality of her situation. When she pitifully calls for the dog from her porch, she tacitly acknowledges what she and Doc must both confront: the smartest boy in class and the prettiest girl in school were never guaranteed the cozy future they thought they deserved, and there is no going back. In her dream at the end of the play, she seems finally to have accepted the brutal truth, finding Little Sheba—the dreams of her youth—dead and "smeared with mud" (69). Her resignation, however, is not made in despair. Even though she admits that Little Sheba is not coming back, the fact that she is "not going to call her anymore" (69) indicates a reality check, a chance to see the world as it is so that she might begin to deal with the facts instead of wasting her life mired in fantasy.

Perversely, Lola is the one who represents Apollonian ideals of common sense, sobriety, and restraint, but who longs to release herself to her passions. In a significant contrast to Doc's appreciation of Schubert, Lola's favorite radio show is the hokey "Taboo," "where pagan spirits hold sway" (22) and which offers its listeners "temptation" (22) and enjoins them to "leave behind your routine ... day-to-day existence ... and follow me where pagan spirits hold sway ... a moon-enchanted isle" (22). "Taboo" is a paean to Bacchus, celebrating the primitive Dionysian rhythms of the deep unconscious. She wants what Doc fears. For all her Apollonian posing, all her frantic, if pathetic, attempts to order the potential chaos in her marriage, she is repressing an intense desire to escape the rigid routine of her mundane life. A former beauty queen, according to Inge, "*She is by nature coy and kittenish*" (14). But she is also no longer capable of having children; thus divorced from her nature, as both an object of desire and as a procreative mother, she craves a return to her mythical essence, to surrender to her dreams, to dissolve her false Apollonian identity in a Dionysian delirium. Desperate for sensual stimulation—to counter her chin-up optimism, her sterility, her forced moral fortitude—she flirts with the postman, the milkman and Turk and resorts to vicarious voyeuristic fantasies by spying on Marie. She is so intense, so "dazed" (23) with Turk that, when he's posing in his track suit, "all his muscles in place" (23), he complains that "she makes me feel naked" (24). Her interest in Marie and Turk borders on prurient. Likewise, her misadventure with the milkman is nothing but an inane ploy for attention. If Doc wants to transcend his desire, a victim of excess, Lola wants to embrace desire, to give herself over to it, a victim of denial.

The atypical characters—Lola and Doc—are surrounded by what at first appear to be conventional types operating as devices by which Doc and Lola measure their alienation—indicative of how divorced they are from themselves and from the society that defines them: Turk, the horny dumb jock; Marie, the manipulative vamp-slash-ingénue; Bruce, the cuckolded "marrying type" (50). These characters, however, do not necessarily fit so comfortably into these neat, two-dimensional stereotypes. The gendermandering is most evident in Turk. For all his superficial vitality, he is a feminized "male model" (23). His name implies Orientalism—exotic, violent and sexually alluring—but he is merely posturing, complaining that he "can't hold this pose very long" (24). Even Lola feels uncomfortable with his gender transposition. When she muses aloud that "The women pose naked but the men don't" (23), Inge's note reads: "*This strikes her as a startling inconsistency*" (23). Marie's last name, after all, is Buckholder, an allusion rich with ambiguity but clearly a reference not only to her sexual prowess but also to the emasculating power she exercises over the men in her life. She allows Turk to talk tough, like his bragging that he "can throw that old javelin any old time, *any* old time" (41), but Marie calls the shots, deciding when, where and, most likely how they will have sex. In fact, Turk's posing with his javelin is just that: posturing, displaying a surrogate phallus. Marie bosses Turk as if he were a puppy, instructing him to "change in there" (22), "get back in your corner" (24), and "get your clothes on" (26). Likewise, without question she has Bruce, her source of freedom, income and security, wrapped around her finger—flashing her engagement ring to prove it—and so suffers no essential loss of power as she feigns deference to him.

If the oppositional Freudian drives in this decidedly Hegelian model thrust the narrative through to its climax, the synthesis implied by this dialectic of desire collapses in Marie. She cannot fulfill Doc's aspirations for purity any more than she can release Lola from her entrenched reliance on living in the past. Her decision to move to Cincinnati and marry Bruce, however, is liberating for Doc and Lola, forcing them to reassess their relationship. Doc's release from his guilt and resentment and Lola's letting go of her impossible romantic expectations imply a restorative synthesis in which they both emerge from their incapacitating delusions back into reality. Juhnke, for example, interprets Lola's dream not as a castration fantasy but as an indication "that Lola does not want a tamed husband, but one who is physically active and very powerful" (106). The other particulars of Lola's dream support Juhnke's reading, suggesting not the neutering, passive capitulation of Doc that Brustein reads into it but a reawakening of the couple's sexual appetite. The javelin Doc hurls into the air, a pointedly phallic Freudian allusion, causes rain, an image classically associated with feminine fertility. Given its context, this fairly crude metaphor can be understood as a nurturing, mutually satisfying reinvestment in their life together. However, the restoration of a balance of power in their relationship also implies a role reversal in which Lola, thanks to her epiphany, assumes a dominant position even as she agrees to play the part of the deferential wife, just as Doc pretends to his position of authority while submitting to Lola's control. The last line, in that case, is even less subtle, when Lola tells Doc, "I'll fix your eggs" (69).

Picnic also relies on gendermandering for its dramatic intensity, exposing characters acting counter to their expected stereotypical sex roles. The play depicts the events before, during and after the annual Labor Day picnic in a small Kansas town. Mrs. Potts, whose marriage was annulled after she eloped, lives with her mother next door to Flo Owens, another husbandless woman, and her two daughters, Millie and Madge. Millie is a bookish tomboy living in the shadow of her older, beautiful sister, queen of the Neewollah Festival. Other women who, significantly, live without intimate men in their lives include three schoolteachers: Rosemary Sydney, Irma Kronkite and Christine Schoenwalder, although Rosemary occasionally dates a local businessman, Howard Bevans. The townsfolk's routine is disrupted by the arrival of Hal Carter, a drifter looking for an old college fraternity buddy, Alan Seymour, the son of a prominent and wealthy banker who is currently "steady" (77) with Madge. After Hal and Alan are reunited, Mrs. Potts invites Hal to go to the picnic that night as an "escort for Millie" (97).

Later that afternoon, Millie shows up dressed for the picnic looking "*quite attractive*" (102), strangely (and suddenly) attuned to her sexuality. (Not so cryptically, her opening line in Act Two is, "Don't quit now, Ernie!" [102]). Soon Rosemary, Howard, Hal and Madge are dancing in the twilight. Rosemary, slightly drunk and jealous of Hal's mesmeric interest in Madge, makes a fool of herself by her rude sexual advances on Hal, and in a fit of self-loathing and self-incriminating indignation, she begins insulting him, trying to humiliate him, until Howard, embarrassed for them both, forcefully stops her. Feeling abandoned in the heat of the argument, Millie drinks Howard's whisky. Discovered sickly drunk by Flo, Millie soon recovers enough to sally on to the party. Once alone, instead of following the others, Hal kisses Madge and tells her, "We're not goin' on no goddamn picnic" (127).

The next morning, Flo and the others realize what Madge has done. Alan, incensed, reports Hal to the police, falsely claiming that Hal has stolen his car. While Rosemary leaves to marry her reluctant sweetheart Howard, Hal shows up to ask Madge to run off with him to Tulsa. At first she refuses, and retreats into the house in tears. But after Alan informs Flo that he is going back to school and leaves without saying goodbye to Madge, Madge appears on the porch with her suitcase and tells her mother she is going to follow Hal.

As in *Come Back, Little Sheba*, the peripheral characters—men-less women and post-adolescent punks—seem at first to devolve into fairly predictable types. Flo is a widow whose husband, after her second child was born, preferred "his wild friends at the roadhouse" (83) to home life. She enters the play like a mother hen protecting her chicks, emerging from within the house "*as though she had sensed Hal's presence*" (78). But with all her matronly concern for her daughters—she is, after all, obsessed with Madge marrying the respectable if boring Alan—Inge notes a "*certain*

Hal (Ralph Meeker) as the archetypal leather boy in *Picnic* (1953). Ostensibly representing an assertive masculinity, Hal actually exhibits behavior typically associated with acquiescent females deferring within certain, often requisite social codes, to male authority. As an object of desire for both gay men and heterosexual women, he also embodies the sort of alpha male swagger straight men identify with, but under Inge's withering gendermandering Hal's exaggerated machismo wilts and his hunky confidence, when challenged by Rosemary, Madge and Mrs. Potts, is exposed as mere defensive posturing. (Photofest)

hardness in her character" (78) that he attributes to 10 years of serving as "*both father and mother to her girls*" (78). It may well be her androgyny that causes her conflicted nature. Having long ago given up sexual interest in men, she now slakes her curiosity through prurient prying into her daughter's affair with Alan. She of all the women is the least interested in Hal and therefore perhaps the most threatened by him. Nor does she understand Madge's reluctance to accept her own beauty, yet she worries that Madge is dissatisfied with Alan's lovemaking. Disparagingly, she admits, "a woman is weak to begin with" (83), but at the end of the day Flo is a direct, independent, no-nonsense survivor. It is no coincidence that Hal ambiguously asks both Madge and Flo "is it all right if I start a fire?" (84), an allusion, of course, to the true source of Flo's discomfort: not the actual trash fire but the simmering passion in Madge that is he about to ignite.

The flip side of Flo, Mrs. Potts, another strong-willed, independent widow, remains very much in line with the behavior expected from a spinster whose mother annulled her marriage on the day she eloped. Mrs. Potts is mischievous, flirtatious, less quick to judge as Flo and so naturally more sympathetic to Madge's irrational urges. Significantly, Madge escapes Mrs. Potts' destiny: she will not be the daughter who sacrifices her life to remain home to look after her "aged and invalid mother" (75). Having no daughters at risk, Mrs. Potts enjoys Hal's company, saying, "I like a man to feel comfortable" (109)—a remark not as subservient as it sounds, given her aggressiveness in pursuing her little guilty pleasures. She defends Hal against the others, even offering to divert the police when they come for him, hinting, "I'll know how to take care of them" (143). After complaining, "old lady like me, if she wants any attention from the young men on a picnic, all she can do is bake a cake" (107), she quickly abandons her pessimism when the party starts: "I can't stay in the kitchen while there's dancing" (118). It is no coincidence that Inge gave Mrs. Potts the two key thematic lines in the play, the first when she corrects Flo's paranoid vision of the picnic, telling her, "we plan picnics just to give ourselves an excuse—to let something thrilling happen in our lives" (107), the second when she tells Flo that Hal "reminded me there was a man in the house, and it seemed good ... reminded me ... I'm a woman, and that seemed good, too" (145).

In contrast, Rosemary, the reserved schoolmarm, goes native. She explodes her teacher's college, prim-and-proper front and reverts to a savage stalking her prey. Her helplessness is ironical and oxymoronic, her effectiveness proved by Howard's capitulation. She pulls out all the stops—sex, guilt, noblesse oblige—and, remarkably—extraordinarily—she convinces him to marry her. But the implausibility at that moment of

Howard's ever again becoming an authentic person obliterates any cathartic consideration for her, as her sacrificing so much self-respect just to land a cad like Howard irreparably diminishes her draw as a sympathetic character.

Rosemary's hidden, passionate life corrupts her, but in this she is no less predictable than the other women around her. Irma and Christine are vain, materialistic, trendy, but in the end they prove to be good sports. Irma, comfortable following her passions, pointedly tells the others, "I'm not going to be a slave all my life" (96), while Christine slyly refers to Irma's "wicked times" (96). Rosemary, recognizing how fast she is slipping out of the game her friends still enjoy, panics, redirecting her self-loathing first at Hal, then in a desperate moment of self-pity, she resorts to emotional blackmail, effectively neutering Howard—who, after all, only wants her for arm candy, to enhance his chances for a promotion, confessing, "folks'd rather do business with a married man!" (139).

Inexplicably, Joanna Rapf, in "The Fear of Loving: Daniel Taradash on His Adaptation of *Picnic*," suggests that the "spinster schoolteacher, Rosemary, is proud of her independence but hysterically throws it away when faced with the prospect of growing old alone" (3). Her use of the word hysterically, of course, must have been carefully chosen (one can only suspect), since its root refers to the womb, and its usage specifically to disturbances of the womb, implying that Rosemary's decisions are shaped by the emotional whims systemic to the childless woman syndrome Koprince outlines in her essay. The idea that she is "proud of her independence" is specious too. Rosemary, like the majority of Inge's most engaging characters, is faking. She tries to establish her own independent, albeit sympathetic context, identifying herself as "an old-maid schoolteacher" (Inge, *Four Plays*, 85, 109) prone to bragging about fictional proposals of marriage, including one "from that man I met at the high school picnic last spring" (85). To cover for her inability to secure a husband, or even a significant other, she claims, "I don't have time for any of 'em when they start gettin' serious on me" (85). She is quick to suggest that because she has lived "this long without a man" (85) she has lost the need for a husband. When Flo asks her about Howard, she lies again, describing him as "just a friend-boy—not a boy friend" (85). These are existential evasions—Sartre's *mauvais foi*. The truth is, of course, that she is not a self-actualized spinster "proud of her independence" but a desperate woman frantic about losing the one thing she still has going for her: sex, and the ebbing but not quite finished passion to provoke a leeching sap like Howard to provide her a veneer of respectability. At the same time she professes to cherish her spinster's independence, she is rubbing in moisturizing cream, checking out Hal, and hypocritically complaining about his "parading around, naked as an Indian" (87) while training Millie in the art of making boys "take notice" (86).

Rosemary's conflict develops between the schoolmarm stereotype she broadcasts—and others expect—and the yearning of her spirit "to drive into the sunset" (125). Even Howard recognizes Rosemary's frustrated spirit, calling her "a poet" (114), but he too would rather deal with her conventional mask instead of the more complex woman behind it. Likewise, he prefers to define himself as a stereotype, adhering to preconceived notions that accompany the self-limiting label of businessman, thus relieving himself of any existential responsibility for creating a self outside of community expectations. He attributes, for instance, his awkwardness on the dance floor to the fact that he is a "businessman" (120), as if that explained his self-consciousness, his lack of passion and inability to relax. Later, when Rosemary dismisses his concern that Flo might be suspicious of their lovemaking, he tells her, "A businessman's gotta be careful of talk. And after all, you're a schoolteacher" (128). As long as their passion can be contained within expected patterns of behavior, Howard feels safe, ensconced in predictability, rendering himself and those around him existentially anodyne.

Even though Rosemary's remedy for her existential angst involves shifting from one convenient stereotype to another, one type she fiercely—desperately—resists becoming trapped in is the socially constructed character Showalter calls the "odd woman" (19). Showalter identifies a *fin de siècle* "construction of unmarried women as a new political and sexual group" (21). "Odd women" were viewed by society as educated, independent—the "initial beneficiaries of the women's suffrage movement" (21)—and therefore empowered and threatening to male dominance by their unwillingness to be "excluded from enfranchisement" (21), averse to the subordinate role required of them in marriage. Showalter identifies a "second factor in the attention devoted to odd women derived from new definitions of sexuality" (21). She explains that celibacy began to be looked upon as harmful, both physically and psychologically, and even though many physicians prescribed, in Freud's terms, aim-inhibited energy diversions stressing "exercise and reading rather than ... masturbation, lesbianism, or premarital sex" (21), these notions further entrapped single women in negative social roles that limited their freedom to create and express themselves outside of community expectations. (Evelyn Wyckoff suffers the same fate in *Good Luck, Miss Wyckoff*.) On the surface, Rosemary appears to enjoy her role as a new (as opposed to odd) woman: literate, financially independent, arbiter of decency and good sense. But beneath the sheen of her stalwart propriety, she longs to reject the pejorative other side of emancipation: spinsterhood.

Until now Rosemary has played her part well, but with Hal's arrival, she finds that she cannot maintain her duality. Her insecurities drive her to compete pathetically with Millie for Hal, then to lash out at both Hal and Madge. She prudishly condemns Millie for reading a "filthy" book (Inge, *Four Plays*, 89)—McCullers' *The Ballad of the Sad Café* (1951)—then initiates an obscene dance with Hal. She pretends to be a teetotaler, but given the chance to taste Howard's bootleg whiskey, she takes a "hearty swig" (116). Rapf explains her dilemma as a gendermandered paradox: "Where in the traditional populist film the schoolteacher is a civilizing influence, in *Picnic* we see the schoolteacher as a victim of civilization from which she must break free" (Rapf, 5). However, it is that freedom "for the uninhibited panorama of nature" (5) Rapf insists Rosemary desires that frightens her and causes her to correct her course, driving not "into the sunset" (Inge, *Four Plays*, 125) but into a degrading marriage of necessity with Howard. Inge hints at the psychological causes of her conflicted nature, the way she profanes with bitterness and whiskey, for instance, the line, "'Cause I was brought up strict by a God-fearing man" (117) so that it sounds like an ironical lyric in a country western song. Indignant at the attention the men are giving to Madge as she dresses in her upstairs bedroom window, Rosemary confesses, "if my father ever caught me showing off in front of the window he'd have tanned me with a razor strap" (117). During the scene where she embarrassingly pleads with Howard to marry her, she allows herself a moment of honesty, telling him, "What do I care what people say?" (129). And when Howard replies, "you're not yourself tonight" (129), she retorts, "I'm more myself than I ever was" (129). In the end, Rosemary is too weak to escape the security of stereotypes, even though to maintain one means to repress her natural, exuberant spirit. She marries Howard to avoid realizing herself on her own terms, and sinks into the luxury of cliché.

Millie flirts with reversing gender roles too, but she finally comes off as a typical tomboy who "cusses like a man" (76) and complains when she has to bathe. She is, after all, the archetypal ugly duckling waiting to metamorphose into the nice young educated modern girl who will marry someone like Alan—another bookish brat who, according to Madge, is "the kind of man who doesn't mind if a woman's bossy" (79). And even though Millie and Alan display, respectively, masculine and feminine tendencies that counter their fixed gender, both are well on their way to assuming stereotypical roles—their cross-dressing is more like optional attire on a window display mannequin, and at any moment they will revert to their expected outfits and settle in.

On the other hand, Hal manages to maintain his surface life—an Apollonian, masculine, public front: he plays a tough athlete impressing the kids with his diving skills (an easy sexual allusion, the phallic diver penetrating the female pool), a ladies' man who, he claims, "never had to pay for it" (116). But he is obviously uncomfortable with the role he is forced to play. In essence, he is a victim in denial, his machismo posturing a mask for his acutely sensitive emotional life. Inge makes the point graphically in three scenes in each act: Hal's reunion with Alan, his dancing before the picnic, and his nocturnal rendezvous with Madge.

When Alan recognizes Hal in the back yard, he initiates a game by asking, "How's the old outboard motor?" (90). Then he mounts Hal, "*clasping his legs around Hal's waist*" (91) while Hal "*swings Alan about the stage*" (91). Besides the homoeroticism of the action, the image recalls Schopenhauer's metaphor of the lame rational man riding on the back of the blind impersonal beast of the will. Hal here assumes the role of the raw sexual impulse driving Rosemary, for instance, and to some degree Helen Potts, while Alan is the tempering force, teamed, as it were, with Flo. In the second instance, during the dancing scene, Hal, as if unsure of himself, feels compelled to remind Millie that he is the boss. "You gotta remember, I'm the man" (118). Millie, of course, is basically a child whom Hal can easily impress and control. But when he and Howard dance together, Hal offers "his version of a coy female" (118). And when Rosemary cuts in, she attempts to ride Hal the same way Alan did in the earlier outboard motor sequence. Hal, clearly uncomfortable, resists Rosemary's advances, as if her aggressiveness threatened his carefully constructed mask of masculinity. But his boots cannot protect him from Rosemary's raw grasp for power. Her story about the janitor who castrates the statue of the Roman gladiator in the school library prompts Hal to pull away from her so forcefully that Rosemary ends up tearing Hal's shirt. In the final scene, Madge has, in effect, literally ridden Hal, sexually, and Hal, his masculine swagger subordinated by Madge's obvious sexual dexterity, acts more submissive than the tough cowboy he has been pretending to be, reduced to pleading for Madge to run away with him.

Hal's attempts to assume the Apollonian role of career man in control of his life are thwarted by his desire to follow his inclinations, to act spontaneously, intuitively, not reasonably—covertly exhibiting the epitome of Dionysian dissolution. He is a romantic, an escapist, good at dancing and romancing. For all his masculine guise of control, Hal finds himself most often the casualty, not the perpetrator, a guilty hedonist prey to his libido. The two women, for instance, who engage him in a casual sexual tryst, also rip him off. The story he tells of his exploits sounds like a male sex fantasy, but on reconsideration it sounds more like the confession of a victim, raped and robbed. Likewise, when Rosemary, the castrating Medusa, attacks him, he pleads for whiskey and tries to disentangle himself from her tentacular snare. And in an ironic visual twist, at the beginning of the play, it is Hal, not Madge, who becomes the passive to-be-looked-at object of desire, the pin-up poster, "*something of a shock to the ladies*" (96). Yet, despite the clearly homoerotic sequence with Alan—which explains as much about Alan's heterosexual inhibitions as it does about Hal's homosexual exuberance—Hal remains the patently heterosexual nexus of desire, to be feared and craved by all the women in the play.

Similarly, Madge is trapped in a surface life of public role-playing with which she is less at ease than she might appear. Whereas Hal is faking his masculinity to mask his feminine urges, Madge has concocted an ultrafemme demeanor to cover her will to control. Beneath her guise of femininity, she is a calculating, reserved, master of make-up, of affectation. It is Millie, not Madge, who readily pays homage to Dionysus, god of inebriation. And though Madge is not academic, at least not passionate for the arts, according to Millie she "cooks and sews and does all the things women do" (99).

Madge's domesticity is ironic, of course, because at first glance Millie is the one set to explode the stereotype: she is aggressive, bookish; she smokes, swears, tries to drink with the men, wants to lead when dancing. But she will conform; after all, she admits she likes Alan. Her female nature is latent, not confused. Madge, on the other hand, must reconcile her public life with her private. Madge appears as the image of the mysterious female, there to be conquered and controlled. But Madge knows exactly what is at stake. Where Hal is impetuous—a primary Dionysian quality—Madge is Apollonian to the core, weighing the pros and cons of each of her decisions. In the dance scene when Hal tries teaching Millie "a new step" (120), significantly Madge "*does it as well as Hal*" (120). Even her sexual tryst with Hal is less a momentary lapse of judgment than a perfectly choreographed plot to capture her prey.

Gendermandering is less evident in Inge's original version of *Picnic, Summer Brave*, and the devolution of the gender-identity issues, which Inge so successfully exploited in *Picnic*, into the clichéd seediness of the caricatures in *Summer Brave* may well account for the unsatisfactory ending Inge preferred in the earlier draft, the one he lobbied for after the original Broadway version went into production (Voss, 131). Voss documents how director Joshua Logan, given the poor receptions of *Picnic* in St. Louis and Cleveland (134), insisted on repairing Hal's image, making him more sympathetic, "a victim of society whose surface behavior masks many deep hurts" (135). According to Voss, Inge "seemed to withdraw his active interest" (133) in the production once the changes in the ending were adopted and participated little in the final revisions. It could be argued that Logan's tinkering helped clarify the gendermandering that ultimately raises the play beyond mere entertainment. Inge disapprovingly referred to his Broadway draft of *Picnic* as a "show" (quoted in Voss, 126–127), insisting that *Summer Brave* represents the "rewritten and final version of the romantic comedy PICNIC" (quoted in Voss, 129). But no matter the sophistry of Inge's polemics, his instincts fail him in *Summer Brave*. The action and sequencing meander; in essence, it reads like a closet play.

But the subtleties of *Picnic* are more significant than mere social engineering—salvaging Hal as a "victim of society"—restoring both the intensity of the dramatic situations as well as the complexity of the characters as they struggle with their identities. In *Summer Brave*, Hal is more con-man and cad than incurable bon vivant, Alan more impotent than sexually confused and effete, and Madge more victim than survivor. While Inge insists that *Summer Brave* is "more humorously true than *Picnic*" (Preface, *Summer Brave*, ix), arguing that it "does fulfill my original intentions" (ix), the absence, in the revised version, of the tight intricacies intrinsic to the gender reversals that made the Broadway production powerful might explain the lack of focus and insight in *Summer Brave*.

Inge's failure to realize this, and to maintain the tense dramatic structure of the earlier play, innervates *Summer Brave*. Part of the problem may be that, as Inge confesses, he only considered reworking it "[a] couple of years after *Picnic* closed on Broadway, after the film version had made its success" (ix). Taking into account Inge's own persnickety complaints about the ending written for the original production (Voss, 129), and his having witnessed the material reconstituted further in the film treatment, one might sympathetically speculate that Inge wished to rejuvenate his original vision, which after all the permutations of Broadway and Hollywood may well have seemed fragile, distant, and all but lost.

But aside from the anemic dialog, unnecessary exposition, and the tendency of characters to analyze themselves (foibles endemic in much of Inge's later work), critical to the weakness of *Summer Brave* is the attenuated stress on sexual identity, as if Inge's inability to see in the Broadway version the powerful dramatic dynamics inherent in subverting expected gender roles blinded him to the truth *Picnic* inspires. This aesthetic myopia is not so evident in the ironic distinctions demarcating the ugly duckling Millie from the full-blown swan Madge, which Inge skillfully retains in *Summer Brave* (not, arguably, as effectively as in *Picnic*) even though in *Summer Brave* both girls seem more tedious, petulant, and sultry. Yet in the revised relationship between Hal and Alan, Inge all but eliminates the gender politics at play between the two men, as much as he does the social reality inherent in the gender expectations of the people around them.

In *Picnic*, Hal is innocent, likeable, less threatening than his reincarnation in *Summer Brave*. He is sympathetic, more a stranger than actually strange, more gullible than dangerous, more victim than perpetrator. In *Picnic*, his friendly repartee with Alan includes the blatantly homoerotic sequence of Alan "*clasping his legs around Hal's waist*" (Inge, *Four Plays*, 91) and riding Hal around the yard like a "*bronco-buster*" (91). Alan shouts, "Who's winkin', blinkin' and stinkin'?" (91). In *Summer Brave*, Inge removes this scene, transforming the banter between the old fraternity brothers in *Picnic* into raw animosity. For instance, instead of merely borrowing $100 from Alan, as in *Picnic*, in *Summer Brave* Hal has already stolen Alan's car, driven it to California and wrecked it. In *Summer Brave*, Hal is callous, coarse and dangerous, more extortionist than extrovert—"blackballed" (Inge, *Summer Brave*, 37), true, but more stereotypical too: a movie-style tough guy, not the conflicted, sensitive *believable* Hal in *Picnic*. And for all his faults, Alan in *Picnic* is likeable, even when his naïveté gets a bit annoying, but in *Summer Brave* he is as cynical and unconvincing as Hal's revised self. The reincarnation of Madge, too, suffers from her devolving into a fixed type. In *Picnic* she is resourceful, clever, and in the end quixotic, but she still manages to break free from her social entrapment. In *Summer Brave* she is merely pathetic. (The misogyny of the revised ending—the original, actually—is echoed later in *Good Luck, Miss Wyckoff*.) The problem for the characters in *Summer Brave* is that they cannot escape their stereotypes. They remain, without the benefit of gendermandering, fixed: Hal the incorrigible shiftless drifter, Alan the spoiled small-town rich kid, Madge the ex-beauty queen shop girl slut.

Inge again uses desire in *Bus Stop* as the key structural device to subvert stereotypical behavior and undercut audience expectations of character types. The setting, a "*street-corner restaurant in a small town about thirty miles west of Kansas City*" (Inge, *Four Plays*, 152), resembles a laboratory where, in Inge's oft-quoted words, "varying kinds of love, ranging from the innocent to the depraved" (Inge, Foreword, *Four Plays*, viii) undergo a clinical examination that even with farcical underpinnings challenges the nature of public gender representations. Not unlike Chaucer's pilgrims to Canterbury, a group on a bus finds themselves stranded during a March blizzard. During the ensuing stay, the four passengers—Bo, a cowboy, and his mentor Virgil; the bus driver, Carl; a chanteuse named Cherie; and an alcoholic academic, Dr. Lyman—ride out the storm along with Will, the sheriff, and two waitresses, Elma, a "*big-eyed girl still in high school*" (Inge, *Four Plays*, 153) and the "*more seasoned*" (153) Grace. As the players begin to form allegiances and rivalries, they pair off into synonymic and antonymic couples that resemble a curious geometrical configuration of sexual symmetry and moral balance.

Grace opens the play by telling Elma that her estranged husband "wasn't much company, 'cept when we were making love" (155). She confesses that she is "a restless sort of woman ... who has gotta have me a man, just to keep myself from gettin' grouchy" (218). Carl, her one-night stand, comes in with the wind, the violent, passionate wind of March, "like a lion" (162). After immediately making a play for Grace, he tells the sheriff he gets "so damned stiff" (167) that only a walk (in the blizzard) "[f]reshens a man up" (167) and that "sometimes I walk for hours" (167). Elma, whose budding sexuality is hardly contained but for her ignorance, is "just curious about things" (154) and wonders if she should "[f]lunk my courses" (155) to attract boyfriends. Lyman, a hedonist philosopher-on-the-lam, like a Baudelaire decadent, connects the gutter to God, so to speak, with his devotion to a failed aesthetics. He claims to "understand everything" (168) he says, but to "despise the way" (168) he says it. Will, the embodiment of judicious behavior, of orderliness and common sense, complains, "A storm like this makes me mad ... like all the elements ... lost their reason" (156). Virgil, too, represents restraint and diplomacy, his integrity reinforced by his name, conjuring both the stern moralist of Dante and the gentle "Virgin" of the New Testament. Ironically, however, Virgil's justice, like Will's, is based as much on his sexual neutrality as on his ability to manipulate the heterosexually coded games the others are playing: disinterested himself, he gives good advice.

These themes of passion and containment, of a necessary human order threatened by natural elements of disruption, are reinforced by Grace's indictment of marriage as a passion-killer. She tells Elma that "makin' love is one thing, and being lonesome is another" (155) and that "me and [her estranged husband] were usually fightin'" (155); finally, she concludes "all married people aren't like Barton and I" (155) and that she was "just as lonesome when he was here" (155). As a representative of the stable community values—along with the curiously cautious Elma and the responsible, even-tempered Will—Grace nevertheless is the one who most appreciates the unpredictability inherent in her job: catering to bus loads of strangers habitually arriving and departing, briefly interrupting the routine of her life. When Will complains that the storm makes him "mad"

Kim Stanley (1955) originated the role of Cherie as a dicey con artist masquerading as a fragile ingénue. (Photofest)

(156) and that he prefers to "see things in order" (156), Grace says, "Let it blow!" (156). And when Elma, still sexually tentative, says, "I'm glad I'm not traveling on the bus tonight" (156), Grace tells her, "Remember, honey, I always serve Carl" (157). The situation, then, in the diner is clear: Will's sanctum of sanity is set against Grace's delight in disorder. And

Barbara Baxley (1955) exposes the vulnerability Cherie must mask to maintain the sexual symmetry that, along with Bo's imperviousness, will ensure their domestic contract. (Photofest)

the message is equally clear: the diner, an image of Apollonian order, also houses the potentially subversive "elements" of Dionysian chaos.

But the central pairing off in the play is, of course, that of the country boy Bo with the city girl Cherie. Ostensibly seen as diametrical opposites—she is refined, he is rough; she is tender, he is tough; she is "citified," he is about as "country" as it gets—they are as similar as they are different, both defined by their masquerades. One way of reading the play suggests that Cherie's "decadence" will be "purified" once she is exposed to clean, simple country living; and Bo's saw-toothed edge will be blunted once he understands the difference between roping cattle and charming women. But a different reading suggests that both characters' decadence is based on their individual impersonations. When Cherie enters the cafe, she is described as "*pretty in a fragile, girlish way*" (157), and her mask-motif is graphically depicted: "*Her lipstick creates a voluptuous pair of lips that aren't her own*" (157). When Bo enters, he is described as "*rumpledly picturesque*" (169) and "*could pass*" (169) as an "*outlaw*" (169). Obviously, Bo and Cherie are not what they appear to be; their essences, in Kierkegaard's terms, are divorced from their phenomena. (Inge's personal library is full of Kierkegaard, Jung, and many general texts on existentialism.)

Bo is the ingénue, Cherie the sleazy demimonde Bo thinks is an angel. She is a child/whore, at once a femme fatale and Shirley Temple, begging to be protected while inured from being abused. Bo's innocence is equally contradictory: he is a bronco-busting tough guy who cries when his toy is denied him. Just as Cherie projects what she denies, Bo's brashness covers his sensitivity. Bo, who acts like a schoolyard bully, is actually a sheep in wolf's clothing, an idea reinforced by his significantly losing the fight with Will. He appears quick to spark, but he is all wet too; he is swaggering and arrogant, but as pliant and submissive as a pet. Likewise, Cherie is vamping to hide from herself, concealing her tough independence with her patented churlish charm. Their dilemma is this: the more Cherie says No, the more she projects Yes; the more Bo says Yes, the more he projects No. The only resolution is for each to penetrate the masquerade of the other, to discover, again in Kierkegaard's terms, the essence behind the phenomenon, the face—the truth—behind the mask. Bo discovers the woman in the girl; Cherie discovers the boy in the man. After she admits that she has led a "wicked" (209) life, he confesses that he is "kinda' green" (210). Their masks are removed; their essences conjoin with their phenomena; they are suddenly what they say they are—all irony gone—so their relationship, now honest, can develop in earnest.

Yet all the passengers operate within the same dynamic: just as Grace and Elma are looking forward to the disruption the bus occasions, the passengers are seeking shelter from the storm of unchecked passion raging on the bus—and just as Will is the marker in the diner against which Grace and Elma can measure the intensity of their emotions, Virgil emerges from the bus as the one left out, a man whose jaded desire leaves him hungering only for his own music, a "t-backy" (170) spitting image

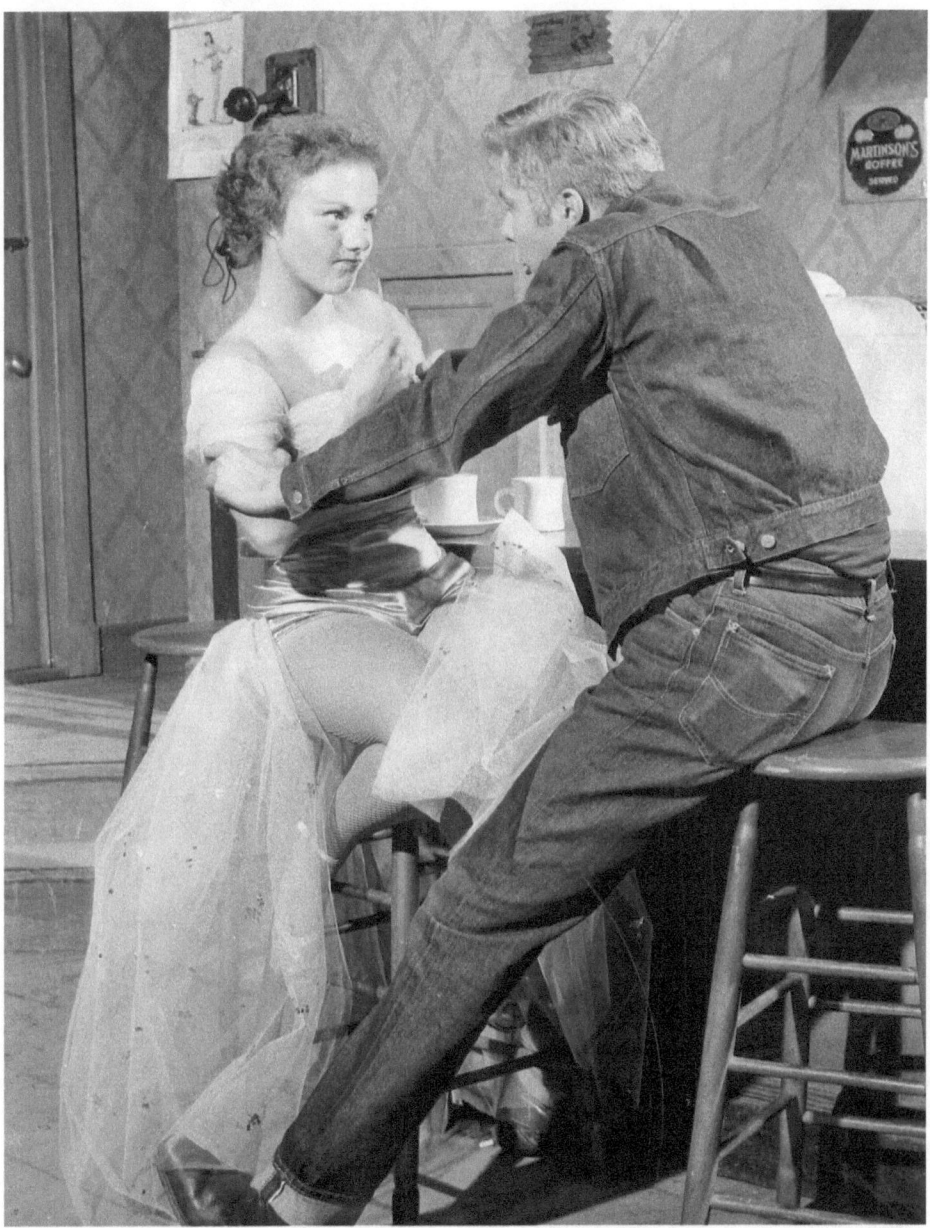

Peggy Ann Garner, with Albert Salmi as Bo (1955). He is the virgin, she the vamp, and knowing full well that she cannot play the dance hall circuit past her sell-by date, Cherie finds a raucous wayward child in search of a mother, tames him, and negotiates their future together on her terms. (Photofest)

Anita Gillette, with John Travolta as Bo (1976). Bo pretends to be a tough bronco-buster, but both his and Cherie's costumes underscore the essential theater in their relationship: hers is a feminine guise, as she hides her hardened core, while Bo in his cowboy duds conceals a soft pliable will. (Photofest)

of midwestern self-reliance. Conversely, Cherie enters disheveled, claiming she needs "protection" (158); but as a torch singer her talent is to provoke and channel passion into expression: to stimulate and control. Bo's job, too, is to bridle the raw animal power of horses and bulls—again, tapping a source of power and at the same time harnessing it. In Bo's case, self-control is more difficult than busting bulls. When he comes up against the implacable moral imperative of Will—"a very religious man" (190) who has "never lost a fight" (190)—and when Cherie sings *That Old Black Magic*, Bo's leash on his emotions snaps, and he must be forcibly brought back into line. Finally, regarding Lyman, Will is told by Carl to "keep an eye on him too" (167). Inge describes Lyman as depraved (Inge, Foreword, *Four Plays*, viii), his depravity neatly expressed by his ostentatious and patronizing erudition, his perversity internally checked only by his drunken self-loathing, checked externally by the authorities hounding him from state to state. And beyond its function to allow Lyman a dramatic opportunity for self-recognition, the scene from *Romeo and Juliet* reinforces the central themes of the play: disruption and reconciliation, thematic pairing, and unrestrained desire as a threat to a traditional values. The tragic and fatal consequences of Shakespeare's drama, however, are avoided in Inge's comedy by the intervention, this time, of the prudent nurses—Virgil and Will—who successfully minister compromise and discretion to the unruly lovers.

In fact, the moral movement in the play is toward conventionality. Aberrant behavior is either corrected or punished. Lyman is recognized for the monster he is, and his attempt to seduce Elma is thwarted. Carl and Grace strike up an affair of convenience, based on what Inge describes as "animal heat" (204) checked only by Grace's sense of modesty; for him, Grace has "everything" (204). Once Bo is tamed, and Cherie pacified, their mutual happiness is all but guaranteed. The winners and losers are identified by how well they adapt their instinctual drives to "normal" civilized behavior, and this perversion creates the most curious dynamic in the play: the pairing off of Bo and Virgil, the replacement of Virgil by Cherie, and the subsequent "punishment" of Virgil for his "unnatural" relationship with Bo.

Virgil's crime is that he lacks passion. His ultimate punishment, finally, is his literally being left out in the cold at the end of the play. Ironically, Virgil embodies an exemplary sense of forethought and even-handedness—virtues Bo lacks, as Virgil intercedes on his behalf—but by the end of the play, the very virtues that secure Bo's success in love doom Virgil to a passionless isolation, outcast and alone. His virtue—reasonableness—is also his vice. Virgil tells Bo that he "gave up romancin' and decided I was just gonna' take being lonesome for granted" (183). He feels "uncomfortable" (185) with women, preferring "the bunkhouse" (185) with his "buddies" (185). In one way, his role is parallel to Grace's: he protects and advises Bo the way Grace does Elma; however, Grace's moderated sexuality hooks her into the community of relations while Virgil's sterility exiles him. Eventually, Cherie assumes the role of mother and wife, displacing Virgil; he stoically accepts his fate by merely commenting, "that's what happens to some people" (219)—meaning, of course, those people who have given up the zest for life, whose uneasiness with passion leaves them emotionally anorectic.

Whereas the play operates within a clearly symmetrical pattern of sexual pairing, the film version of *Bus Stop* (1956) dramatically diminishes the dynamic sexuality in the play (certainly in part to comply with the acceptable moral film codes of the '50s) and by doing so cancels the gendermandering that makes the stage version more subversive, relevant and powerful. The incorrigible Lyman is eliminated altogether. The libidinous liaison between Grace and Carl, explicit in the play, is reduced to sophomoric flirting and locker-room insinuations. Virgil is likewise transformed from a latent-gay big brother to a harmless, if lecherous, grandpa gallant. Even Elma's impish curiosity is whited-out. But of all the characters, Cherie is the one most changed from play to film. Whereas Bo remains as goofy in the movie as he is "green" (210) in the play (but somehow more cartoonish, his antics more exaggerated), Cherie is nearly stripped of character (as it were), half-naked most of the film, the sexual vitality she embodies in the play perverted into pure icon: a centerfold center-screen, her essence proportionally diminished by the degree to which she is overexposed, exploited as much by the audience's expectations as by the relentless pursuit of the camera's eye. So that, in one of those pernicious ironies which seem to punctuate her career, the producers set up Marilyn Monroe as a sort of sexual scapegoat: if anything unseemly happens, it must be her fault. They allow her to play to her salacious reputation while salvaging the moral integrity of the film. Thus the play is democratic, its sexuality equally distributed among all the characters, while the film goes out of its way to neutralize everyone but Monroe, all the overt sexuality safely wrapped up in her image.

In his Foreword to the Random House collection *Four Plays*, Inge writes that he "never sought to write plays that primarily tell a story" (vii), preferring instead to create "extensions of meaning beyond the immediate setting" (viii). And he explicitly acknowledges the allegorical pattern of *Bus Stop*, writing that "the cowboy's eagerness, awkwardness, and naiveté in seeking love were interesting only when seen by comparison ... with

Mary-Louise Parker plies her ruse with Larry Pine as Virgil (1996). (Photofest)

the amorality of Cherie, the depravity of the professor, the casual earthiness of Grace and Carl, the innocence ... of Elma ... [otherwise] the characters may have been interesting, but not very meaningful" (viii).

Inge's attention to the patterning processes of human existence—gendermandering in a metafictional sense—fits well within the tradition of idealist philosophy. Inge echoes Kant's notion of the mind's activity imposing order on the raw material of sensation when, in the same essay, Inge writes that "a play's merits can exist, not in the dramatization ... but in the over-all pattern and texture of the play" (viii). His use of Bo to represent irrational desire in need of meaningful context similarly reflects Kant's idea (later refined by both Schopenhauer and Freud) of the conflict between will and inclination (between Schopenhauer's blind desire and reason; between Freud's id and superego). After all, the most controlling force in the play (perhaps not coincidentally) is Will, and this naming of the sheriff recalls Kant's contemporary, Fichte: "Will is in a special sense the essence of reason" (viii). And it is by this moral imposition of a framework on desire, the very structuring process—perhaps the most ethical activity of man—that *Bus Stop* survives as more than just an entertaining romantic comedy. Its significance and perennial value exist in its ultimate moral imperative: the ability of people to order their passions, and of the artist to marry design to desire.

The Dark at the Top of the Stairs (1957) is more problematic. Many critics complain that, because the characterization at the heart of the play relies too heavily on fundamental psychological types, the play, of all Inge's work to date, was the one most lacking in sound aesthetics and dramatic tension. Still, Inge's use of gendermandering—the employment of ironical subversions, the way characters as types reveal the opposites from which they create themselves—redeems the play as one of Inge's most intricate. As Voss reports, "Most of the next-day critics considered *Stairs* Inge's best play yet" (Voss, 173). But this verdict was not unanimous. The reviewer in *Time* magazine noted that "[t]here is no enveloping mood to the play because there is recurrent parlor comedy and domestic vaudeville" ("New Play in Manhattan," 42) and that "the general effect has a somewhat ploppy, India-rubberlike impact" (42). Later critical evaluations bear out the more tempered view taken by the reviewer from *Time* more than they validate the initial raves from the dailies. Even Shuman, at least as sympathetic to Inge's work as Voss, tries, not so successfully, to defend the play against what "has been referred to as a patchwork" (70), including an "inconsistency in tone" (71) and "the divided emphasis in the play" (71). One of the more sober analyses was by Tom Driver in "Hearts and Heads," published in January 1958, in which he decries the play as "a specimen of the kind of drama our theater in mid-century provides" (18). The core of Driver's complaint—that Inge's plays, especially evident in *The Dark at the Top of the Stairs*, had become overly psychologized at the expense of dramatic action—foreshadows the hostility Inge will confront from both the critical and popular reception of each of his subsequent box office failures. Driver writes:

> In the first place, since it is [or wishes to be] a science, psychology produces a clinical effect. That is, it changes our attention from the essential *what* or the meaning of an action to the *how* of it. It prevents us from thinking of ultimate concerns or ultimate realities and encourages us to think in terms of cause and effect. The result is the belittling of actions, for where we think we understand an action through knowing its psychological causes, we must perforce feel superior to it, since knowledge is power and the deliverance from fear. The spread of psychology in our drama has gone hand in hand with the disappearance of the hero [18].

In fact, the play deals with what is conveniently called, as noted above, the family romance: obviously, the Oedipal and Electra complexes act as the matrix to the action. In this context, the characters, to satisfy the psychological patterns necessary to the dramatic structure, must maintain their gender roles, yet their inability to do so—their resistance to this neat psychological profiling, confronted as they are with the messy human truth of life—creates the dramatic tension that drives the action: the people in the play cannot subvert their expected gender-specific models without disrupting the symptoms and prescribed resolutions that the psychology underpinning the design of the play demands.

Unlike the squalor of the Delaney's neighborhood in *Come Back, Little Sheba* (the play *The Top at the Dark of the Stairs* most resembles), which served as a rather overt metaphor for the shabbiness of the shattered lives within their house, Cora and Rubin Flood live in a "*comfortable and commodious*" (Inge, *Four Plays*, 225) home among "*symbols of respectability and material comfort*" (225), indicative of the pretensions to status the Floods seem determined to maintain in the face of economic hardship. Rubin cultivates his cowboy image, cutting an impressive figure, looking, as Aunt Lottie recalls, like "a picture of Sin, riding down the street on a shiny black horse" (254). A traveling salesman stubbornly sticking to his harness business in a time when the country is rapidly adapting to the automobile, he spends most of his time on the road, leaving Cora home with her two children, Reenie, their pathologically shy 16-year-old daughter, and Sonny, their effeminate 10-year-old son.

Rubin is a machismo poser, a tough-talking bully dressed in cowboy boots and a Stetson, who "din wanna marry nobody" (247). He compensates for his perceived lack of freedom and his increasingly precarious economic situation by having affairs with women he meets on his sales trips, or, as Cora puts it, "frisking over the country like a young stallion" (246). She, on the other hand, puts up with Rubin's dalliances until one day he hits her and she makes plans to leave him and move in with her sister Lottie and Lottie's husband, Morris. But Lottie and Morris have troubles of their own: they have not made love in three years. Perversely, Lottie even envies her sister's marriage, telling Cora, "I wish to God someone *loved* me enough to hit me" (279). Meanwhile, Rubin loses his job and, cowed, his boots symbolically covered in mud and left on the porch, he returns to Cora to ask her forgiveness. Cora has been dealing with tantrums by Sonny and Ree-

In the 1959 Music Box Theatre production of *The Dark at the Top of the Stairs*, directed by Elia Kazan, Sonny (Charles Saari) exercises an acute Freudian cathexis as he clings to Cora (Barbara Baxley), his object of infantile desire. Inge's obsession with the Oedipus complex and his exploration of its dramatic possibilities dovetail naturally with his use of gendermandering: the son overidentifies with the mother as the dominant figure in the home, causing in Freud's view (and Inge's) the son's homosexuality. (Photofest)

nie, the suicide of Sammy (her daughter's prom date), and disturbing revelations from Lottie, but she allows Rubin back into the home, the family feuds are settled, and the play closes with the dark at the top of the stairs transformed into "*the warm light*" (304) of familial understanding, love and loyalty.

For all the saccharinity of the play's resolution, the action opens on a dysfunctional family. Rubin is a wayward husband and absent father. Cora compensates for her abandonment by doting on her children, especially her son. In turn, the children are maladjusted and withdrawn, neither

Sonny nor Reenie having worked through to a proper resolution their respective Oedipal and Electra complexes. Sonny overly identifies with his mother, treats his father with ambivalence, and displays all the classic Freudian indicators of homosexuality. But he too is typified as an effeminate sensitive male child who prefers reciting poetry, going to movies and filling scrapbooks with photographs of movie stars rather than playing with the neighborhood boys his own age. Reenie, who achingly wants to please her father, defers to his authority at her own expense, and already exhibits traces of spinsterhood though she is still in her midteens. She cannot form relationships with other men, and as a result retreats from engagements, moping around the house and complaining that she is happy only when she is "alone, practicing at the piano or studying in the library" (287).

What appears reductive—this tidy psychological typing—illustrates the main problem with Inge's play. Ostensibly set in the '20s, the play nevertheless conforms to the typical gender behavior codified by the social milieu prevalent in the '50s. In fact, the date of *The Dark at the Top of the Stairs* seems artificial, established more for dramatic conventions—prohibition, the transition from horse-based to automobile-based jobs, the midwestern bigotry toward Jews—than to inform the psychological dilemmas facing the characters as they make choices that actually shape the action of the play.

The types the characters represent were as well established in the collective cultural imagination of the time of the play as they are today. Rubin is "the traveling salesman," happier on the road visiting the Mavis Pruitts along his route than he is at home offering the Apollonian core of order and stability around which his family will thrive. Cora is "the doting mother" left home alone, less wife than the mother of Rubin's children, who, from her own insecurity, has created children ill equipped to confront the world. Reenie, "the introverted daughter," is too shy to go to the dance and would rather read in the library or play Chopin alone. Brother-in-law Morris is the "henpecked husband." Lottie is his "nagging wife." With characters as tightly pigeonholed as these, the moments of madness are few as the characters cling to their masks and conform to the expected patterns of each type. Even Rubin's slapping his wife seems predictable, and her forgiving him equally so. And the suicide of Sammy, the "nice Jewish boy," intended to shock, has such weak psychological grounding, seems so forced and abrupt, that the effect is merely to highlight the action as a contrivance.

The real tension in the play, as often happens with Inge, relies on gendermandering, even of characters tangential to the central action of the play, like Lottie Lacey, for instance, Cora's sister. Many critics see her as a pathetic creature trapped in a childless marriage with her passionless husband, a dentist (reinforcing yet another stereotype). Shuman is especially harsh in his evaluation: "Lottie represents the unhappy combination of vulgarity, puritanism, self-righteousness, and bigotry which is so often found in severely repressed individuals" (79). Such psychological generalizations make for nifty pigeonholing, but this surface vision of Lottie proves much too superficial for Inge's intentions and does little to elucidate the dilemma faced by a character as complex as Lottie. Shuman fails to separate Lottie's theatrical life from her essential life. Her vulgarity, bigotry, and self-righteousness are the products of a protective persona, similar to Rosemary's, that she uses to shield herself from the existential angst of having to create an identity instead of allowing others to determine her character for her. Her remarks about sex to Cora and the Catholics to Morris—satisfying Shuman's prognosis of "sex-starved" (78) and bigoted—are less inflammatory than inflationary. Lottie presents one self to Cora, another to Morris, both mutually inconsistent. She acts more solicitous about the feelings of others than she does about her own shortcomings, allowing Cora to believe that she envies her wife-beating adulterous husband and her spoiled, irascible children, while remaining sensitive to Morris' moods and keeping him in her confidence. Instead of lingering to assuage her supposed misery, she hurries home at the first chance for escape, lamely going along with Morris' excuse that it might rain. She has unrealized expectations in her life but this hardly qualifies her as abnormal. Shuman even cites the fact that she "indecorously removes her corset" (78) as a sign of her instability, when all she wants to do is to "ride back home in comfort" (Inge, *Four Plays*, 281), which sounds more like common sense than any evidence of a neurosis. The scene is more plausibly designed not to expose Lottie's "vulgarity" but to provoke Cora's nearly pathological overreaction as she "[r]uns protectively to Sonny ... to prevent his seeing this display" (281). Regardless of what she tells Cora—as she'll tell her sister whatever she wants to hear—Lottie may well be rather satisfied with "a house full of cats" (275) and a husband who leaves her alone.

Koprince follows Shuman's argument in making prescriptive assumptions about Lottie, describing her as "trapped in an unsatisfying marriage" (Koprince, 255). She reads Lottie as being "deeply jealous of her sister, Cora, who, in her view, possesses everything a woman could desire—a home, a handsome, virile husband, and a son and daughter to care for" (258). Again, a review of Cora's situation—with the bratty children and the violent, unpredictable and now unemployed husband—does not require a stretch of the imagination to see that Lottie's comments to her sister are designed to placate Cora's anxiety and are not necessarily indicative of any jealousy. Koprince's assumption that Lottie is self-conscious about "what people will think of her if she is childless" (259) is certainly warranted, but that merely confirms that "Lottie has indeed been cross-examined by society about her childlessness" (260) and is sensitive about how to respond to this public prying into her own preferences. The problem with Koprince's observations—as well as Shuman's—is that these types of normative statements about what is "unsatisfying" regarding Lottie's marriage are as dogmatic and authoritarian as the judgmental community standards to which Lottie feels she must measure up. Her inconsistency undermines Shuman's and Koprince's attempts to explain her motives by assigning her a stereotype: her "slippage" is actually proof of her defiance. As a gendermandered character, she illustrates a recognizable stereotype, but simultaneously she resists being branded and refuses to perform as expected.

Further evidence of gendermandering is especially evident in Rubin's public resistance to his feminization. Gendermandering in this case allows him privately to maintain his machismo and to rule, within the haven of his house, from the stable, as it were. Cora calls him a "wild horse" (Inge, *Four Plays*, 226) and tells Lottie his sex is "animal" (276). Rubin asks if she expects him "to stay home here to pleasure you every day?" (227). His gratuitous grubbiness mirrors another macho poser, Hal, who "left every towel in the bathroom black as dirt ... left the seat up, too" (104). But unlike Hal, who was fairly clueless and uncouth by nature, Rubin intentionally violates house civility, baiting Cora. This explains why, in the first scene, he allows himself to be trumped during his initial exchange with Cora. She needles him about his time away from home, reminds him of the travails of the children, but then settles for a payoff of $20. To be fair, instead of relishing the sport of trading insults, which seems to be her habit, she is genuinely concerned about their financial future, acutely aware of their economic backsliding as their neighbors move into affluent socioeconomic status spheres. Her recognizing the situation, as much as her reminding Rubin about it, only works to aggravate Rubin's gender identity crisis. But when the neighborhood bullies mock and threaten Sonny, Cora flies to his defense while Rubin insists Sonny "fight it out for himself" (231). By this time, what began as a petty deflation is becoming ontological. Rubin has allowed Cora to usurp his authority in the family, leaving him control over only the sex and the money. What he considered his machismo triumphs humiliate him when Cora repeats the details she knows about his affairs and how he squanders money on cheap gifts for his mistress while denying his own children their movie tickets and prom dresses. Humiliated, left with nothing but his butch cowboy outfit and a date with a whore, Rubin slaps Cora, and the separation is complete.

When Rubin returns home, chastened and apologetic, he has literally cleaned up his act, confessing, "I din wanta track up your nice, clean house" (295)—emphasis on *your*—so he leaves his boots on the porch. Nothing in Rubin's character has changed, of course, only his circumstances. When Cora asks, "What made you decide to come back?" (295), he answers, pragmatically, "I lost my job" (295). And with the job, of course, goes the whore. When she pointedly asks, "Did you get my message?" (295), he responds evasively, "What message you talking about?" (295). She drops it, but clearly their reconciliation is one of mutual survival. Whereas he beat her before, now he merely excuses her accusations, calling them innocuous "li'l digs" (296). His response to her allegations elicits a strategic apology from Cora, who seems, finally, to understand that Rubin's main complaint is his worry that Cora might blow his cover. When she tells him about job openings and insists he "go downtown first thing Monday morning" (196), Rubin objects, saying, "Don't you realize that every time you talk that way, I just gotta go out and raise more hell, just to prove to myself I'm a free man?" (296). Even if they all know Rubin is desperate for work and must compromise his old-fashioned values and adapt to a new economy, as far as his acting the role of breadwinner and loyal family provider, Cora's dialog is not part of his script. There is no sign of romantic epiphanies, only a salesman hawking a new and improved version of himself and a wife who will put up with beatings and infidelity for a steady squeeze and the semblance (at least) of paternal authority guaranteed to stabilize the household and miraculously ease the children suddenly out of their Oedipal/Electra limbo.

No soulful conversion clutters the inevitable and wholly implausible resolution of the plot. Their compromise is one of convenience. In an embarrassingly effusive confession, Rubin admits to his great fears and doubts, all of which amounts to a culturally created masculine fear of being exposed as afraid or weak. Cora promises, "I'll never envy Peg Ralston another thing" (297), and Rubin swears to keep "doin' the best I can" (298). They profess their love for each other, and then Rubin expresses his need for the masculine control only Cora can provide him. She is "clean and dainty" (299)—satisfying the wife-not-a-slut requirement—while she also provides him "a feeling of decency ... and order ... and respect" (299). To crown his superficial, self-serving sales pitch, Rubin confesses that his greatest fear is "endin' up" (299) like Morris, sexual impotency supposedly the *coup de grace* for the proverbial red rooster. Rubin and Cora, instead of realizing an essential renewal in their relationship, experience only a temporary shift in control, accentuated by Rubin's calling Cora to bed, which hardly rates as submission for Cora. After all, with Rubin temporarily consigned—and content—to stay at home "pleasuring" her, Cora, at least for the immediate future, is on top.

Cora emerges as one of the most curious characters in Inge's oeuvre. As the driving moral normative force at the center of the family, and at the center of the play, her overriding motivation is not to escape typified behavior but to enter into it, to conform to it. Oddly, her salvation, and that of the family, seems to rest in her ability not to subvert a stereotype, but simply to become a different one, signed by Norman Rockwell, a hunky-dory white bread mid–America picture-perfect archetype. Aside from the faulty structure of the play, in which most of the dramatic action—Reenie's trauma at the dance, Sammy's suicide, Rubin's being fired—occurs offstage, the ironic desire of the mother to displace her existential individual self with a representation, to enter the symbolic as spiritual suicide, may be the primary reason for the play's sappiness, as it bogs down in sentimentality and set bits of moralizing speeches, replete with lines like "There are all kinds of people in the world" (294) and "Times are changin'" (298).

Still, Cora is formidable as she dramatically shapes the Oedipal skeleton of the play. Her skill at bargaining, bickering and playing for advantage—the emotional bedrock of their marriage—is evident from the first scene. She complains that Rubin has dirtied her clean towels, reeks of bay rum, goes off too often, for too long—in short, she nags him over what by now has become routine. What she really wants, from her honest sexual need and intuitive territoriality, is for Rubin to stay the night. It does not take long for her to invoke the children as another reason for him to stay, updating him about the children who have become strangers to him. Reenie has "no confidence at all" (227) and Sonny "doesn't know how to get along" (227) with the boys who "tease him and call him names" (227). Rubin identifies the problem, in his inimitable way, as Cora's fault, describing, though he would not know it, classic symptoms of unresolved Oedipal and Electra complexes. He reminds her how, "when those kids was born, you hugged 'em so close to ya, ya made me think they was your own personal property" (228). As for Sonny, Rubin graphically accuses her of "kissin' and makin' over the boy until I sometimes wonder who's top man around here" (228). After a feeble attempt to get Rubin to consider working a job in town, she finally relents, settling for extorting some money from him for Reenie's prom dress. She defends her son against bullies, colludes with her daughter to dress elegantly for the prom, and confronts Rubin with his philandering. When Rubin slaps her, it is a kind of perverse victory for Cora.

True to the role required of her as the template for the Oedipal/Electra family romance around which the play is designed, Cora coddles Sonny, her "speckled hen" (234), telling him that she loves him "[m]ore than anything else in the world" (234), and antagonizes Reenie, warning her that she is "not going to make friends just staying home playing the piano" (241) and chiding her for only practicing the piano, not playing in public. She admits to spoiling the children, illustrated by an oblique (if pointed) allusion: when she offers Lottie some leftover fried chicken, she explains that her children "won't eat anything but the breast" (260). But as if to mitigate her responsibility for the children's behavior, she tells Rubin, "If I kept the kids too close to me, it's only because you weren't there, and I had to have *someone* close to me" (228). Still, she admits to Reenie that "maybe I've hurt you more with pampering" (285) and tells Rubin that Reenie's "eyes light up like candles every time you go near her" (227). When Rubin leaves, she says to Sonny, "You're the man of the house now" (283). On the other hand, Cora's relationship with Reenie is strained. Reenie lashes out at her mother and brother, blaming Cora and her passion for Reenie's new dress for provoking Rubin. She worries about what they will do if "Daddy doesn't come back" (248), refuses to consider moving to Oklahoma, and even after witnessing Rubin slapping Cora Reenie confesses how much she loves her father and asks her mother why she had to "say those things to him" (248). During the reconciliation scene in the aftermath of the party, Cora tries to wean her daughter away from holding her father in the center of her life, which presumably prevents her from establishing normal sexual attractions to other men. Trying to counter her daughter's reclusion, which Reenie blames on her parents' fighting, Cora advises her, "It's perfectly natural if a boy wants to kiss you, and you let him" (286). As for Sonny, she finally insists that he "mustn't come crawling into my bed anymore" (289). Her attempt to distance herself from an inappropriate intimacy with her son seems to work, as Sonny declares, "I don't like you any more" (290), which is, of course, the point. Afterwards, all seems to be forgiven. Cora suggests that the fight with Rubin was her fault, telling Morris she thinks she has "failed" (261) her marriage and confessing to Reenie that she is not mad at Rubin anymore, "can't blame him" (284). By the final scene, Reenie has tempered her anger at her mother, just as Sonny has moderated his animosity toward his father. Cora, satisfied with the arrangement, sets out to restore order in the house, even as Rubin, in a pathetic attempt to reassert his masculinity, blusters, "Just don't get the idea you can rearrange *me* like ya do the house" (299). Of course, by now it is obvious who has won this skirmish.

The motivation for Cora's accepting Rubin back into the house, and for her forgiving him—actually blaming herself for the fight—is clearly a result of how she interprets the visit by Lottie and Morris. In Cora's view, Lottie is living in bad faith. She lies to Morris, in reference to Rubin, telling him how she is "glad I'm married to a nice man I can trust" (254) but later confiding to Cora that her desire for a "handsome buck like Rubin" (276) precludes fidelity. "Who cares if he's honorable?" (276) She tries flattering Cora, insisting that Reenie and Sonny are "the two nicest kids in the world" (257) while conspiring with Morris to keep them from moving in with her, confessing, "we'd be in the loony bin in less than two days with them in the house" (253). For Cora, who must discount other readings of Lottie's situation to ensure her own final reconciliation with Rubin, Lottie's inconsistencies and *mauvais foi* can be traced back to her unsatisfactory sex life with Morris and the fact that in bed with Morris "[n]othing ever really happened to me while it was going on" (280). Lottie's revelations force Cora to reevaluate her situation, comparing her circumstances to her sister's and realizing that other marriages can be even less idealized than her own. Inge, needing a straw man as a foil for Rubin, describes Morris as a *"man of wrecked virility"* (251) and allows Lottie to testify how, given her impotent and frustrating relationship with Morris, even marriage to an ogre like Rubin can seem inviting. Whereas Cora once envied Lottie's "having a husband you could boss" (278), Lottie, spiritually resigned in her frustration with Morris, wonders about "all the things in life I seem to have missed out on" (280), a disclosure that triggers in Cora an intuitive truth: it is better to live with a roughneck stud than a passionless eunuch.

As implausible as the children suddenly working through their Oedipal and Electra complexes is their encounter with the mysterious Sammy, a meeting through which the children are magically transformed: Reenie turns into a beaming young teen coming out on the arm of her date, Sonny into a reasonable young man cured of his tantrums. But with *The Dark at the Top of the Stairs*, Inge seems to have become more comfortable dealing with issues he might earlier have felt taboo, especially homosexuality. And as if predicting some of the material Inge would present in his next three plays, the scene between Sammy and Sonny is one of Inge's most explicit. The action creates some of the strongest dramatic tension in the play by threatening to unravel, publicly, the carefully constructed stereotypical tapestry into which the family weaves its private drama.

When Sammy, Flirt and Punky arrive to pick up Reenie for the party, they wait downstairs as she frets in a nervous panic upstairs. Punky and Flirt dance at the back of the room, and Sammy asks Sonny if he wants a "wild West ride" (266). Sammy "kneels on the floor" (266) and lets Sonny sit on his back, then he bucks around the room. To underscore the subtext of the scene, Sammy then gives Sonny his sword, which Sonny feigns to stick into himself. Further emphasizing the impact of the action, after Sonny is told he cannot go to the party with Sammy—covertly as his date—he has a tantrum fit as intense as any lover's spat. The juxtaposition of the heterosexual couple who "indulge in a little private lovemaking" (267) with the overtly homosexual action of Sonny riding Sammy and the symbolic phallic swapping of the sword rips the fabric of convention, as the sensitive effeminate child announces his homosexuality. The action exposes a truth behind the facade, a glimpse beneath the mask. Of course, in the moral context of the play, Sonny's latent homosexuality is a sign of the normative breakdown that results from the father's absence. In this sense, Sammy's suicide is sacrificial: killing the scapegoat cures the family of its own deviance.

Significantly, Aunt Lottie is more concerned about Flirt and Punky and is not upset by the much more subversive literal horsing around of Sammy and Sonny. As she is accustomed to seeing only what she expects to see, she becomes at that moment a victim of her own impulse to stereotype. She affirms the nice Jewish boy as a peculiar child, while the gendermandered action reveals exactly the opposite: a breakdown of stereotypical behavior that reveals a contrasting vision of a truth beyond any of the characters' experiential scope.

The play, however, does not sustain such moments, as the other three major plays of Inge manage to do. The action reverts to a normative payoff in which the return of the father means the reestablishment of the family unit; the family becomes normal, comfortable in its stereotypical sanctity. Sonny is "cured" in the end of being a so-called mamma's boy or a sissy by simply reverting to another stereotype: the son who triumphantly makes the Oedipal break from his mother. Cora forbids him to sleep with her any more, then his father returns to displace him from his mother's bed. As if to compensate his son, Rubin sets Sonny up with a girl who is an accomplished whistler, and the son, comfortable in his sudden new role, rejects the final proffered embrace of his mother. Reenie, too, after Sammy's suicide, emerges from her shell of emotional hiding, shedding her introversion and her bitterness toward her brother: their final action is to go off to see a movie together, like best friends. Rubin has apologized for slapping Cora, and has promised to get new work—on his own terms, of course, because as the man of the house he has to assert his Apollonian prerogatives, reminding his wife that she can't "talk to a man like that" (296). The action affirms their moral worth as both acquiesce into their culturally determined roles as a normal—or typical—husband and wife. Still, Cora's final sexual innuendo—"I'm coming, Rubin. I'm coming" (304)—is hardly satisfying, as it strains to provide the climactic closure to her sense of restoration. If she is "coming" her satisfaction is all too neat to be either plausible or convincing. Yet, perversely, that is her achievement: to become predictable.

Considering Inge's big four plays collectively, one is tempted to agree with Robert Brustein's indictment that Inge is a "fiddle with one string" (56). Brustein's point is twofold:

> The man who hides fundamental insecurities behind an exaggerated show of maleness ... will end up in a filial, dependent relationship with his wife. What is suspect is the ambiguity and the persistence with which Inge presents the same situation. Depicting this limited brand of healthiness as fanatically as Williams depicts his limited brand of sickness, Inge seems to ignore all other possibilities for happy family life [56].

The first part of Brustein's complaint echoes Kauffmann's more irascible accusation about the "disguised homosexual" (1) forced to "masquerade" (1) because Broadway producers (and the paying audiences) required them to write "a two-sex version of the one-sex experience that he really knows" (1).

Whether Inge's homosexuality resulted in "distorted" family portraits is arguable, but viewed in the context of Brustein's observation of men hiding "fundamental insecurities behind an exaggerated show of maleness," it seems self-evident that the need to masquerade unites Inge's leading men. Doc pretends to be a benevolent humanist, an idealist interested in art, music and platonic love, although he often acts more like an officious, pedantic boor. But once Marie's behavior gives the lie to the illusion Doc projects onto the veneer of his life, he reverts to a dangerous realist, raw and mean as reality. Of course, because it takes Doc a sufficient amount of alcohol to break through the stifling Apollonian mask behind which he suffers, he is not beyond redemption: the AA salvage company rescues him. After an appropriate time of penitence and some serious drying out, Doc resumes his masquerade, this time as a repentant, docile "sad-looking old bird dog" (Inge, *Four Plays*, 68). As Lola explains, without necessarily understanding the symbolic context, "women pose naked, but ... the man always keeps covered" (26). Doc pathetically responds:

"A man, after all, is a man, and he ... well, he has to protect himself" (26). Worth noting is how, in the beginning of the play, Doc fixes breakfast for the others, but by the end, after the transition he has undergone from playing at being a sensitive domesticated male to rebelling against the "sluts" (56) who have ruined his life, Lola promises to prepare Doc "a nice big breakfast" (67) of, significantly, scrambled eggs. This image of emasculation combined with the seeding of the clouds caused by the javelin "that never came down again" (68) in Lola's dream creates the sense of threat in the last line of the play, when Lola tells Doc, "I'll fix your eggs" (69). Ironically, the roles have been reestablished, but Doc, emasculated, can assume his imaginary role as the masculine head of the household, with his wife ready to please him as long as he can acknowledge, when necessary, that the arrangement itself is theater, or, as it were, a play within a play.

Hal is another poser, a typical Inge cowboy, full of apocryphal tales of derring-do and bravado, but in the end he is nothing but a hotshot clotheshorse, a hunk "naked as an Indian" (87), another beast undone by beauty, more than willing to be taken hostage by a woman who can reinforce his image of himself. But when a real ball-buster like Rosemary gets her fangs into him, Hal retreats, playing coy and asking for a drink of whiskey. Rosemary's story of the janitor chiseling away the phallus on the school statue, directed as much to Howard as to Hal, exposes Hal as another tough-guy impersonator. The truth is that Hal, as much as any of Inge's pretenders, desperately wants to give up his posing. As if to undercut his own romantic image of himself, he tells Madge, "I'm a bum" (126) and, "When I was fourteen, I spent a year in the reform school" (126). This honesty, naturally, only impresses Madge all the more, and the night takes its inevitable course with Madge and Hal skipping the picnic for the proverbial roll in the hay. His feminine shame at her distress, however, calling himself "a no-good bum" (132) and admitting that he "ought to be shot at sunrise" (133) for what in the argot of family values is called taking advantage of her, or, worse, euphemistically, compromising her integrity, only endears him, this time, fatally to her. Madge tells him, "After all, you're a man" (143), to which he responds, "And you're a woman, baby" (143). It does not get any simpler than that, but this is merely more theater: her submissiveness is as conditional as his acquiescence. He can be as studly and coarse as he wants as long as he respects her, because they both know that once Madge has been allowed a peek behind his masculine mask, there is no going back.

No question Bo is as archetypical as any of the machismo clowns in the first four plays. He is brash, pompous, physically and vocally hyperbolic. But he is no match for Cherie once she unmasks him like a skillful diplomat trained in the art of painlessly filleting an adversary while allowing him to profess publicly that he is impervious to knives. Like Doc and Hal, Bo uses his disguise to protect himself, as if he knows he must soon replace Virgil with a more appropriate sidekick—implying, not so subtly, that he must swap his homoerotic (if Platonic) playmate for the real thing, and this, to Bo, represents a threat to his culturally imposed, socially reinforced image of manliness. At least a century removed from the dangerous, mean, unglamorous and gritty world of real range-riding cowboys, Bo insists that he is "the prize bronco-buster, 'n steer-roper, 'n bulldogger, anywhere 'round" (170), which, in his mind, qualifies him to "a little more respect" (170). His line to Cherie, "thass no way to talk to your husband" (172) is by now a familiar refrain in Inge's plays. After conferring with Virgil, Bo decides to tell Cherie the truth: "I'm really a very *tender* person" (193). Inge treats a man's asking forgiveness from a woman as a weakness the tough guy must admit—like a reality check—so that he may resume his ontological machismo theater, but with the woman's permission. Of course, this capitulation has its consequences. As soon as he admits his confident swagger is merely a runway pose, she begins to control their lovemaking. She says, like an instructor, "when ya kiss me, it oughta be different" (212). He replies, all trace of machismo gone, "it's kinda scary" (212), and later, deferring and excusing her experience, he confesses, "I'm virgin enough for the two of us" (214).

Rubin, another cutout cowboy seduced by his own image, walks the walk, his costume replete with "a big Stetson, boots, narrow trousers, colorful shirt and string tie" (226), and talks the talk, telling Cora when she challenges him about his lover Mavis Pruitt, "Can't ya understand how a man feels, givin' up his freedom?" (247), and "There'll be ice-cream parlors in hell before I come back to this place and listen to your jaw" (247), threatening to "raise every kind of hell I can think of" (248). But, alas, he does come back, contrite, hat in hand, boots on the porch, asking forgiveness just like Doc, Bo, and Hal, singing the same tune, too. After running through a litany of ego-driven, socially constructed male fears—not having a job or enough money, being apprehensive about a change in his career, finding himself "a stranger in the very land I was born in" (298)— he confesses, "I still shouldn'ta hit ya" (299), but his contrition is qualified with a wink and a nod to Cora, as he adds: "It wasn't manly" (299). After her revelation (that Rubin is human), Cora gushes, "I never realized you had such doubts" (297). She typifies Inge's matriarchal mavens, willing to allow their men to play cowboys and Indians as long as Custer admits his fundamental fear of Medusa. In essence, the women enable the men to indulge in behavior each woman actually craves, admires and respects ... on her terms.

Brustein's second complaint is that Inge creates happy endings promoting a "limited brand of healthiness" and in so doing ignores "other possibilities for a happy family life." Actually, at the end of each of the big four, no one is sure of anything. Doc is between binges, Lola is murderously attacked, Hal and Madge are precariously employed, Bo and Cherie are locked into an imitation Las Vegas wedding, Cora and Rubin balanced delicately between his need for a job and her need for sex. Inge's endings are negotiated settlements, détentes between war weary partners, rapprochements that are hardly ideal.

Lola, less a self-sacrificing martyr than a practical self-preservationist, narcs out Doc to Mr. Anderson. When Doc comes back from the hospital, Lola remains disengaged, withholding her recommitment until Doc breaks down, pleading with her, "*Please* don't ever leave me" (67). But after Doc retreats into self-abasement, Inge notes in Lola's face "*a new contentment*" (67). Having confessed his utter dependence on her, he is free to indulge his self-centered (alcoholic) life and babble on about his need for vitamins, his health problems, his doctor-prescribed need for a hobby. When he asks, "About Little Sheba?" (68), Lola recalls her infamous emasculation dream, which Doc dismisses, saying "Dreams are funny" (69). But no more "funny" than their marriage truce.

Hal also needs a front of heterosexual "normalcy" as much as the semblance of respectability within the shifting mores of a rapidly urbanizing midwestern social milieu. Having never been able to make it alone, he has finally found someone as desperate as he is, and figures that together they might have a shot at legitimacy, if only for a few months. Madge, equally frantic to escape the confines of her home life, chooses the lesser of two evils: to shack up with Hal in a "crummy ... room in the basement of the hotel" (143) or become the town slut. Flo warns her, "After a while, there'll be other women" (147), and in Inge's world, that is guaranteed. But to Madge, living with each other in a pretense of love beats the small-town life she is doomed to endure otherwise (her fate in *Summer Brave*). Again, no idealization here.

Cherie, down and out, fed up and anxious, agrees to move from urban Kansas City to outback Montana, swapping her chanteuse act for a role as a pioneer wife. But she is not giving herself away, exactly. In a classic gendermandered coup, Cherie, the woman who in a calculatedly understated euphemism explains to Bo how she has led a "wicked life" (209) and "had other boy friends 'fore you" (209), scores the virgin, Bo, who actually admits that she is his "first girl" (210). Bo, hardly the studly man-of-the-world he pretends to be, is so determined to keep the charade alive that he dismisses Cherie's past, sacrifices Virgil, and pathetically tries to convince himself that their marriage is the inevitable consequence of an irresistible love. A marriage concocted out of such false pretenses is surely not evidence of an auspicious beginning to their budding romance.

Finally, given the threats, emotional blackmail, mutual survival instincts and flat-out viciousness tinged with lacrimation that bind Cora and Rubin, one must wonder exactly what Brustein means by "healthiness." Rubin is a callous, bullying, self-centered cheapskate who ignores his children as much as he does his wife. A stranger to them at the outset, he remains a stranger at the end, grafted to his wife by sex. She, a conniving opportunist, feints or strikes but gets her way. As soon as Morris and Lottie exit, for instance, her son tries to open a moment between them: she shushes him with, "I'm trying to think" (282). Her instinct is to calculate, Rubin's is to react: a volatile combination.

But more often than not, in Inge's major Broadway plays, women are from Mars (in contemporary cant) and men from Venus. Think of Marie's baiting Bruce, Rosemary's extortion of Howard, Grace's orchestrations, Lottie's hypocrisy. The men, plumed in deference, assuming arrogant poses, prove utterly dependent on their mates. But the women are Machiavellian, masters of sophistry. They masquerade too—appropriating, underscoring, and challenging sexual stereotypes, and by doing so again call into question what Brustein means by "healthiness."

It is this question of healthiness Koprince addresses. For her, childless women in Inge suffer socially imposed stigmas, and are considered "abnormal and inferior" (251). She portrays the childless women in Inge, judged against acknowledged sexual stereotypes defining the cultural norm in the '50s, as damaged, "defective and perverted" (254). She focuses on Lola Delaney, Helen Potts, Grace from *Bus Stop* and Lottie Lacey, arguing that "social pressures to have children have contributed to the instability of women such as Lola Delaney and Lottie Lacey" (258). She describes Helen Potts and Grace as "lonely, and frustrated" (259). According to Koprince, their childlessness portrays them not only as being "lonely and sexually frustrated, but even worse—as psychologically maladjusted" (257). The '50s, Koprince concludes, "was not a Golden Age for everyone—certainly not for those women who were childless, and who were branded by society as unfeminine" (262). Rapf makes the same point: "Inge's work ... is about loneliness, failure, and the problems of love" (Rapf, 3). For her, the focus of Inge's work is "sexual hypocrisy in middle-America" (5). His resolutions, hardly fantastical, work not to offer euphemistic solutions—"the bittersweet security of family life" (Brustein

53)—but to expose the social stress and conditioning that illustrate how "happiness of the family bosom is only a social illusion" (Rapf, 5). Far from proving Brustein's idea, that of the characters overcoming "fear, need, and insecurity only through the fulfillment of domestic love" (Brustein, 54), Inge's plays tend to reinforce the negative impression of "what happens to people when they live in a restrictive social environment that denies them the freedom to express their feelings" (Rapf, 3).

Koprince and others, including Brustein and Voss, rightly emphasize that "to understand Inge's dramas, one must appreciate the family-centered culture of the period in which they were written" (Koprince, 252). But few critics recognize Inge's talent not only to present realistically the stereotypically marginalized characters of the white middle-class American experience of the '50s, but to present them in both the raw and homogenized versions, the one hosting the cancerous other.

Splendor in the Grass depicts the ruinous schemes of two meddling parents, Ace Stamper, a wealthy self-made Kansas oilman, and Mrs. Loomis, a social climber warped by class envy. Ace is determined to prevent his son Bud from marrying Mrs. Loomis' daughter Deanie, expecting him instead to attend Yale and take charge of his father's business, while Mrs. Loomis is equally determined that Deanie will marry Bud and secure for her family the wealth and status she expects. By manipulating the canned social mores of a small-town community, and driven by a need to live vicariously through their children, the parents succeed only in destroying their children's innocence.

The story involves two typical high school sweethearts coming to terms with their sexuality, guilt and passion. The psychological conflict explores the struggle between the repressive superego and the blind driving will of the id. Both lovers crave sexual release but fear the social and psychological consequences sexual consummation implies, and the tension results from their frustration, trying to reconcile their desire with the expectations of their parents. Bud, trapped in the classic either/or fallacy inherent in the Madonna/whore complex, longs for sexual satisfaction with Deanie but senses that by having sex with her outside of marriage he will sully her perceived purity and paradoxically spoil the image of the girl he cherishes. As long as she is a virgin, he can idealize his love for her, but were she to consent to sex with him she would be reduced to one of the pick-ups like Juanita or his sister, Ginny. Deanie tries to play the dating game according to the rules established by her mother—in which so-called nice good girls do not "enjoy those things like a man does" (Inge, *Splendor*, 4)—and she thus finds herself in a similar predicament as Bud: if she has sex with him, she fears he will no longer respect her and will consider her unworthy of marriage, but by not having sex, she risks driving him away, losing him to girls less inhibited about sex and social decorum. While Bud's father cajoles him and warns him "not to do anything you'll be sorry for" (8), her mother keeps Deanie in the impossible situation of balancing not going "too far" (4) with preserving her relationship with Bud, whom her mother considers "the catch of a lifetime" (5).

The action opens with Bud and Deanie making out in a clearing by the river. Even though their *"kisses are so long and fervent"* (1), their frustration is painfully evident when Deanie rejects Bud's attempts to *"gratify his desire"* (1), confounded by *"a fulfillment which they fear"* (1). When Bud drops her off at home that night, Deanie asks her mother, "is it so terrible to have these feelings about a boy?" (4). Her mother merely reinforces her feelings of guilt and confusion, telling her, "No nice girl does" (4). Bud faces a similar grilling when he arrives back at his house. His father is celebrating a "new gusher" (7) with his field hands, serving aphrodisiacal oysters and "home brew" (8). Alone with Bud but with talk of sex and oysters among the men in the background, Ace warns his son, "You get a girl in trouble and you pay the consequences" (9). Ace reveals to Bud his plans to send Bud to Yale and implores his son not to disappoint him.

Bud's mother has just returned from Chicago where she was sent by Ace to retrieve Ginny, whose resume of failure now includes being kicked out of finishing school, flunking out of college, and at art school having gotten pregnant and marrying what her father disparagingly calls a "cake-eater" (13). Having annulled the marriage, her father vows to keep her home to teach her a lesson, but Ginny, an insouciant, nymphomaniacal drunk, has other plans.

At school Bud and Deanie are the perfect couple, envied by the others, except another girl commands equal attention, but for different reasons. Juanita, the "school pick-up" (15), literally comes between Bud and Deanie as they stand at the entrance to a classroom, squeezing by with a coquettish smile. Bud's acute awareness of the dissimilarity between the virginal Deanie and the sexually active Juanita only compounds his frustration. He walks down the hallway slamming lockers. Later, playing football, his aggression overcomes his discretion and he is flagged for unnecessary roughness. But his attraction to Juanita, or, at least, to the mysterious knowledge she offers, increases, and is so obvious he makes Deanie uncomfortable. In a fit of anger and insecurity, Bud forces Deanie to her knees and commands her to pledge that she loves him and will "do anything" (24), as if the assurance that she would have sex with him will somehow compensate for not having actual sex. After Bud leaves, Deanie's eavesdropping mother maliciously tells her that Ginny had an abortion, and that is "what happens to girls who go wild and boy crazy" (26).

At the Stampers', Ginny rebels against her father, making it clear that she will not be domesticated or become a hostage in "the ugliest place in the world" (27). Bud is more acquiescent, even as he tries to explain to his father that he is not interested in Yale, would prefer to attend an agricultural college and settle down with Deanie on one of his father's ranches. Desperate to keep his son from marrying her, Ace promises Bud that if he will only finish Yale he will consent to the marriage and send them to Europe for a holiday. He suggests Bud find "another kind of girl" (29) for sexual gratification, advice Bud rejects, protesting that he loves Deanie too much to do something like that. When Bud tells Deanie of his father's promise, she assures him that she will "wait forever" (30).

Ace recruits Bud to chaperone Ginny while he is away on business, an impossibly difficult task given her penchant for booze and promiscuity. During a double-date with Ginny and one of her boyfriends, Ginny mocks Bud's prudery, telling him what he has known since he first tried to persuade his Dad to let him skip Yale and marry Deanie. "You never do anything. Except what Dad wants you to" (38). She teases Bud and Deanie about their abstinence, asking Bud, "Why don't you take her upstairs and get it out of your system? Why don't you both just quit trying to pretend you're so pure and righteous?" (38). At Christmas, the friction between Ginny and Bud finally explodes. When Ginny decides to go off with a married bootlegger instead of joining the family for Christmas dinner, Bud tries to stop her and she slaps him. Her father dismisses her as a "trollop" (43), but Bud still feels protective, and at the New Year's Eve party, he tries to prevent her from both embarrassing the family and succumbing to her self-destructive impulses. "Dead drunk" (44), she admits to Bud that she "has a bad reputation" (45). Later, he finds her in a car in the country club parking lot, sexually servicing a group of young men. Bud starts a fight, Ginny drives away, and Deanie rescues Bud from a beating. Seeing his sister so debased has a profound and instant effect on Bud, and when he takes Deanie home he refuses to kiss her goodnight, then tells her they should "stop kissing and fooling around—maybe forever" (49), news which devastates Deanie, leaving her exasperated and in tears, unsure of how to remedy her moral conundrum.

Their break-up proves difficult for both of them. Bud is distracted from his schoolwork and sports activities. He finally collapses on the basketball court with a dangerously high fever and is hospitalized. He recovers, but when he tries, in a sense, to ask for the doctor's permission to seek sexual release, complaining that "a guy can go nuts that way" (55), the doc-

Repressed beyond redemption, Deanie Loomis (Natalie Wood) teeters on the edge of madness in *Splendor in the Grass*, directed by Elia Kazan. Unable to counter her abstinence with masturbatory fantasies, she dissolves in a baptismal ritual, trying symbolically to immerse herself in the amniotic fluid of femininity, prefiguring her later attempt to drown herself in the river. Forced to live against her nature, she is displaced from her chthonian self and, in this sense, her retreat into madness is an attempt to recover her primal authenticity. (Photofest)

tor's answers are as inarticulate and evasive as Bud's stammering questions. Soon, however, Bud takes matters into his own hands, as it were, by literally picking up Juanita in his new Buick roadster and initiating a sexual liaison with her, news that spreads like a prairie fire around the school. When Deanie overhears the gossip, she suffers a nervous breakdown that soon becomes so serious her parents consider sending her to a psychiatrist. Concerned that Deanie is squandering her privilege of marrying into a wealthy family, Mrs. Loomis confronts her daughter, threatening to "call that boy and tell him what I think" (65). Deanie, lying "*in the bathtub ... full of very hot water ... turns suddenly ferocious*" (65). Her mother exacerbates her panic by asking what she has feared all along might happen: "did he spoil you?" (66). Deanie becomes hysterical, shouting, ironically, ""I'm not spoiled at all. I'm just as fresh and virginal as the day I was born. Oh, I'm a lovely, virginal creature ... who wouldn't think of being spoiled ... a good little girl" (66).

Dismissing Deanie's hysterics, mainly because she does not want to spend any of the family's new wealth realized from a sudden spike in Ace Stamper's oil stock, Mrs. Loomis refuses to send Deanie to a psychiatrist. Deanie does recover enough to accept a date to the Junior–Senior prom with a friend of Bud's. She and Bud meet, dance, and then go outside to talk, but their rendezvous ends with Deanie begging Bud to have sex with her, and when he refuses, telling her, "this isn't the way it should be" (76), she runs off and tries to drown herself in the river.

After her suicide attempt, she is institutionalized, leading to her complete, ineluctable separation from Bud. During therapy she meets her future husband, a doctor from Cincinnati. Bud, miserable at Yale, is relieved of his obligation to his father (as well as his fortune) when Ace, after his stocks collapse, commits suicide. Bud marries an Italian girl he met in a New Haven speakeasy and moves back to the ranch in Kansas. At the ranch, Deanie and Bud meet one last time—she the poor girl now married to a successful doctor, he the former wealthy scion now a dirt farmer with a homely wife. The two concede they "don't think much about happiness" (119) and agree that "[t]hings work out awfully funny" (119).

The central gender reversal occurs not between Bud and Deanie, as might be expected from the pattern in most of Inge's other successfully gendermandered works, but between Bud and his sister, Ginny. Of the two siblings, Bud exhibits traits commonly associated with the cultural constructs defining women. He is sensitive, deferential, moody and spiritual, subordinating his instinctual life to the moral dictates of his conscience. He suffers from an acute sense of guilt, which Freud identifies as

Above and Opposite: The wanton and the chaste in *Splendor in the Grass*. For Ginny Stamper (Barbara Loden) sex precludes abstractions: she is raw physicality, giving herself freely to anyone who fits her needs for the moment, including this unidentified suitor in the parking lot at the country club dance. She is one of what her father calls "the other girls" men use to satisfy their carnal needs but then discard as being unfit for marriage. Ironically, her sexual aggression masculinizes her, freeing her from the gender expectations reinforced by the social codes of the community and thus making her a dangerous subversive force exposing the town's hypocrisy while undermining community standards.

In contrast to Ginny's open licentiousness, Deanie and Ginny's brother, Bud (Warren Beatty), strain to maintain their parents' standards of decency and propriety, even as their confusion leads to a debilitating sterility. Because their parents' ideas are skewed, the children's values are equally flawed. Bud feels compelled to abide by his father's belief that a wife must be pure to be worthy of marriage, while Deanie is confused by her mother's opinion that sex is an unpleasant duty a wife performs for her husband. The contrast between the couples' idealized concept of love and the need to release their natural sexual energy eventually perverts their desire and channels their passions into self-destruction and withdrawal.

originating from two origins: "one arising from fear of an authority, and the other, later on, arising from fear of the super-ego" (Freud, *Civilization*, 759). Certainly, Bud's deference to Ace resembles a daughter trying to please her father rather than a rebellious son working through an Oedipal conflict. His father's constant pleas for his son not to disappoint him only feed Bud's sense of moral duty, restrict his natural desires, and pervert his essentially feminine self. This psychological trap creates the tension that ultimately destroys his relationships with both love objects: Deanie and Ace. As Freud notes, "what is bad is whatever causes one to be threatened with loss of love" (85). Bud risks losing his father's love if he consummates his passion for Deanie. On the other hand, he risks losing Deanie's love if he obeys his father. This dilemma constitutes the source of his and Deanie's frustration. Bud lives against his nature, and suffers for it because his sense of decency has become exaggerated by the constraints inherent in the either/or fallacy operating throughout the social code defining the small-town community: a Manichean view of righteousness in which people are either good or bad, right or wrong, virgin or slut, pure or filthy.

Such reductive moral categorizing restricts Bud's response to the reality of his relationships. As Paglia points out, "At some level, all love is combat. We are only *for* something by being *against* something else" (Paglia, 14). At play is what she (paraphrasing Nietzsche) terms the "amorality of the instinctual life" (14). After all, "love comes into opposition to the interests of civilization [while] civilization threatens love with substantial restrictions" (Freud, *Civilization*, 745). In Paglia's paradigm, Bud suffers from Apollonian rationality while tempted nearly to the point of madness by his essential Dionysian nature. In this, he is cross-dressed, gender-bent, a woman playing at being a man. Unlike his father, whose massive egoism projects purpose, strength and, above all, ambition, Bud prefers his mother's life, quietly withdrawn from the masculine bouts and conflicts of competition. He plays sports mainly to satisfy his father's nostalgia, Ace per force reminding Bud of the injury that cut short his own high school football career and insisting that Bud is "running for both of us now" (Inge, *Splendor*, 8). But for Bud football is just another outlet for his pent-up sexual aggression, a way to release the anger created by his resistance to the punishment he suffers from the demands of his super-ego. Sublimating his instincts leads Bud into aberrant behavior: he slams lockers, commits unnecessary roughness, acts out violence against Deanie, attacks the young men lined up for sex with his sister. What he craves most, it seems, is displacement, the dissolution of his self. Bud equates sex with either marriage or naked carnality: even when Deanie is willing,

Bud is the one who insists on not having sex before marriage—at least with her: she is his cherished love ideal that sex would spoil, but with Juanita sex is permitted because she is spoiled already. When Bud returns to Kansas from Yale with his wife and children, sex has clearly become less an expression of passionate arousal than the agent of family bonding. Safely domesticated, he is obviously comfortable, even if he is unsure about being happy. He has settled for the security of home, hearth and family. Stoically resigned, he tells Deanie, "You gotta take what comes" (119).

Whereas Bud takes after his mother, Ginny favors her father, though Ace would loathe admitting it. She is willful, bossy, direct and materialistic, qualities associated with the cultural constructs defining masculinity. She represents an Inge archetype—the gendermandered woman—like Cherie but without the disguise—boisterous, manipulative, sexually aggressive. She, like Bud, lives against her nature, and her resistance, like his, is rooted in her conscience, but in her case, she opts not for the sublimation that keeps Bud, no matter how frustrated, playing by the rules, but for intoxication. When her conscience strikes, she dulls it with liquor. Her inebriation is palliative, the "crudest, if most effective" (Freud, *Civilization*, 730) defense mechanism available for a psyche refusing to confront the hardships of reality. As if jealous of her father's overt masculinity, she becomes what Ace calls "another kind of girl" (Inge, *Splendor*, 29), the ones Ace and his friends "never mentioned" (29) but used to "get a little steam outa our system" (29). She fits Paglia's revisionist notion of the femme fatale, embodying "the spectre of the west's bad conscience about nature" (Paglia, 13).

But the psychical role into which she has been cast is self-destructive. While she refuses to play within the strictures of society, she nevertheless punishes herself, as if at some intuitive level she understands the nature of her transgression. The implication is that Ginny lacks a fully developed conscience, that her mechanism for self-restraint—guilt—has not been sufficiently internalized, so her father must impose physical external restraints. She complains that her father is "going to make me stay home all year just to punish me" (Inge, *Splendor*, 26), but she inevitably turns the tables and becomes the punishing agent for the town's hypocrisy. Though reluctant to assume the role the town has forced her into, she recognizes her function in the moral framework of the community, identifying herself as "a freak" (27), her brutal honesty challenging the pretense and duplicity of the codes that allow the town to believe itself a harbor of goodness and sanctity. When Ace chastises her about smoking in the churchyard while he has just slept through the sermon, she asks,

"You want me to be a hypocrite?" (33). Without pretense, she is free to represent the embodiment of what the others ignore or fear.

Ginny, more masculine than the men she dates, cannot find men who satisfy her. When she brings Glenn home, he acts like a demure schoolgirl: awkward, hesitant, so unsure of himself that she feels compelled to answer for him when her mother, attempting to be polite, inquires about his background. After Bud tries to interfere, objecting to her dating a married bootlegger, she slaps him and warns, "Don't try to be Sir Galahad with me, Buddy boy" (43). The reference to Bud's inability to realize the masculine ideal of a knight gallant, coupled with the diminutive sobriquet "Buddy boy" reinforces her masculine drive and his feminine impotence. The reference to Galahad ironically underscores the lesson Mrs. Metcalf imparts to her class, in which the Knights of the Round Table are admired for chivalry and upholding "a very high regard for womanhood" (19). Ginny could not care less for chivalry, as her sense of love precludes abstractions. Insatiable, she demands physical, carnal satisfaction. She tells Glenn, a filling station attendant, "Fill me up, please" (37), and in the parking lot at the country club, one man is not enough: she needs a gang, perhaps indicating a general lack of masculinity in the (supposedly) virile heartland. In the end, she fulfills her mission, becoming the succubus who reveals, in Paglia's words, "the chthonian realities which Apollo evades" (Paglia 5). In her final confession, she tells Bud, "The only place they'll speak to me is in the dark. *In the dark*" (Inge, *Splendor*, 45)— the dark of shame and mystery, intrigue and danger, the shadows where linearity dissolves. Her last action implies self-recognition as much as self-disgust and atonement, as she "*can be heard crying*" (47) before she drives away, leaving Bud to fight for his pathetic dignity against the sex opportunists he envisions sullying his sister.

Deanie's situation is synonymous to Bud's: she too is a victim of both external and internal restraints that overwhelm and stifle her instinctual life. Oddly, her conscience seems derived from her mother, illustrating a much too neat symmetry in the Oedipus/Electra cycles linking the Loomis and Stamper families. Bud is plagued by an overidentification with his father, Deanie with her mother, and because the "models" of behavior—the parents—are flawed, the products—the children—are equally damaged. Bud's father's sense of sexuality is recreational, and he brags about his experiences with "another kind of girl" (29). Deanie's mother's ideas about sex are dutiful and unpleasant, as she advises Deanie, "Your father never laid a hand on me until we were married" (4).

Just as Bud implodes from his father's impositions, Deanie tries to free herself from her repression by subordinating herself to Bud, as if by releasing herself from the responsibility implied in making a decision she can erase her feelings of guilt about her actions. When Bud forces her to her knees in front of him (in the film, their positioning implies subservient fellatio), she admits, in a fit of self-abasement, "I'd do ... anything ... for you" (24). But what she fails to realize at this point is that by relinquishing her will to Bud's command she diminishes her authentic self. Yet later, after pleading with him to have sex with her in the parking lot at the prom (mimicking Ginny), her recognition of this self-debasement drives her to attempt suicide. Bud tells her, "You've lost your pride" (76), in his clumsy fashion merely underscoring how she has lost her soul, her vital choosing self. His hesitancy to satisfy their sexual attraction may be pathological, but his action is based on a sound moral precept (via Kant's categorical imperative) because he does not take advantage of her desperation. She, however, is too addled by whiplash, jerked between restraint and desire, to discern the fine distinctions of such psychological insight, even if her dilemma is woefully formulaic: unable to control herself, she cannot control Bud. Her breakdown in class, prompted by her reading of Wordsworth's *Ode: Intimations of Immortality*, the poem from which the title is taken, underscores her resistance and frustration. The passage she reads reinforces her fear that her chance to enjoy "splendor in the grass" (59) has been ruined and that she must accept the sterile stoicism of finding "strength in what remains behind" (59). In short, she feels cheated.

Her tantrum in the bathtub resembles a baptismal ritual initiating her passage from youthful idealism to the adult realities of compromise. She is literally dissolving, finally trying to drown herself in a symbolic immersion into amniotic femininity. (Significantly, water imagery implies sexuality throughout the script, and in the film she is portrayed masturbating in the steamy bath.) She tells Bud, "I've changed" (75), but the implication is ironic: her desire is no different, only her willingness to express it, so she is still acting in bad faith because her motive is to please Bud, not herself. When she brags, naively, "I can do anything [Juanita] can do, and a lot better, too" (75), she only proves how little she understands about her own conversion: for Bud, Juanita is simply one of his father's other girls. Deanie's plunge into the river expresses her need for some sort of salvation, a final attempt at cleansing herself from her degrading self-abnegation.

In the hospital, Deanie explains her attempt at redefining herself, telling the doctor, "I have to grow up all over again" (93). Part of her recovery includes pacification of her expectations, as she learns stoically to accept the fact that "[l]ittle girls must grow up" (109). She sees her vision of an uncomplicated perfect union with her childhood sweetheart for what it is: childish dreams. However, by understanding the limits of her own expectations, she learns to accept others. She does not blame her mother, though Mrs. Loomis treats her daughter abominably, and she realizes, perhaps most importantly, that the way she "worshiped Bud like he was a god" (120) was unfair to both of them, and to accept him as a man like "other men all over the world, trying to get along" (120) humanizes her too. She settles into the truth of life, that endurance may diminish spontaneity, but survival does not preclude comfort.

Perversely, while Bud's father and Deanie's mother try to raise what they—and the community—consider decent, upright children, their attempts at control cause their children to become the odd ones, the extremists, allowing Juanita to emerge as a normative value against which the motives of the others can be measured. Whereas both Ginny and Deanie are self-destructive, the one nihilistically unrestrained, the other clinically repressed, Juanita enjoys life, has a good attitude, a healthy sexuality, and compared to her peers, an enviable *joie de vivre*. For Deanie, water implies frustration. She never relaxes by the river: parking with Bud there is never satisfying, and she plunges in only to try to kill herself. In contrast, the water for Juanita is inviting. She frolics in the waterfall, as if nourished by the river, in touch with her essential self. As one of Bud's friends explains, "Juanita is the only girl in the whole school knows what it's all about" (20). Her vitality makes her a threat to the other girls who resent her comfortable sexuality. Compared to Juanita, the other girls seem petty and vicious. They attack her for dating Bud, but her simple explanation—she claims she likes him because he is not "a snob" (57)—is refreshing. Unlike Ginny, who indiscriminately consumes whatever she desires, and Bud, who obsessively tries to preserve his precious ideals, Juanita gives and takes with an easy balance. With her, "*Bud is enjoying the simplest joy he's ever known*" (57).

4

Minor Works

A Loss of Roses; Natural Affection; Where's Daddy?; Good Luck, Miss Wyckoff

To say that Inge's last three major attempts were tainted by his psychotherapy would not be a mischaracterization. The Oedipal obsession that nearly derailed *The Dark at the Top of the Stairs* continued to plague Inge after his first four Broadway hits. Shuman identifies the period as the "most difficult years since his arrival on Broadway" (86). Voss is convinced that Inge's early encounters with psychotherapy, "particularly the Freudian analysis most common at the time, eventually gave him insight into himself that enhanced his writing and extended his human understanding" (68). Voss's biographical interpretation may well be true, but clearly, in Inge's case, what began as a tool for introspection later became a Kafkaesque apparatus from which Inge could not disentangle himself—at least, not aesthetically, to the detriment of his craft. And although, as Voss suggests, late in his career Inge began to doubt the efficacy of psychotherapy (204), the damage to the playwright's dramatic art had already and irreversibly been done.

The aesthetic problems with Inge's last three Broadway plays—*A Loss of Roses*, *Natural Affection* and *Where's Daddy?*—clearly arise from his near obsession with the Oedipal conflict that Shuman so thoroughly explicated (even as a euphemistic way to avoid addressing the homoeroticism in Inge's work), and, in the case of *Where's Daddy?*, Inge's disenchantment with psychotherapy. Part of the failure of his appeal may be attributed to a shift in focus from his interest in stereotypes and gendermandering to a narcissistic concern with psychological role-playing, and so his characters tend to reinforce stereotypes instead of subvert them, and the dramatic action in the plays serve only to promote the theme instead of allowing the theme naturally to arise from within it.

What seems to interest commentators most about *A Loss of Roses* is the impact the failure of the play had on Inge's personal life. Inge helped provoke this sort of critical prurience by remarks he made shortly after the play closed on Broadway and then by the Foreword he wrote for the 1960 Random House edition of the published play. That Foreword is arguably more interesting and certainly more revealing about Inge the playwright than the play itself. Voss, ever sympathetic, characterizes it as contradicting what he told interviewers just after the Broadway debacle (Voss, 192), concluding that it was written by "an Inge who was deeply hurt and rather confused" (193). A more accurate and less considerate accounting might describe the piece as a bitter, self-righteous, self-serving tantrum by a juvenile prima donna temperamentally unsuited for professional critical assessment.

A brief piece of less than a thousand words, the Foreword allowed Inge a forum in which he managed not only to question the very nature of theater, but also to disparage the collaborative, ensemble efforts of Kazan and Clurman and Booth and others that had in the past served him so well but which, as in the spat he had with Logan concerning the ending of *Picnic*, betrayed in Inge a crippling insecurity, a paranoia and stubbornness—evidence of an aesthetic megalomania, a severe disconnect between his clear-eyed craft and his blinding narcissistic needs.

Inge opens the piece sounding more like a writer of so-called "closet plays" than the author of four major Broadway hits. Like a spoiled child reluctant to share his toys, he finds it "comforting for the author to get the manuscript back into his own hands" (Inge, Foreword, *Loss of Roses*) so he can "clear from his mind all the confusing experiences he has had to cope with during production" because otherwise "it is very difficult for an author to remember the play, to hold onto the essential parts without which the play's meaning cannot be expected to be clear." What is clear is that Inge failed to accept his own contribution to the failure of the play, in the case of *A Loss of Roses* a calumny that certainly cannot be blamed on the production no matter how weak the staging or quarrelsome the personnel.

He follows with a disclaimer, of sorts, reiterating his contempt for theatrical collaboration and again dismissing any of his own responsibility for what he calls "a complete failure." He writes, "working under the pressure that exists in theatre today, people become excited and mistrust their best instincts." In a bizarre exercise in deflection, Inge claims that his concern for "dramatic values" forced him to rewrite so much of the material that he was unable "to hold onto the essential parts without which the play's meaning cannot be expected to be clear." It is in fact his loss of instinct for dramatic values that wrecks *A Loss of Roses*, a play that would have struggled for relevancy under the best of productions. That he was "too confident of the play" testifies to his waning sensibility, a breakdown of that critical faculty T.S. Eliot identifies as "a continual extinction of personality" (Eliot, "Tradition," 527).

As he did with *Picnic*—restoring the play's original ending and publishing it as *Summer Brave*—Inge rewrote the ending of *A Loss of Roses*— "to end with the parting scene between the mother and son" (Foreword, *Loss of Roses*)—claiming that by doing so he was "able to right the wrong that was done" to Lila because, he writes, "it is really Lila's play." But this assertion underlines the problem: the play is nobody's and everyone's, as if Inge could not make up his mind which character should be the focus of the dramatic action, so that in the end none of the characters is able to be seen as more than a two-dimensional mouthpiece for Inge's simplistic study of what amounts to Freudian straw men.

Among other problems (and there are many), Inge expresses a weird sense of what he must have come to expect from worthwhile art. As if responding to his critics and their harsh (albeit accurate) evaluation of the play, or to answer some particular deficit that he thought could be corrected by merely clarifying its context, Inge calls the play "timely" then defensively qualifies his description, claiming that even though the play was not "representing any class or race struggle, not living with any consciousness of the atom bomb or of rockets to outer space," it nevertheless "deals with individuals who, like many people today seeking an inner peace in the midst of terrifying social change, must come to deal with evil in their lives." Fine sentiments, except the problem is not with the theme or the story but with the rendering. He uses exposition to present what should be dramatized and dramatizes what would be more effectively rendered in exposition. Inge seemed to have forgotten that great art, according to no less a preeminent critic than Horace, should both entertain and edify, and Inge, with *A Loss of Roses*, misses on both counts. His statement, "in *A Loss of Roses*, I have been able to make clearer than in any of my other plays an existentialist view" should raise the hackles of even the kindest of his critics.

But while most detractors cite the static plotting, the trite, clunky dialog and the predictability of the action, the central problem of the play may more acutely be attributable to Inge's faulty characterization. The people in the play, instead of reversing or subverting expected gender roles, remain true to type, and so besides being predictable they lack the dramatic irony that made the characters in his first four plays so fascinating, complex and relevant beyond Inge's topical context. But because in *A Loss of Roses* the characters must conform to the prescribed parameters set by Freud, their actions dictated solely by the necessity of satisfying strict psychological types, they lack the illusion of spontaneity, so that the personalities of the people in the play stem from consequences of the action, not from predetermined codes of behavior that illustrate more theory than life.

Inge waves the Freudian banner early in the stage directions when, after introducing in the very first line "A mother and her son" (Inge, *Loss of Roses*, 3), Inge notes that Kenny "bears some secret resentment that he has never divulged, that he has perhaps never admitted to his consciousness" (3). And though the Freudian scope of the play has been well documented, it may be worth reviewing it within the framework of gendermandering, as it is specifically the lack of gendermandering in the play that attributes most to the collapse of its theatrical viability. The play attempts to dramatize Freud's ideas regarding a son suffering from his inability to abandon his mother as his initial object-cathexis, or love-object, and the ramifications of this psychological malady as it retards the son's development into a "normal" young man capable of forming bonds with other nonmaternal love objects. Kenny acts according to this prototype, and what little action occurs in the play involves his attempts to detach his libido from his mother. Kenny's dilemma explains both his rejection of Miriam Caswell, the "nice" (14) girl whom his mother admires and has chosen for his wife, in favor of the girls "who hang out at the drugstore ... who don't expect anything from a boy but his *physical* attentions" (14), and his easy attraction to and subsequent rebuffing of Lila. These patterns are derived from Freud's theories on the neurotic characteristics of love expressed as symptoms of neuroses. Freud writes, for instance, of two prognostic aspects in a boy's problematic struggle to detach his libido from his mother. In the case of Kenny, "the libido has remained attached to the mother for so long, even after the onset of puberty, that the maternal characteristics remained stamped on the love-objects that are chosen later, and all these turn into easily recognizable mother-surrogates" (Freud, "Special Type," 390). Kenny further demonstrates Freud's other observations regarding the mother-son cathexis by dividing his sexual life between his mother—"a person of unimpeachable moral purity" (391)—and the girls he casually sleeps with and that satisfy "the phantasies formed by the boy in puberty" (392) of actually consummating sexual relations with his mother. Finally, Kenny conforms to Freud's notion of the "rescue-phantasy" (392): "All his instincts, those of tenderness, gratitude, lustfulness, defiance and independence, find satisfaction in the single wish *to be his own father*" (392). As for Helen, Freud types her behavior too, as she treats Kenny "with feelings that are derived from her own sexual life: she strokes him, kisses him, rocks him and quite clearly treats him as a substitute for a complete sexual object" (Freud, *Three Essays*, 288–289).

The simple plot details the events of a month in the lives of Helen Baird, a widowed woman in her 40s, and her 20-something son, Kenny, who live together in their modest house during the Great Depression. Lucky enough to have jobs, as members of the underclass they are nevertheless striving to make ends meet. The immediate calamity involves Lila, a young friend of Helen's who needs a place to live for a few weeks. Helen has offered her Kenny's room, displacing him, much to his chagrin, from his bed to the davenport. Lila functions like the typical disruptive element that proved so effective in *Picnic*. But instead of an overheated male like Hal dropping into the sexually charged back yards of Helen Potts and Flo Owens, Lila arrives like a femme fatale promising fireworks of a different kind, offering Kenny both the mother-figure love-object he craves along with an available sexual partner with which he can satisfy his Oedipal desires. As a morally lax, minor actress in a traveling circus, Lila establishes a strong and immediate contrast to Helen, a prudish churchgoing woman of conventional piety. Accompanying Lila is her racy crew of misfits: Ronnie, a closet gay serving as a gigolo for Olga, a washed-up poseur, and Ricky, Lila's pimp and lover. While the others are satisfied to set off to find work in Kansas City, Lila tells Ricky she would prefer to settle down, especially if they were married. Ricky mocks her and aggressively shuts off any further discussion of marriage but promises to return if he finds her work. He leaves with a warning: "Don't foul up the nest" (Inge, *Loss of Roses*, 33).

Lila settles in, catching up on old times with Helen. She tells how her marriage turned into a degenerate farce when her husband's father, masquerading as his brother, tried to sleep with her (with the encouragement of his wife), and after detailing her family's milieu—a string of unpalatable marriages and affairs—she explains how she finally escaped, running off with a traveling show and ending up in North Dakota where after trying to kill herself she spent time in a mental institution. Helen, for her part, tells Lila how her husband died a hero, having saved "the brightest girl in the whole school" (38) from drowning in a swollen river. She then confesses how much Kenny has been affected by his father's death, and the trouble she had raising him as a fatherless child. She also tells Lila that Kenny is a pathological thief, that he refuses to move out of the house and take a career job in Wichita, that she worries he is incapable of forming a loving bond with women suitable to become his wife, and that when she nearly married a man named Swede, Kenny was so angry she called off the marriage.

That night Kenny comes home drunk, but Lila agrees to keep his escapade a secret from Helen. The next morning Lila makes Kenny breakfast, initiating a pattern of mothering that rivals Helen's. After Kenny tells her that he has bought his mother an expensive watch as an anniversary present, Lila initiates a game, role-playing two young lovers, but Kenny quits playing and confesses that he wants to make love to her, saying that he might marry her, but Lila resists his advances. Helen interrupts them and, confused by her suspicion, infuriates Kenny by rejecting his gift of the watch. Meanwhile, Ricky calls to tell Lila that he has work for her, but it turns out to be a job making pornographic films. Lila refuses to go with him, and when Ricky gets violent, Kenny shows up to help her. Inevitably, at this point, Kenny and Lila sleep together, but the next morning Kenny reneges on his offer to marry her, and Lila, after a half-hearted suicide attempt, resigns herself to a life with her scurrilous manager, Ricky. Kenny leaves home for Wichita, successfully making the Oedipal break from his mother but leaving Lila at the mercy of Rick, with whom she leaves for a humiliating life of sexual degradation.

The play opens with Helen and her son, Kenny, painfully navigating Kenny's Oedipal dilemma. His stunted progress through the complex, now that he is 21, has clearly prevented him from becoming an independent adult, and also from moving away from home or finding a suitable mate to settle with into a responsible sexual relationship. Whereas Kenny's frustration, befitting his Freudian caricature, stems from his half-understood sexual desire for his mother (that later Lila satisfies), Helen's anxiety is rooted in her desperate desire for her son to outgrow her. Neither knows how to resolve the crisis, and both are hesitant to confront the cause of their misery, mistrust and anxiety—possibly because they are not trained psychologists, so they can hardly be expected to articulate their problems.

One unintentional effect of their squabbling in the first scene is that Kenny and his mother resemble a bitchy sit-com couple whose marriage survives on petty bickering—Ralph and Alice Kramden, for instance, without the levity, unless the dialog is read with an ear for camp. (Melodrama in Inge nearly always risks slipping into self-parody.) But Helen and Kenny's imaginative connubial relationship needs reinforcement early so that the rest of the action suits the dictates of Freud's theory. And it is that proclivity to allow theory to determine the action instead of result from it that separates *A Loss of Roses* from Inge's other work and underscores, by contrast, the fatal flaw in the play.

In *A Loss of Roses* (1959), directed by Daniel Mann at the Eugene O'Neill Theatre, Kenny (Warren Beatty) realizes the ultimate Oedipal fantasy: an affair with Lila (Carol Haney). Unable to match his father's machismo, Kenny settles for the consolation prize, a willingly submissive surrogate to his indomitable mother who offers him both maternity and sex. Mistaking Kenny's id-driven fantasies for love, Lila plays the damsel in Kenny's romantic rescue fantasy. Empowered after bedding Lila to detach his libido from his mother, Kenny makes his escape, but his supposedly successful Oedipal break is qualified by his innate ingenuousness and *mauvais foi*. (Photofest)

Essentially, Kenny and his mother are living like a couple without sex, affirming Kauffmann's complaint about Albee, Williams and Inge: "the marital quarrels are usually homosexual quarrels with one of the pair in costume" (Kauffmann, 1). And in this romance, Helen eagerly assumes the Apollonian top. But Kenny, named after his father, with his father's looks, but hardly capable of matching his father's heroics, resists his passive, feminine role. Unlike his mother, whose faith in good works—especially restraint—keeps her anchored in a concrete world of action, Kenny strives symbolically: trying to assume financial control over his mother, taking her to movies, celebrating her anniversary. Lila innocently points out the irony, reminding Helen: "It must make you feel sometimes that he *is* his father" (Inge, *Loss of Roses*, 39). But when Lila asks if Kenny will "sit at the table where his father would be" (81), Helen says no, that she will "sit at the head" (81) because Kenny, according to his mother, in the most enigmatic line in the play, "never learned to carve" (82).

Helen is a mother desperate to wean her son from, in Freudian terms, maternal plenitude. She "*no longer strives to make herself sexually attractive*" (3); in fact, she conscientiously works at making herself sexless, dowdy and pious. Cursed with a weird mix of mystical empiricism, and intuitively aware of Kenny's positivist predicament, Helen demands only one special commandment (with, of course, a Freudian twist): "You've got to pay me respect as your mother" (6). When Kenny refuses to eat the store-bought pie, Helen says, "I just can't feed you like I used to" (11). She pushes Kenny to date "the little Caswell girl" (13), and when he says he will "look after *everything*, if you'd stay home" (15), she responds, "I have to show my love for you now in different ways" (16). She feels compelled to remind him: "you're *not* your father" (16), an unfortunate turn of phrase, as its ambiguity highlights Kenny's insecurities, which is the last thing he needs, but it may also drive him away from the family romance, which is what Helen has already decided would be best: to force the boy from the nest. When Kenny ostentatiously dresses for Helen's anniversary dinner like a "fashion plate" (87), and then presents her with an expensive watch (hers significantly malfunctions throughout the play), she rejects him. The effect is as if she rejected him as a lover. He lashes out in a tantrum and leaves. Lila again delivers the clinical, technically ironical line, "He just wanted to do what big Kenneth would have done" (90). Exactly. But Helen is finally determined to force the issue. She tells Lila: "I can't let him do the things his father did.... There are some ways that can't be allowed" (90). The problem, dramatically, is that Kenny has shown no proclivity or even articulated a concrete desire to sleep with his mother, so his revelation that "Dad was the only man in this family you ever loved" (119) remains a symbolic epiphany, never an actual threat.

Kenny is a pampered mama's boy who will not cook but neither will he eat store-bought pies. He intentionally upsets Helen, swearing and teasing her with his petty thievery. The longer he lingers at home, getting drunk and dating what Helen calls "the trashiest girls in town" (54), the more frightened she is of his dependency and compensatory lifestyle. She has given up home cooking because "it makes Kenny more dependent on me" (84). She pleads with him to accept that he is "too old to still be making love to me like you did when you were a baby" (15). Complicating her fear is Kenny's atavistic need to replace his father, a hero whose status is so unimpeachable that Kenny will never match, supercede or even come close to meeting the standards of manliness his father set. His father drowned saving a bright, beautiful, successful girl—one his mother would certainly approve of—a wifely type—just the sort of girl Kenny's vapid sidekick Jelly is afraid of. Jelly says, "I'm gonna hurt a girl like that, or get her dirty" (21), and when he asks Kenny if he knows what he means, Inge's note indicates that Kenny "*knows too well*" (21).

In the note above, Inge, binging on pop psychology, frames (and thus condemns) Kenny as another psychological type suffering from what has been identified as the Madonna/whore complex, a phenomenon (stemming from the Oedipus complex) where some men categorize women as either mothers or whores. In the complex, a man's idealization of the mother combined with the unconscious fear of incest as the husband recognizes his mother in his wife—especially after they have children—can lead to impotency and drive the husband to seek sex with prostitutes in order to maintain the categorical distinction that elevates the status of his mother and wife.

For Kenny, then, Lila is a godsend. As his former nanny—his surrogate mother—who seems even now motivated only to please him, Lila provides the (barely) acceptable sex partner through whom he can play out his Oedipal drama: both whore and mother, she is sexually pliable, but she babies him too. Plus, she has been primed for Kenneth Jr. since she was a teen. Helen reminds Kenny that he was "crazy about her.... It used to make me feel a little jealous" (7). In a classic case of transference, Lila confesses to Helen of having had "the wildest crush on your husband" (36) and of idolizing him as a model of responsibility. So for her, Kenneth Jr. becomes the blood image of her icon. Trouble is, her dependence on men is pathological: she is too weak a presence for Kenny. She readily admits, "lotsa times I've tried to talk myself into thinking some guys are better than they really are" (36). She tells Helen, "I just die if I don't have someone to kinda lean on" (39). For her part, Lila needs a man who can control her. No wonder: like Lola and Doc in their détente, Lila calls Ricky "daddy," and he calls Lila "baby." While Lila manages to approximate the mother-as-sexual-object, enough at least for Kenny to accept her as a whore, she is too fragile and ruined to replace his mother as the image of purity in which Kenny has invested his life. So instead of identifying with her subjective self in a sort of epiphany resolving Kant's categorical imperative (i.e., to treat her as an end in herself, not as a means for self-gratification), Kenny plays to type and burns her in a ritualistic *auto-da-fé*.

Helen, of course, is as ready as Kenny to sacrifice Lila. She certainly has no qualms about turning her over to Ricky just after Lila, acting out some obviously incapacitating psychological issues, has in short order slept with Helen's son, tried to kill herself, and is now willingly entering into a contract with Ricky as debilitating as suicide. When Lila tells Helen that except for her fur coat Kenny "can have everything I've got" (55), she opens the door for Helen to transfer her allure. After some perfunctory demurring, Lila eventually succumbs to Kenny's rescue fantasy and plays the romantic femme to his errant knight, until he dumps her and his mom and hits the road to Wichita and a swinging single's life circa 1960. For Helen, Kenny's departure provides parental closure—the bird flying from the nest—but for Lila, Kenny's escape amounts to abandonment and betrayal. Lila, of course, is battle-scarred. When Helen refers to men as beasts, Lila responds, "I get the feeling all men are like that" (51). And in a heavy-handed bit of symbolic innuendo, Lila portentously recalls a play she did with Ricky where in the last scene Ricky shoots her "right through the heart" (64).

Lila, in Inge's nod to naturalism, has been bred to be a scapegoat. Her family name is, after all, Green, and she ingenuously admits to a fatal naïveté, confessing to Kenny, "I like anyone who's good to me" (61). She tells Helen that the doctor in North Dakota labeled her "emotionally immature" (52). Helen implies that as a child Lila had to cope with a stepfather and older stepbrother who did not, as they say, have Lila's best interests in mind. Her desperate idea of freedom was to run off with Ed Comiskey, a circus impresario. After escaping that farcical marriage, Lila endured a string of affairs with con men and transients and a butch actress named Daisy Curtis (61). All of her life she has lacked discretion, and true to form, knowing better, she allows herself to mistake Kenny's id-driven fantasies for love, Helen's self-righteous piety for trust, Ricky's exploitation for respect. She lives, after all, in bad faith. Kenny's dreaming that "someone died" (108), within the Oedipal context of the play, could be interpreted as his eliminating Helen as a sex object, as he is now ready to pursue a "normal" life sexually independent from his mother. But the alternate, *complementary* implication is that Lila is the one who "died," and it is she who is condemned to maintain a life of masquerade while Helen and Kenny settle into what for them (and presumably for Freud and Inge) passes for authenticity.

Inge insists that "it is really Lila's play" (Inge, Foreword, *Loss of Roses*), but the problem with this reading (even by the playwright himself) is that Lila does not change. Born a victim, she is victimized during the play and promises to reprise the role with Ricky and their new gig in "blue movies" (Inge, *Loss of Roses*, 99). In a nice twist, Jelly brags to Kenny that he has seen "a lot of dirty pictures" (20) from Kansas City, the kind Ricky reminds Lila she "posed for that time up in Grand Rapids" (101). Lila is Inge's *deus ex machina* rescuing Kenny and Helen from a life bonded by mutual guilt. But because she is only a stand-in, she is expendable. The real action arcs between Kenny and Helen, climaxing in Kenny's penitential outburst: "Dad was the only man in this family you ever loved" (118). His statement is both literally and figuratively true, but so is Helen's rejoinder: "If I'd loved you any more, I'd have destroyed you" (119). Lila's epiphany is less sanguine. Before she catatonically saunters off with Ricky into a world of peep shows and petty prostitution, she acknowledges that she has lived optimistically in "another one of those childish 'illusions' the doctor up in North Dakota warned me about" (124) and concedes, "I'll be happier now that I don't expect [a man to marry her] any more" (124).

Although critics justifiably disparaged the play, and audiences shunned it—Voss says it "staggered to a close after only twenty-five performances" (190)—*A Loss of Roses* nevertheless illustrates Inge's willingness—not so successfully here—to exploit and undermine gender stereotypes. Even in this messy attempt, one of the most curious aspects is the image Inge presents of the so-called nuclear family. Helen, having usurped big Kenneth's position of authority in the household—she does, after all, sit at the head of the table—assumes the role of hubby. Lila willfully fills in for the mom, and Kenny is cast as the ideal androgynous child: beautiful, spoiled, virile, desperate to replace his father but woefully ill equipped for the task. But Kenny's bisexual compromise, allowing him to escape into anonymity and mediocrity, seems inviting compared to the extreme choices of Helen and Lila, Helen preferring a monastic life punctuated with sallies into charity work, Lila the self-abnegation of industrial sex and exhibitionism. But for the women, the choices, in the end, are existential: Helen restores order and purity to psyche and nest while Lila condemns herself to some pagan/Christian hybrid of martyrdom. Only Kenny seems to retain his *mauvais foi*: supposedly cured by that patented Inge remedy—sex—Kenny saunters out with the false confidence of post-coital swagger, seemingly buoyed by bedding Lila but actually as tentative as Mrs. Mulvaney's child on her first day of school.

In *A Loss of Roses*, Inge flirts with the idea that the ideal father is a strong woman the son *wants* to sleep with, and the ideal mother a subservient woman he *can* sleep with. But Kenny is already domesticated, destined to become a good wife to a strong mother—a wife like Claire Brinkman: a lay-about promiscuous tart in a box. But Donnie, in *Natural Affection*, is still wild, having spent his young adult life in the penned-up jungle of reform school, surviving sadistic attacks from prison screws, exploitative whores, being abandoned in the first place by his parents. He is truly dangerous: feral and needy—signifying a new Inge archetype, a Nietzschean spirit condensed from the tamer ghosts of Doc, Hal and Bo.

With *Natural Affection*, Inge writes through a confluence of influences: the effects of his psychotherapy, a new readiness and boldness by American playwrights to explore explicit and graphic material, especially involving sex and violence, and finally an emerging interest on Inge's part in American literary naturalism. Inge's involvement with Freudian psychology, both clinical and theoretical, has been well documented by Voss and others, and the turn in mainstream American theater, at least the impact of Williams and Albee regarding the violent psychosexual content of contemporary theater in the late '50s and early '60s, is a matter of record in the history of American theater. More pertinent to this study is Inge's embracing literary naturalism as a praxeological frame by which he organizes his response to what he perceived as a society suddenly in crisis, reeling from "outbreaks of the most bizarre and irrational killings and acts of desperation" (Inge, Preface, *Natural Affection*, viii).

Traditionally, the writers associated with American naturalism, following the French example of Flaubert, Zola and the Goncourts, were "pessimistic and deterministic, and they chose materials from the sordid, ugly side of life: sex, hunger, poverty, disease" ("Realism," 829). They decried the fraying of the social fabric and viewed men as suffering animals, economically determined, trapped in a hostile environment, prey to passions they can neither control nor understand, consumed by degradation and mayhem. Foerster, in *American Poetry and Prose*, identifies the American naturalist writers as adhering to a loose philosophical doctrine involving "a biological determinism in which man was conceived of as controlled by his primitive, animal instincts; …a sociological determinism whereby the weak were destroyed and the strong survived in a world of struggle and chance; ...the search for reality, not in the average, but in the violent and the sensational, in war, murder, disaster, poverty and strife, and among the lower orders of mankind" ("Realism," 830).

And while Inge lacks the poetic decadence of Williams, and the symbolic architectonics of Albee, his naturalism resembles the unflinching voyeuristic eye of Arthur Fellig (Weegee) and the particular strain of Social Darwinism exemplified by Crane, Norris and Dreiser. Most unusual is Inge's naïve pessimism, evidenced in his Preface to the 1963 Random House edition of the play, a whiny tract every bit as defensive and self-serving as the Foreword to *A Loss of Roses*. Inge sounds rather patrician, as if he woke up one morning to discover that "the newspapers were so full of violence that the morning headlines were an assault upon one's breakfast digestion" (Inge, Preface, *Natural Affection*, viii). He opens the Preface with an excuse, appealing to the clichéd notion of artistic license (that smacks, more accurately, of artistic temperament) to rationalize the critical rejection and commercial failure of the play. Inge points out that life can be ugly but "beautiful, too" (vii), then he cites a New York City traffic jam and roadwork with jackhammers as causes for the "animal hostility all of us felt but were cautious enough not to display" (viii), distilling violence down to anything that causes inconvenience, as "all violence ... comes from our feeling of rejection in a world that continues to make man feel less and less important" (viii). He concludes by complaining about how *Natural Affection* "was a very difficult play for me to write. I wish I could have written a comedy, but I couldn't at the time" (ix).

Instead of exposing the raw nerve of the beast in man, *Natural Affection* exposes the dull toothache of ordinarily miserable lives enhanced by Freudian archetypes and paint-by-numbers behaviorism. Yet the play cuts a fine edge: throughout his *noir* melodrama, Inge subversively works gendermandered characters into action challenging cultural assumptions of gender types and patterns of power. Otherwise, the play, with its roots in naturalism, if derivative, is fairly typical. But in Inge's hands, the surface text bends into gender role reversals, undercutting the first deductive principle of the play: the destructive nature of primitive masculine desire. Donnie fits all the clinical attributes of Freud's homosexual (noted elsewhere in more detail), but in this stereotype Donnie is not actually free—he realizes freedom in submitting to his mother's masculinity, allowing him to luxuriate literally in the lap of passivity. Even though his homosexuality is latent, he expresses his frustration in textbook fashion. Inge's using the knife as a surrogate phallus is clumsy, but in conjunction with mixing milk and blood, the integrity of the imagery remains intact, even while Donnie's acting out his instinctual urges in a ritualistic murder is as aesthetically suspect as it is psychologically pat. Still, *Natural Affection* follows the pattern connecting all of Inge's plays: the dramatic possibilities in gender role reversals.

The action begins a few days before Christmas in "*a small but comfortably furnished apartment of the near North Side*" (Inge, *Natural Affection*, 3), a posh area of Chicago where Sue Barker, "*an attractive business woman*" (3) lives with "*her lover, Bernie Slovenk*" (3), a car salesman. Sue and Bernie are struggling in their relationship. Sue longs for marriage, but Bernie claims he cannot "marry a broad who can brag she makes more money'n I do" (15). Sue tries to reason with him but finally concedes, "I only wish ya loved me enough to marry me" (18). Her pleading and bargaining with Bernie only infuriates him and complicates the imminent arrival of Donnie, the son she gave up for adoption when she was 18 and who has spent his youth in foster homes, reform school, and "shacking up with some old whore down on Division Street" (13). Across the hall from Sue and Bernie live Vince and Claire Brinkman, a slovenly, ill-matched couple who both harbor sexual interests in Bernie, Claire having slept with him numerous times before, Vince allowed only to hint overtly at his homosexual desire.

By the time Donnie arrives with Gil, his psychopathic friend from reform school, Inge has established his usual dialectically symmetrical relationships: Sue and Bernie, Vince and Claire, Claire and Bernie, Donnie and Gil, Sue and Donnie, Vince and Bernie. Donnie is clearly fascinated with Sue, as "*he is drawn to his mother's bedroom, cluttered with her most personal items: a slip and a pair of panties*" (27) that Donnie "*lingers over*" (27). Gil, a tough who dabbles in drug dealing, murder for hire, and gay prostitution, offers to line up Donnie with some work, but Donnie declines, suggesting that he could kill a certain guard who abused him at the reform school but prefers to "make things with [his] hands" (31). Gil gives Donnie a number where he can be reached in case Donnie cannot "make it straight" (31) then slips away as soon as Sue and Claire return to the apartment.

Donnie is painfully aware of the other man in his mother's life and frets that Bernie might not "*like* me" (39). When Sue dresses him in Bernie's favorite Oriental robe, Donnie worries that Bernie might "get sore" (39), but Sue pacifies him, telling him, "He better not. I bought it for him" (39). Mother and son review their separate histories, Sue explaining her abandonment by Donnie's father, Donnie relating his abuse at reform school. Then Donnie tells Sue that if she agrees to keep him, he does not have to return to the reform school and can stay with her indefinitely. Sue says she cannot commit to anything without first talking to Bernie, but when Bernie comes home he is livid. Having crashed one of the company cars and likely now to lose his job, he is humiliated and much too angry for Sue to mention the possibility of Donnie's staying.

To make matters worse, Donnie has infused Bernie's treasured kimono with the smell of "disinfectant they use at the farm" (48), left the tub filthy, and has gone shopping wearing Bernie's expensive cashmere jacket and *vicuña* shirt. When Bernie calms down, he initiates sex with Sue. At first she responds reluctantly, then she is filled with "*sudden desire*" (55) and rushes to lock the door, but Vince interrupts them to give Bernie a gift—a bottle of cologne. Frustrated, Sue complains, "it's just not natural for a man to be as thoughtful of another man as he is of you" (59). Bernie counters, "Vince gives me a gift, so he's a queer. Is that the way you reason?" (59). After Vince leaves, Bernie and Sue take another stab at sex but are again interrupted, this time by Donnie. He shows off his expensive new clothes and turns a rock 'n' roll record up much too loud, dancing provocatively. Bernie tries to connect with him, but painfully insecure and jealous Donnie can only mutter in monosyllables.

By Christmas Eve, the friction between the couples—Sue and Bernie, Bernie and Donnie, Donnie and Sue, Vince and Claire—is acute. Recognizing the strain, Sue bargains with Bernie, suggesting that after a year she will lease a furnished room for Donnie "to make up for all the years when I wasn't able to do anything for him at all" (73). But Bernie's losing his job has crushed him, and while exchanging presents he feels even more inadequate when Sue gushes about Donnie's handmade gift to her. Donnie catches Bernie kissing Claire in the kitchen, while Vince drunkenly dances around the living room, stripping off his clothes before passing out. The others decide to go out to the Playboy Club without him. When they return and wake Vince, he goes off on his own to continue his binge, and Donnie takes Claire into her apartment. Sue confronts Bernie about sleeping with Claire, and after trading insults and accusations she slaps him. In response, he slaps her back, accusing her of stealing "a high-paying job from some man" (102). The violence escalates when Donnie returns, having aggressively resisted Claire's advances, and the night ends with Bernie going to spend the night at the Brinkmans'.

Early the next morning, Vince staggers in with a few strays he picked up to party with in his apartment. Bernie returns to Sue's claiming not to have slept with Claire, but he packs to leave anyway. Sue says she will get a bigger place to accommodate them and Donnie, but Bernie responds, "They don't make apartments big enough" (108). After Bernie leaves, Donnie suggests in overtly sexual terms that he and Sue can live together. He promises to "take [her] places, to shows and things, and to all the swell restaurants, and we could even take a trip together" (112). He tells her he considers her "the most wonderful woman in all the world" (112) with whom he might "sail off on a cruise" (112). But when he tries to kiss her she is repulsed. She tells him he must return to the reform school and that she is going to find Bernie. Donnie becomes more forceful, desperate not to be sent "back to that place" (113), but in a sudden spasm of anger Sue tells him she is "not going to give up the rest of my life to keep a worthless kid I never wanted in the first place" (114). Stunned, Donnie releases her and she runs after Bernie. Donnie collapses on the sofa, "*shaking with the traumatic pangs of rejection*" (114). When a woman from the party staggers in and "*kisses him on the mouth*" (115), Donnie "*grabs the butcher knife from the kitchen table and stabs her several times*" (115). His anger temporarily slaked, Donnie "*plays the twist record full blast*" (115), drinks some milk and "*walks out of the apartment forever*" (115).

Besides the soap operatic plot mechanisms interlocking the relationships, the various couples share another overriding symptom: resistance to the gender realities that constantly intrude on their self-presentations. Instead of adhering to their expected roles in passive deference, the women are sexually straightforward, even aggressive. Sue seems inclined to tolerate Bernie's abusive malingering because he pleases her in bed. Claire, though emotionally infantile, is sexually confident and unabashed in her pursuit of sexual pleasure. The young woman from the party Donnie murders sexually dominates him as he sobs pitifully on the sofa, and his violence towards her stems more from resistance than the hatred of women with which Inge tries to associate him in the Preface. The men, on the other hand, are sexually conflicted. All three—Bernie, Vince and Donnie—fear being labeled a "queer" (31, 59), a "fag" (84) or a "faggot" (90, 91) yet each exhibits stereotypically effeminate behavior—this during a period in American social history when the contemporary concept of "metrosexual" was unheard of, and men who displayed femininity were clearly considered homosexual or, more charitably, merely odd. Donnie confuses his desire for maternal plenitude with incestuous sexuality, Bernie desperately clings to the props of manliness while fussing over his clothes, his bath and his financial dependence on Sue, and Vince's alcoholism seems more a result than a cause of his not being able to satisfy Claire sexually, a self-medicating reaction to cover his homosexual tendencies.

Gendermandering is most acute in the relationship between Sue and Bernie. Sue's all-consuming need to marry Bernie stems from her belief that marriage—even, in this case, a bad one—will somehow correct the transgendered role she has assumed as head of the household, conventionally a role reserved for men. She is older than Bernie, more responsible, successful and economically independent, a self-made woman who overcame the traditional, perennial problems of a pregnant teen, an abandoned single mother, and a woman rising through self-determination to a position of power in the male-dominated world of business, yet she still manages to cope with the dual expectations of working women: satisfying the roles of homemaker *and* breadwinner—cleaning, cooking and shopping while maintaining her professional status and income. Even though she recognizes her situation, explaining to Bernie, "I can't hold down a good job like I do, and take care a the house like women used to" (7), she nevertheless longs for a more conventional life, pleading with Bernie to marry her, lamenting, "At my age, a woman gets to feeling kind of desperate" (16). But her concern about getting too old to marry is actually an excuse to keep her from confronting the true dilemma in her life: her reluctance to accept the gender role reversals that place her in the dominant position over Bernie, just as he resists the truth of his subordination. She clings to the notion that Bernie will assume the traditionally male function in the household, fully aware, however, that in her experience the men in her life shirk responsibility. And though she criticizes both Bernie and Donnie's father for their lack of commitment, bragging to Bernie, "I faced my responsibility, and it was the making of me. I've been strong ever since" (16), she romanticizes her conflict, describing her situation to Donnie by comparing herself to "the Mama Lion who goes out and bags the supper while the Papa Lion sits back on his haunches, looking handsome and regal" (39). But she constantly checks her assertiveness, sensitive to how prickly Bernie becomes whenever she reminds him that, in fact, in their relationship he amounts to little more than, in his words, "some goddamn gigolo" (7).

Papa Lion Bernie, no matter how much energy he expends trying to project a sense of masculinity, is feminized. He lazes about the apartment in his silk Oriental robe, impressed with the gift of cologne Vince brings him, as sensitive about his clothes as he is about his economic dependency—his chief excuse for resisting Sue's proposals for marriage. Like Sue, he pretends to want a traditional relationship, complaining, "My old lady *made* her own bread. Women today can't even slice it" (6), yet he wallows in his role of the fussy wife, griping about his wardrobe, working out at the gym, keeping himself fit and available for sex. He downplays his dependence on Sue while simultaneously expecting her to comfort him like a doting mother, satisfy his sexual needs like a compliant wife, and provide for him economically like a generous father. Whereas Sue is a pragmatic realist, Bernie lives a pipe dream of independence, unrealistically hoping one day to own an exotic car dealership and envying Sue for, in his fantasy, being able to "tell everyone else to go to hell" (8), braying, "By the time I'm thirty-six, I'll be makin' better dough than you" (7). Sue plays along with Bernie's machismo posturing, well aware that, dressed in his kimono, pampered by Sue, sexually satisfying but otherwise—socially and professionally—impotent, Bernie essentially fulfills the cliché of a kept woman. (Incredibly, Shuman finds Bernie "a likeable enough character" (113) and even thinks he is "sincere" (113) in his love for Sue, easily dismissing, it seems, Bernie's infidelities, threats and actual violence against her.) In fact, Bernie is reduced to sheer physicality. Sexual and combative, as crass as he is dandified, he threatens to "beat hell out of [her]" (6) if she reminds him he is a sycophant, an accusation that, in his hyperawareness, amounts to taunting him for living off her.

Complicating Sue's relationship with Bernie is her equally conflicted relationship with Donnie. She feels guilty for having abandoned him and hopes to expiate her shame by dutifully satisfying what she considers her contractual social obligations to her son, but she finds herself trying to balance her maternal instincts with her natural desire as an adult woman hungry for sexual companionship. The impossibility of Sue's idealized expectations (that she can harmonize a relationship between her adult son and her lover) compared to her reality (that her criminal son, suffering severe psychological damage, is locked in a primeval competition for security and pleasure with a hot-tempered, cock-sure, aging but still virile crypto-queen) explains why Bernie and not Donnie surrenders in the end: Donnie's pull is anthropologically stronger, viscerally more compelling. Bernie can always find another benefactor, but Donnie has only one mother. Unlike the subtexts in *A Loss of Roses* and many of his short plays, in *Natural Affection* Inge uses the circumstances of the Oedipus complex less essentially and more existentially. Donnie's choices result more from his immediate needs rather than his psychological makeup. This freeing of the subjects from determinism runs counter to the intuitive naturalism of the play, suggesting that the action implies meaning Inge did not intend. Nevertheless, the effect is to allow Sue a decision made freely between the two men in her life. That she chooses Bernie signals a triumph of self-determinism over innate behavior: she follows her sexual, not maternal, instincts.

Claire, as a counterpoint to Sue—Inge's masculine ideal—ostensibly defies gendermandering. She appears to be a typical sex kitten, one of Boucher's nudes, part child, part whore, but in fact she is a calculating empiricist, and though she mirrors Bernie's amorality, she is even more free, an obligate opportunist with no fidelity beyond herself. Like Bernie, with no money sex is the only currency she has to bargain for kicks. Unlike Bernie, though, she is more aggressive, faithful to her instincts: ironically, she can luxuriate in being kept, as that is the stereotypical expectation of the little lady at home. While sycophantic Bernie suffers anxiety attacks about being a gigolo, public performance favors Claire: she is expert at her various roles: committed to nothing particular, she commits to everything. She confuses nostalgia with optimism, missing her childhood Christmases because as the "baby of the family [she] used to get just loads of presents" (23), but she enjoys Chicago—sleeping around on her husband's account while dreaming of a modeling job, preserving her body by avoiding having children. But for all her deference, she is confident enough to take risks to satisfy her desire. She opts for craft, constructing her theater in a masculine context.

Claire's problem with Vince is not her dissatisfaction with him per se, although he is a mess of a lush and an ornery sentimentalist. He at least gives her a platform from which she can operate, providing her the motive and the means to pursue her trivia. Indications suggest that she will not be faithful in any monogamous relationship, so Vince is not, in her mind, singularly worthless: the main issue for her is that Vince cannot be directed. Opposed to her fetish for Apollonian form, Vince stays inebriated, lost in ecstatic Dionysian improvisation. He may be a cuckold whose wife sleeps with his friends; an alcoholic in analysis; a tax cheat facing fines and jail; a sap who tries to buy friendships with ostentatious presents and cheap flattery; a paranoid who, according to Bernie, "is so mixed up, he don't know what he is" (59), but he is also an Inge archetype: a man incapable of maintaining the mask of order and rectitude expected of him by the norms of American society. His wife, morally irresolute, nevertheless maintains a fairly consistent view of reality. She is nearly all surface: cunning, good at masquerades. Vince, however, is beyond role-playing. He is terrified of the sober act he must maintain between his drug-and-alcohol induced erasures. Most significant, perhaps, is how appalled he is by the castration scene in Tennessee Williams' *Sweet Bird of Youth*. Whereas Claire's objections reflect the mock prudery of a practiced hypocrite—"the characters in it were *sick*" (82)—Vince's reaction is visceral, instinctual. And even though Vince is a product of the bourgeoisie, conditioned to rely on euphemisms to ease his sudden confrontation with primal fear—he warns the group: "They cut off his paraphernalia" (82)—his exaggerated response indicates problems grounded in Freud's castration complex: "he now sees the notion he has gained of the female genitals in a new light; henceforth he will tremble for his masculinity, but at the same time he will despise the unhappy creatures on whom the cruel punishment has ... already fallen" (Freud, "Leonardo," 460).

The fear of castration, however, is not reserved solely for Vince. In fact, Freud's complex connects all the male characters. Bernie's hair-triggered anger at Sue stems from his being reminded of his subservient position in their relationship. From the opening scene when he tells Sue to "Toss me my robe" (Inge, *Natural Affection*, 5), he is defensive about his emasculation. Ironically, Bernie's implicit homosexuality is evident in the fact that his admiration for Sue results not from her typically feminine traits but for her typically masculine qualities. He admits, "Ya nosed out one piece of competition after another to get where you are. I've seen you down at the store. You're hard as nails" (50). A classic narcissist, he measures success by his sexual prowess, seeking in Sue the man he can never become and basically making love to the self-image he conjures in her. Significantly, after Sue asks him to be "a pal" (13) with Donnie, he prescribes the same remedy that has worked so often for him, asking Sue, "How 'bout me fixin the kid up with a nice chick?" (13) When he reminds her that "a man don't like his own li'l contribution to be overlooked" (18), referring to his ability to satisfy Sue sexually, he means for his use of "li'l" to be, in the context of the situation, taken sarcastically, as an understatement, but given his gendermandered position in their *pas de deux*, the diminutive is explicit: because his self-worth is determined by her sexual responsiveness, he constantly suffers from an existential paradox that frustrates his natural attempts at self-definition.

This ontological symbiosis also explains his misogyny. By envying Sue, as the man he cannot become, he projects his self-loathing onto her, trying to diminish what he actually admires. He qualifies her achievements, telling her, "you got pretty far for a woman" (8), and then he castigates her categorically, complaining, "You dames can never leave well enough alone" (18). His misogyny, of course, is not restricted to Sue. His disregard for Claire, even though he enjoys sex with her when it suits him, again stems from his awareness that he and she live synonymously: they are both unfaithful sluts, but because Bernie is the one who disrupts conventional expectations, he acts out of resentment, incensed by the truth of his situation. When he wrecks the car, he blames the accident on "a crazy dame" (45) and curses "women drivers" (45). He slaps Sue, then accuses her of stealing jobs from men. As if to level the playing field, he tells her, "No dame slaps me without getting the same thing in return" (102). But in the end, he leaves her because he realizes he cannot compete with her, asking her in a phrase redolent with self-pity, "Do ya know how a man feels ... when he finally wakes up and realizes he's not gonna make it?" (109). His retreat, like his misogyny, originates in his identity crisis.

Donnie's misogyny, equally acute, also stems less from his problems with the Oedipus complex than from his confused sexual gender role identification. In his Preface, Inge writes:

> There was one story I read of a boy who, rejected by his mother and sent back to a work farm, ran out onto the street and killed the first woman he saw for vengeance. In his heart, he could never admit how much he hated his mother. He had to kill a substitute [ix].

What appears to be a neat summary of the play—at least regarding Inge's intention for writing it, and the ostensible motivation driving Donnie—actually misrepresents the more intricate patterns of gendermandering that complicate the action. That Donnie would become so upset that he would murder a surrogate mother figure because she left him in an orphanage is hardly plausible, and throughout the play there is scant evidence that Donnie hates his mother, although his infatuation with her as a woman and potential sexual partner coupled with the impossibility of his incestuous desire certainly establishes the foundation for his extreme disappointment when she rejects him, but to base his murderous reaction on such a tenuous motive—the disillusionment of a jilted lover—oversimplifies his predicament. His violence toward women is indisputable. He was sent to the reform school in the first place because "he beat up some woman" (Inge, *Natural Affection*, 12). He also hits Claire and, of course, murders the woman from the party. Conversely, he is afraid of Bernie, only suggesting to his mother out of teenage braggadocio that he "could lick Bernie" (104). Still, his misogyny seems more a product of his confused sexual identity than any psychological complex—especially the Oedipus conflict. Indeed, he hardly fits the classic Freudian profile. Though his father abandoned him, he never lived with his mother long enough as a child to develop the unhealthy bonding and overidentification with the mother typical of people suffering from Oedipal conflicts. More likely, his treatment by the Division Street whore he lived with when he was 14 and the sadistic guard at the reform school probably did more to shape his perception of sex as a bargaining strategy than any childhood trauma in the Freudian playbook. Sexually abused by both men and women, he views his mother as a means to a very specific end: he can avoid being sent back to the work farm only if she agrees to take him in. Because of his confusion about sex, which he has experienced only as a tool of manipulation, he comes on to his mother out of a last-chance effort to persuade her to keep him home.

Sue, inadvertently, bears some degree of responsibility for Donnie's expectations. When Sue first meets him in her apartment, she "*hugs him affectionately*" (35) and brags, "you weren't so shy about kissing me then" (35). Donnie responds by "*[s]quirming out of her embrace*" (36) and complains, "Mom, you're suffocating me" (36). In the penultimate scene, just before Sue rejects Donnie and runs after Bernie, Donnie is "*[t]rying to embrace her*" (113) while Sue is "*[t]wisting violently to get free of him*" (114). In the first encounter, Donnie is self-conscious of Bernie. When Sue reminds him how "[i]t used to be you couldn't get enough of my huggin' and squeezin'" (36), Donnie asks, "Where's the guy you told me about?" (36). By the end of the play, Donnie is all too aware of Sue's sexual ties to Bernie, and so he desperately resorts to the one thing he thinks his mother will respond to: sex. Sue, who seems unaware of her contribution to Donnie's Oedipal fantasies, is nevertheless self-conscious about displays of affection with Bernie (and even more so about sexual activity) while Donnie is present. She insists that she and Bernie "not have any love-making while he's here" (14) and chastises Bernie when he complains, telling him, "If I couldn't control myself for a few days, I'd be ashamed to admit it" (15). Bernie and Claire are more casual about sex, as if, given their promiscuity, it means less to them than to Sue. For Vince, sex is just another escape mechanism, like his alcoholism. And Donnie, trained to view sex as a strategic weapon by which to punish or reward, naturally tries to emulate the role Bernie plays in Sue's life. But having been emasculated, feminized and kept in a cage for most of his formative years, he is impossibly miscast in his attempt at virility. Sue's choice in the end to submit to Bernie's sexual control illustrates her attempt to escape her masculine gender-determination, imposed by necessity, and to restore her "natural" femininity.

The critical and commercial failure of *Where's Daddy?* is well-documented, and most commentators agree on the reasons for the flop: the sappy plot; the pontificating of Inge's mouthpiece, Pinky; and the pious theme trumpeting social conservatism and conventional values. Voss documents the gamut of these complaints, citing critics as diverse as Stanley Kauffmann, Walter Kerr and Norman Nadel, among others, representing both the daily press and the magazines, who describe the play as "'gross and unattractive ... obvious ... burdened with stereotypes ... preposterous'" (Voss, 232–233). Voss attributes the failure not only to a lack of ironic distance between Inge and his material, especially through the figure of Pinky, but also to "Inge's gathering disillusionment with psychotherapy" (229) and the shifting aesthetics of the theater audience. With *Where's Daddy?* Inge "takes a swipe at existential absurdism ... 'contemporary thinking and philosophy' ... 'method' acting" (229) and, it seems, the entire character of the '60s' youth movement, creating an unrecognizable straw man, a veritable *piñata* he beats with the self-righteous fervor of a censorious virtuecrat nostalgic for a never-never land of social simplicity and "heartland" values.

But aside from Inge's reactionary moralizing and his puerile petulance—combined, of course, with the plausible, accurate and justifiable aesthetic caveats detailed by his contemporary critics—something more insidious may explain the lack of dramatic dynamics in the play: a marked lack of gendermandering. In all of his successful work, including the best of his short plays, Inge skillfully manipulates gender role reversals, exploding stereotypical behavior and challenging social expectations based on conventional notions of sexual identities. Recall the pretentious machismo machinations of Doc, Hal, Bo, and Rubin exposed as masquerade, complementing the matriarchal masculinity of Lola, Madge, Cherie, and Cora masked by their calculated feminine charades. But in *Where's Daddy?*, not one character plays against type. Tom, a young husband and father hesitant to give up his bachelor's freedom for the responsibility of family life, has a sudden (and dramatically unfounded) epiphany and rediscovers his purpose in life as head of the nuclear family. Likewise, Teena is content in her role as the needy, deferential wife, but as soon as she experiences childbirth she is quick to recognize motherhood and her nesting instincts as the essence of her existence. The black couple next door, Helen and Razz, are appropriately civilized to qualify as token exemplars of educated African-Americans, supposedly thereby undercutting the stereotype of blacks (manifest in Mrs. Bigelow's attitude) as ignorant, uncultured, violent and purely Other. Yet after Teena has the baby, they become nothing more than nannies, predictably espousing liberal dogma while reinforcing the negative portrait of blacks as useful caretakers, more in touch with nature and their instinctual lives than the ineffectual ofays. And though it is ironic that Pinky, Tom's pompous homosexual mentor (and serial child molester), is the prime advocate for the virtues of traditional marriage, spousal fidelity and heterosexual parenthood, his sexuality is fixed and his behavior consistent with his anal social type.

The action resembles a Joe Orton farce. Tom's banging in and out of the apartment is punctuated by Pinky's more sedate but no less arbitrary boomerang appearances, and Mrs. Bigelow's cameos balance the faithful visits by Razz and Helen. All the arbitrary comings and goings in this hurly-burly are neatly anchored by Teena's tense hesitancy. The characters, partitioned from each other, operate like magi *manqué* offering their puny epiphanies. Tom and Teena realize their essence as parents.

Mrs. Bigelow recognizes that blacks are as capable of snobbery and shoddy expectations of upward mobility as anyone in Andover. Pinky drops his cerebral façade and connects with his emotional core. Helen and Razz discover their innate "whiteness"—translated as normalcy—manifest for Helen in her crass materialism, for Razz in his unmitigated bitterness. Their discoveries are personal and self-justifying, and in the end, implausible, or at least unbelievable, because none of their experiences is grounded in action. As mannequins, their performance is limited to mouthing platitudes about social issues relevant to newsworthy items of the day. Clearly with *Where's Daddy?* Inge was intent on revisiting, with the same peevishness, the complaints he outlined in the Foreword to *A Loss of Roses*: the world is a cold, mean-spirited place where children hate their parents and parents hate their children and inexplicable violence is visited upon the innocent. For Inge, as for Yeats, another stodgy traditionalist (and cryptofascist), "Mere anarchy is loosed upon the world, / The blood-dimmed tide is loosed, and everywhere / The ceremony of innocence is drowned; / The best lack all conviction, while the worst / Are full of passionate intensity" (Yeats, 91). But no matter how self-righteous Inge's sentiments, echoed perhaps more effectively in Yeats' tight phrasing than in Inge's play, his rendering of the issues barely rates above a sentimental inveighing against modernity and a sniveling resentment for the loss of modesty and respect in a society Inge regarded as decadent, degenerate and debased. Given Inge's awareness of his own homosexuality and the irrational social animosity toward gays, his complaint in *Where's Daddy?* represents a classic case of the chicken voting for Colonel Sanders. But as Voss notes, "The 'confounding present' was seldom pleasant for William Inge, and it was to become even less so" (179).

The "confounding present" in this play opens on Tom and Teena, who started shacking up after they met in acting class. Tom is a former homeless hustler who was befriended and saved from the street by an older benefactor, Pinky. When Teena got pregnant, Tom married her—allowing Inge, in a meta-narrative, to marry a typical dialectic: Teena, a disingenuous child of Rousseau—suicidal, pampered, cursed with an affluent Andover family—slumming on a bohemian kick in the less salubrious but culturally rich environs of Manhattan, ends up with Tom, a narcissist psychoanalyzed into paralysis who now aspires to some transcendental yuppie stag ideal. But Tom has decided he and Teena should separate after the child is born, and that they should put it up for adoption. Teena, who obviously does not feel as certain about this arrangement as Tom, nevertheless parrots Tom's point of view, even while he whores his questionable acting talent out to an ad campaign for vanity items (specifically, hair tonic for jocks). In Tom's view, his career and residuals will pay off more than any investment in a wife and child. After all, as his logic goes, he only married Teena because he "wanted the baby to be legit" (Inge, *Where's Daddy?*, 49). His motives are purely selfish.

The play begins with Tom practicing his lines for a television spot he assumes will secure him an income while he pursues acting classes in hopes of a more substantial role. Teena, ignoring him, offers practical advice on how to take care of his laundry when he leaves her for life on his own. Together they have been practicing for a different scene, however, the one in which Teena tells her mother that she and Tom are not only separating and probably divorcing but that she is also giving up her baby, due any second, for adoption. Clearly reluctant to follow through with this plan, Teena tries her best to follow Tom's direction as he prepares her for the performance, and true to form, Tom slips away at the last moment, leaving Teena to confront her mother alone.

Mrs. Bigelow arrives good-naturedly with a bag full of bottles and toys to celebrate her daughter's pregnancy, but Teena's responses, as prepackaged and vacuous as Tom's philosophy, only add to her mother's bewilderment. In response to her mother's consternation, Teena recites the patented textbook psychobabble she has rehearsed with Tom, and her justifications sound as forced and insincere as they are ludicrous and rote. It is clear, however, that Teena only half-heartedly believes what she is saying, prefacing her assertions with qualifiers such as "Tom insists" (8) and "Tom says" (9), concluding, "Tom *always* is right" (9). When Mrs. Bigelow questions Tom's authenticity, Teena defends Tom, saying he "can't talk to people who are parents" (10) because he "didn't even know who his real parents were" (10). But, she hastens to add, Pinky "was very good to Tom" (10). She confesses that she was pregnant before Tom married her, but that he had chosen to go through with the marriage because "he didn't want the baby to be illegitimate" (11), neatly illustrating the convoluted logic Tom and Teena (tentatively) use to rationalize their decisions. Obviously, they ignore the fact that abandoning their child could lead potentially to the same traumas that psychically damaged Tom, and how this retreat from responsibility exemplifies a disingenuousness that strains credulity.

As Mrs. Bigelow tries to reconcile Teena's actions with Tom's philosophy, Helen drops by, and Mrs. Bigelow suffers another cultural shock: her daughter's best friend is an African-American, a successful gallery agent, no less, dealing in rare, expensive art (that afternoon having sold a de Kooning). Mrs. Bigelow, struggling in practice to apply her theoretical limousine liberalism, is uncomfortable around Razz and Helen. Before leaving, she expresses her concern about her daughter's fragile mental health—reminding Teena of her youthful suicide attempt—but Teena angrily dismisses her mother's apprehension, refusing to reveal her hospitalization to Tom because she does not want him to pity her.

Alone, Tom and Teena review their plans. Regarding the child, Tom thinks it best if he "didn't know if it's a boy or a girl, or how much it weighs, or what color eyes it has, or any of those things" (24). Tom, as callous as he is self-centered, frets that he is "prostituting" (25) himself by acting in the television commercial. Even Razz ribs him mercilessly, sarcastically wondering, "Why don't you make an *honest* living? Like in kidnaping [sic] or counterfeiting. Something with a little dignity" (23). But Teena, ever faithful, comforts Tom, assuring him (incredibly, but in an effectively light bit of foreshadowing) that he is "just being practical" (25) and that one day he will "get a good part in a wonderful play" (25). They slip into a sort of impromptu therapy session, exemplifying exactly the kind of analyst-dependent drivel that has helped create their current crisis, at one point arguing about whose analyst is better, his or hers, proving to what extent their analysts dominate their lives. They have become, in effect, existentially neutered, having given up their autonomy and their ability to make decisions, deferring instead to their therapists. When Tom insists that his residuals will earn him enough money "to pay my analysts and to help you out" (24), his priorities are clear: privileging his analyst, he subordinates his wife and the mother of his child.

Tom tries to reassure Teena that through her acting skills she, too, "may become famous" (25), explaining her difficulties by blaming her upbringing, claiming that her childhood with her loving parents and a strong family environment was somehow inferior to his experience of abandonment and displacement, bragging (ironically) that he "never had parents ... who forced me to go to church ... and filled me with inhibitions, and—repressions" (28). Teena concurs, suggesting that maybe she would have been better off if her parents had physically abused her, wondering at one point "if it wouldn't have been better to have been beaten" (26). Their values are inverted, the implication being that she is so spoiled she resents "Mother and Father ... being *nice* to me" (26). Tom hems and haws about how he is "very fond" (27) of Teena, claiming that, if not for the baby he would stay with her, continuing to control her—still directing his play—until, inevitably, the conversation turns to Tom's decision to move back in with Pinky. In one of her few honest outbursts, Teena tells Tom, "you won't have to worry about Pinky's having a baby" (30).

Conveniently (and appropriately, given Inge's farcical plot), Pinky arrives, summoned by Tom in his desperate retreat from marriage and parenthood. Pinky, punctilious, pedantic and pesky, chastises Tom like a moralizing aunt, discounting what he calls his "occasional indiscretions" (36) (which, presumably, include pederasty with teenage boys) and bemoaning Tom's notion that "you have to be sordid to be real" (40). Then masquerading as a perverse caricature of Matthew Arnold, preaching a panacean litany stressing reason, tradition and righteousness, Pinky exchanges therapeutic cant and pointlessly reductive sociopolitical polemics with Tom. But when Tom tries to pass himself off as an existential individualist striking out to "make a life of my own" (44), and pretends to justify leaving Teena and turning the baby over "to parents who have been selected by a committee" (48), Pinky scoffs, accusing him of self-sanctimonious "martyrdom" (48). Pinky then challenges Teena's acquiescence, but she proves as inauthentic as Tom, merely parroting Tom's sophomoric ideas, using the same empty phrases Tom employs euphemistically to cover his insecurity. Instead of honestly expressing her perspective, Teena abnegates her existential self, luxuriates in passivity, and, free from responsibility, is actually afraid to admit or confront her feelings. Disappointed and not a little disgusted, Pinky disavows Tom and refuses to let him come home with him, and Tom collapses in tears. After lecturing Teena on the merits of emotional maturity and personal responsibility, Pinky exits, leaving Tom to explain to Teena the difference between his relationship with her and what he shared with Pinky, at one point wondering, "Do you suppose I'm really homosexual ... and just can't face it?" (55). But before the couple can pursue this peculiar twist in their otherwise perfectly dysfunctional marriage, Teena feels the baby kicking in her womb. When she tells Tom, "he can't wait to get out" (57). Tom *looks absolutely sick*" (57) and immediately flees the apartment, ditching Teena. She tries to engage Helen and Razz in a diversionary dinner party, but finally unable to contain her emotions she desperately chases after Tom. Razz follows, and returns to the apartment with Teena's "*limp, unconscious body in his arms*" (62).

The design of Act II mirrors Act I. It opens with Teena, recuperating from having given birth to a boy, being cared for by Razz and Helen. The interruptions begin, as in the first act, when Mrs. Bigelow enters. Tom makes a series of appearances, and Pinky overlaps Mrs. Bigelow's exit. She leaves after enduring, and he after delivering, sagacious lectures and lessons in life (but not, as in Act I, griping about poor grammar). The main difference between the two acts is that in the end of the play Tom decides to stay with Teena and the baby. But this psychological turn is so implausible and unwarranted that Tom seems as spineless for staying as he did for running off. His motivation for suddenly wanting to be faithful hinges on Teena's calling his bluff, as it were, and rejecting him on her own terms, his change in attitude attributable only to his need egoistically to reestablish himself in one of the few sympathetic mirrors he knows: Teena.

Act II begins with Razz and Helen literally babysitting Teena, illustrating the imposition, hardship and sacrifice Tom's irresponsible absence has provoked. Helen resembles both Sue from *Natural Affection* and Rosemary from *Picnic* when she wistfully presses Razz to marry her. His response echoes Bernie's from *Natural Affection*: he refuses to marry a woman before he can support her economically. It seems, for Inge, a man's using income to assert control over a woman—indicating a complementary fear of emasculation—transcends race, as does Helen's belief (like Rosemary's and Sue's) that marriage itself, not the quality of the commitment, will suffice to satisfy her essence. Helen tells Razz, "[e]ven after watching all the agony she went through, I want to have [a child] too" (66).

Helen, worried about Teena, desperately tries to locate a representative from the adoption agency, in part to speed up their intervention but also because she needs to free herself so she can go to work. Meanwhile, Tom shows up to find Razz practicing lines from Shakespeare's *Othello*, a scene intended to draw a sharp contrast between Tom's crass commercialism and Razz's artistic aspirations. Gutless and incorrigibly egoistic, Tom tries to explain his return by claiming he has decided to care for Teena "until the baby's born" (73), justifying his actions by using typical narcissistic logic: "a matter of two weeks can't have a serious effect on my career ... I've got to make something of myself ... who can make it with a wife and child hanging around his neck?" (74). Tom explains that when he began to doubt his decision to leave Teena, he naturally made an appointment to see his analyst who pointed out that because Tom had kept the key to Teena's apartment, subconsciously he "was just not ready to break off our relationship" (74). His keeping the key indicated, in Tom's words, "a real Freudian slip" (75). It is, his analyst told him, "the key to her heart ... to her body" (75). He confesses to Razz that he did not, as he had planned, stay with his boss, a woman at the agency, but instead spent the night wandering around the city wallowing in self-pity, torn between his desire to pursue his career and the comforts of "the only real home I've ever had" (77). All of his concern, however, is centered on himself, and even his fond memories of life together with Teena are based on what she has done for him, not what he might do for her.

Through this exercise in self-rationalization, Tom talks himself into a ludicrous epiphany—that "a woman's not a slot machine" (76)—and then he delivers a disturbing, gratuitous, simple-minded, reactionary opinion in which he justifies denying the reproductive rights of women and equates abortion with murder. His reasoning is, of course, self-serving. In a speech that could today be delivered by the most radical Republican moral alarmists in government, he says, "I don't like the idea of taking a life once that life is started ... I think preventive measures are O.K., but when a baby's almost three months along, I think you're taking a life" (77). Though these sentiments, uttered by a mollycoddled shirker, may appear comical given the incongruity of Tom's theoretical perspective and his actual behavior toward Teena, they are nevertheless distressingly relevant and illustrative of an entrenched privilege enforced by men determined to use sex and biology to manipulate women. Tom concludes, "I'm glad I was born" (78).

When it comes to dealing with a live baby for whom he is responsible, Tom sings a different tune, panicking when he discovers that indeed Teena has already had the child. With the baby crying and Teena pleading for him to embrace it, Tom again proves his impotence by running out of the apartment to call Pinky, then he leaves the building. Teena sobs hysterically at first, but when the adoption agency calls, as if inspired by Tom's cowardice, she resolutely refuses to give up the child. She says, "I'll show him. I can raise a baby without him" (82). She confides to Helen that when she was younger she tried to kill herself, but since giving birth she has found a reason to live, a purpose in her life.

Helen gives Teena sleeping pills and heads off to work, leaving Razz to care for the baby. When Teena's mother shows up this time she finds Razz holding the baby, which makes her nervous because, as she puts it, "I've never really known a Negro before" (89). She is cautiously pleased that Teena is keeping the baby, but she seems more concerned about proving her progressive credentials to Razz than actually accepting her grandchild. Hopelessly white bread, she prattles on about how progressive she is, but her experience of minorities is limited to her membership in the Urban League and her acquaintance with "a very nice Negro lady ... on the P.T.A. Board" (89). But mere minutes after confessing her ignorance of and discomfort with cultural Others, she feels cozy enough with Razz to ask his advice about what she considers her daughter's "unconventional lifestyle" (90). Razz listens sympathetically, but remains understandably noncommittal and distant. Mrs. Bigelow treats him like a priest to whom she can confess her sins and, by doing so, relieve the guilt she feels about her shoddy parenting and unearned affluence. She admits how she had Teena "very late" (91) and that she was not a good mother, more confused than loving. Razz, however, resists playing the role of confessor, and realizing her lapse, Mrs. Bigelow cancels her indiscretion and returns to form with a platitude: "Everybody today has problems" (93).

At this point, Pinky enters and reinforces Mrs. Bigelow's condemnation of Tom and Teena's lifestyle, stressing their common faith in what might be called "traditional values." Mrs. Bigelow prefers to think of Pinky as "different" (96) rather than gay—which her social circle likens to being "immoral" (96)—and she compares Pinky to one of her cousins who she felt was "the nicest person in our family" (96). They carry on espousing family values—including the therapeutic benefits of knitting—until Tom rushes in, prompted by his analyst who suggested he should "see the baby [and] stay for a few days ... to see if I can become adjusted" (100). But this time Teena refuses his casual commitment and delivers her *coup de grace*: either Tom stays "for good" (100) or, otherwise, as she tells him, "I can get along all right without you" (101). Tom refuses to be blamed for their situation, but Teena, uninterested in his evasions and petty justifications, refuses to let him see the baby, reminding Tom that he told her he "never wanted to see him" (101). Tom, thrown off-balance by Teena's sudden independence and confidence, cannot reestablish his control: for Teena, the baby has rendered Tom irrelevant unless he commits to the family. Pinky then berates Tom for his indecisiveness and egoism, a bit unfairly labeling "your entire generation ... selfish little beasts who have no concern for anyone in the world but yourselves and your own selfish pleasures" (103). Tom's response is simply to retreat again.

After being rejected by her daughter and suffering a tongue-lashing from Razz—"I'm sick of being a dumping ground for everyone's confessions" (106)—Mrs. Bigelow exits, leaving Pinky and Razz to figure out how to cope with Teena's postpartum dilemma. But as soon as she leaves, Tom reappears, again brandishing his Freudian key, this time claiming, "I'm going to stay" (110). He professes his devotion to Teena, his repudiation of his analyst, and his rejuvenated faith in the nuclear family. The play ends in a series of harmonious resolutions, the characters having coated their individual traumas in a sugary altruism: Tom embraces fatherhood, thereby establishing his legitimacy as an adult; Teena fulfills her desire for stability within a traditional family structure; and Pinky drops his pedantic cynicism, his parenting skills justified now that Tom has accepted the responsibilities of adulthood. Razz and Helen revert to afterthoughts, token functionaries in a story that never really needed them.

In Inge's successful plays, stereotypes are undermined by his gendermandering. In *Where's Daddy?*, instead of questioning conventions, the characters reinforce them. The play predicts the sort of current neo-con discourse exemplified by David Brooks, a conservative columnist for the

New York Times. In the face of the 2003 decision by the Supreme Court of Massachusetts allowing homosexual marriage, Brooks writes:

> Anybody who has several sexual partners in a year is committing spiritual suicide. He or she is ripping the veil from all that is private and delicate in oneself, and pulverizing it in an assembly line of selfish sensations.... But marriage is the opposite. Marriage joins two people in a sacred bond.... Marriage is in crisis because ... individual choice is held up as the highest value: choice of lifestyles, choice of identities, choice of cell phone rate plans. Freedom is a wonderful thing, but the culture of contingency means that the marriage bond, which is supposed to be a sacred vow till death do us part, is now more likely to be seen as an easily canceled contract [A29].

Noble sentiments, it seems, from a fellow virtuecrat reflecting exactly Inge's point of view (Voss, 226–233). In parts of the play, Voss argues, "there is no distance between Pinky and William Inge at all" (230). Yet given even Inge's unintentional self-parody, as he pontificates through Pinky, it is hard to imagine Inge sympathizing with Brooks' conclusion:

> The conservative course is not to banish gay people from making such commitments. It is to expect that they make such commitments. We shouldn't just allow gay marriage. We should insist on gay marriage. We should regard it as scandalous that two people could claim to love each other and not want to sanctify their love with marriage and fidelity [A29].

Perversely, far from promoting legal gay unions—much less marriage—Inge in *Where's Daddy?* seems conflicted, condoning and condemning the homoerotic paradigm Pinky shared with Tom, suggesting on the one hand that Tom's life with Pinky was better than life on the street but not as valid as the sanctity of heterosexual parenting. Pinky and Tom's bond is clearly based on the idealized man/boy Greek ideal of pederasty, technically referring to an asymmetrical relation between an older and active partner, the lover/*erastes*, and a younger, passive partner, the beloved/*eromenos*. As the young man matures, he moves on from the relationship with the older man into a mature relationship with a woman, while the mentor seeks out a new young companion. But in a neat twist, Tom must make the Oedipal break from a homosexual mother figure, Pinky, to whom he has a powerful attraction, both sexually and emotionally. Still, Inge fails to address the issues Pinky brings to the table—gay parenting and man/boy sexual relationships—instead using Pinky to preach a rigid puritanical morality couched in familiar, all-too-predictable rhetoric.

Even more perverse, in *Where's Daddy?* Inge allows his characters to remain true to form, stereotypically static, while he manages to gendermander himself: speaking through Pinky, he becomes the schoolmarm moralist, nostalgic for traditional order, respect and good old-fashioned family values—no matter how, exactly, such values may be defined, isolated or identified. Of all the targets in this Sunday school lesson of a play—psychoanalysis, racism, "alternative lifestyles," commercial television, existentialism (all presented more as parodies than realistic situations)—he addresses neither the bigotry of homophobia nor the reality of pedophilia. In fact, by creating a bizarre role model out of a virtuous deviant, Inge seems not only to excuse Pinky's idealized pederasty, but also to condone it while, incredibly, railing against a supposed social degeneracy caused by the collective derogation of nuclear families.

Good Luck, Miss Wyckoff suffers from all the faults that plagued Inge's worst writing: clumsy shifts in point of view, stilted and artificial dialog, strained similes, awkward allusions, and clumsy use of flashbacks that weaken the narrative drive. Voss concedes that Inge "overreached into the realm of the sensational and the phony" (261). But the one saving grace, paradoxically indicative of the flaws in the less successful attempts Inge made in his later work in both theater and prose, involves his attention to gendermandering that made his early work so powerful. In *Good Luck, Miss Wyckoff*, a common first reaction is to assume that, instead of challenging expected behavior based on male and female stereotypes, Inge reinforces socially and culturally determined gender roles, reducing the two central figures in the story—Evelyn Wyckoff and Rafe Collins—to effigies of types: she the frigid, submissive female, an intellectual divorced from her instinctual, sexual life; he the well-hung black male, dominant, feral and finally sadistic.

But actually, Evelyn reveals herself as a strong-willed, masculine survivor who emerges in the end not as a victim but as a victor who fulfills her desires, faces the consequences, and demonstrates an admirably capacity for taking charge of her life on her own terms.

Inge structures the narrative like a palimpsest, with the past dramatic action sandwiched between Evelyn's present *a posteriori* situation. Both the place—Freedom, Kansas—and the time—April—are ironic. The town of Freedom is anything but free, the inhabitants representing the myopic values of small town midwestern America as intolerant, prejudiced and bigoted as any insulated community of John Birchers. Likewise, the spring, a season for renewal, fresh beginnings and second chances, proves to offer Evelyn no sense of rejuvenation, only humiliation, rejection and isolation. Her situation, for both her fellow boarder and friend, Beth, as well as her landlady, Mrs. Heming—who once referred to the ladies as "my girls" (Inge, *Good Luck*, 10)—remains, in Evelyn's view, "impossible to understand" (10). The disconnect between her social standing and her actions with Rafe not only confuses the townsfolk but allows them a sort of smug revenge on Evelyn, whose liberal ideas were often at odds with the local consensus. A midwesterner, she nevertheless attended Columbia University, "would rather die than be considered a 'right-winger'" (85), and was suspected by some in the town to harbor communist sympathies for being "one of the most outspoken opponents of Joe McCarthy" (119).

Inge works the narrative from the immediate present, when Evelyn prepares to leave town after being disgraced for having a sexual affair with a local black junior college athlete, Rafe Collins, to the immediate past, when she reminisces about the events that led up to the discovery of her affair with Rafe, her being humiliated by some of the students at school and subsequently being fired by the principal, Mr. Havemeyer. While she waits for a taxi to take her to the train station, "full of guilt and remorse and humiliation" (6), she reviews her situation: dismissed from her lodgings, ostracized by the townspeople and those she considered her colleagues and friends, she recalls resisting, after she "set up for herself a series of additional social amputations" (40), thoughts of suicide. Inge then shifts to her distant past, reviewing her visits to Dr. Neal, a general practitioner who attributes her anxiety on "premature menopause" (81) brought on by her still being a virgin at age 35, and to Dr. Rubin, a psychiatrist who gives her the moral cover to consider sexual affairs, but only if she makes "decisions with a free will" (125). She also recounts her clumsy, abortive attempt at flirting with a bus driver which causes her to reevaluate her sexuality, and her futile, frustrating visit to her parents where she discovers, as they baby her, "how difficult it can be to break the infant relationship with one's parents" (104). Inge then moves the narrative to the immediate past, beginning when Evelyn first has sex with Rafe, detailing the devolution of their relationship from sexual intrigue to sadomasochistic violence, action culminating in Rafe raping and torturing Evelyn. Inge returns to the immediate present to finish with Evelyn's final moments before catching a train out of town.

The novel begins with an image of Evelyn's acquiescence to male authority conflicted by the hesitant female desire to appropriate masculine power, expressed symbolically by the description of Mr. Heming's chair. Evelyn sits, as if deferential, "on the footstool that belonged to the big overstuffed chair ... considered Mr. Heming's chair" (3), but when Mr. Heming was away on business during the week, she and the other women in the house "used the chair with the knowledge that they were usurping another's rightful seat" (3). This opening image of her diminutive status—sitting on the footstool as if at the feet of authority—embodies the central issue of the story: Evelyn's encounter with brutal, literally naked male aggression, dominance, and control, and how she survives her initiation into sexual subservience with her sense of self intact, undefeated and stronger for the experience. Until her encounter with Rafe, Evelyn "never challenged [Mr. Heming's] title to the chair" (4). Now, "her breasts greasy with the ointment she had spread on them after the burns she had incurred" (5) when Rafe sexually assaulted her on a hot radiator, she wonders why women, in the presence of a man, especially a head of the household like Mr. Heming, "were like children suffering a loss of freedom to play at the games they liked to play when an authoritative father is present" (5). The implication is that Evelyn's resistance to sex, and by extension to dissolving her carefully constructed self in the miasma of her instinctual, ecstatic life, was so severe, only an extreme act of violence could liberate her from the safe, insular prison she had walled herself in, represented by her intact hymen—her "maidenhead" (74). She not only resents her virginity, she indulges in typical (if not stereotypical) rape fantasies, reflecting, perhaps, her anxiety regarding too much control over her body and her inability to reconcile the demands of her reason with those of her desire. She tells her psychiatrist how she "wished that some attractive man had raped her at puberty [because] it would have been better than no experience at all" (107). Having realized her rape fantasies in the flesh by submitting to Rafe's reductive, sadistic control, she concludes that she "could even feel grateful to Rafe for giving her the experience of being used. If she had also been misused, it was the fault of her innocence, which had to be destroyed" (174). Beyond mere justification, she understands, subjectively, a core existential truth: she is alone in a harsh and meaningless world where only an absurd faith in hope can sustain her. Though she retreats into anonymity, she is more prepared to encounter her existence—her sense of her self, her being—on her own terms.

Inge presents the process of Evelyn's gradual sexual awakening—from voyeurism, through vicarious engagements, to her complicity in pornographic degradation—though a series of events that illustrate the difficulties of a single woman in a small community trying to come to terms with her sexuality while maintaining her sense of social propriety. Remarkably, her first encounter with sex is both voyeuristic and vicarious. She witnesses a young heterosexual couple in a car in the school parking lot engaged in oral sex, and the incident left her with "sympathetic pains ... enough to add desire to her curiosity" (15). Next she submits to a physical examination by Dr. Neal, on whom she has developed a schoolgirl crush but who keeps the examination clinically professional. As bizarre as his diagnosis might seem (that her depression is caused by her celibacy), research indicates that this sort of pathogenetic opinion is not without medical precedence. Showalter identifies "sexual anesthesia" (21) as a condition by which "late-nineteenth-century thinkers acknowledged women's capacity for sexual pleasure and discussed the psychological and biological harmfulness of celibacy" (21). After examining her vagina and anus, the "tight-fitting doors to the unentered vaults of her body" (Inge, *Good Luck*, 75), Evelyn cannot ignore the "irony that she should be told by this man, whom she could love and give herself to with abandon, that a sexual experience would be therapeutic to her condition" (79).

Abandoning fantasies of an affair with Dr. Neal, she refuses the proposition from a bus driver, objecting (she hopes) "out of a genuine feeling of moral disapproval" (117) while being flattered by his frank expression of a sexual interest in her. Frustrated, she seeks solace in therapy and tranquilizers until, as if unable to push herself into sexual activity from her own volition, she allows herself to accede submissively to the demands of Rafe, a sexual predator who strips from her any pretense of propriety. He manages to reduce her from a sentient subjective being to an object existing only for "the practice of the sexual act" (159). Not until her submission devolves into masochism, when Rafe begins to "brutalize his victim's pasty white flesh" (161), at one point convincing Evelyn to crawl on her knees and beg, does she finally recover her subjective self. Once her former self has been completely destroyed—discovered with Rafe burning her breasts on the radiator—she is more fully able to reconstitute herself, reassessing her life within the context of the extremes— frigid virginity and absolute sexual abandonment—with which she now has experience.

The trouble with a conventional reading like the one above, in which Inge appears to work away from gendermandering toward affirming, in fact, stereotypical behavior—Rafe, the virile, implacable alpha male of Andrea Dworkin's nightmares forcing Evelyn, the repressed hysteric, to discover and accept the submissive woman within—is that even in her submissiveness Evelyn remains perversely in charge, maintaining control of the affair the same way Inge's other seemingly subversive women do: Lola, Cherie and Madge, for instance, who through their feigned subservience manipulate their men, allowing them to pose and parade in their masculine props while the women get exactly what they want or need. Likewise, for much of the novel, Evelyn plays a masculine gender role. She is well educated, logical, assertive, asexual rather than sexually deprived—

until, of course, her doctors decide that she is sexually repressed, creating (arguably) the sense of incompleteness she then tries to correct. When she meets with Mr. Havemeyer, knowing that she must resign for her transgression, she is the one who, as they say, takes it like a man (a phrase indicative of the normative prejudice inherent in Western cultural assumptions), accepting responsibility for her actions and making no excuses. Mr. Havemeyer's response, in contrast, is feminine. He seems incapable of respecting his own principles, and he uses euphemisms like "blackout in your behavior pattern [and] deportmental problems" (30) to buffer his discomfort with the situation. She admits that she is "bored by the talk of women, the smell of women together ... [t]he sickening smell of them when they were careless about padding their menstruations" (133). She complains, "Even a stupid man was more concerned with more fundamental things than women were" (133). And though her chance encounter with the couple in the car enjoying oral sex sparks her curiosity, not until she is told by Dr. Neal that it is abnormal to be a virgin at 35 does she begin to panic about her lack of sexual experience, "of making a complete surrender" (117).

But throughout her transition from uptight schoolmarm to sexual subordinate, a process initiated by Rafe but directed, as it were, by Evelyn, she submits willingly, as excited by the desire she provokes in Rafe (a desire that imperils him as much as her) as she is by the satisfaction she derives from actual copulation. Rafe, of course, is meant to represent the epitome of a sexual terrorist, primitive and Other, yet it is Evelyn who retains the power—not physically, certainly, but essentially—causing Rafe to act against his own best interest, jeopardizing himself legally as well as risking his scholarship and future viability for both jobs and any other collegiate assistance. Evelyn likens herself to "prey" (134), a victim, as she submits to Rafe—the frightening bestial image of raw desire, the id incarnate. (The naturalism throughout is heavy-handed, with references, for instance, to Rafe's "animal cunning" [136].) But Rafe might well be seen as a victim of his own animal needs, as much a prey to desire as Evelyn. She could have ended the flirtation at any time, and though her anxiety regarding the affair is real, it is caused more by her fear of exposure than any hesitancy to instigate Rafe's performance. Though she worries about being discovered, taking heavier does of barbiturates and losing weight, she only superficially objects to Rafe's stalking her, and her protestations when he is rough with her have no conviction. Only when, in a rare moment of self-actualization, Rafe acts on his awareness of his own duplicitous subservience and lashes out at Evelyn in revenge does she indicate any hesitancy or displeasure with their arrangement, and even then, once she is discovered and the affair perforce must end, she seems to regret losing the power she wielded over Rafe, and admits, "'Maybe Rafe Collins was the only man strong and stubborn enough to break down her resisting will" (174).

Evelyn is gendermandered to the degree that, while submitting superficially to the culturally conditioned behavior expected of a single woman in small-town America after World War II, she actually exhibits patently male behavior: control, dominance and aggression, occluded by her feminine masquerade. And even in her willful submission to Rafe, as she tries to appropriate proper female behavior that might qualify her for the gender-role mantle of "woman," she emerges from her crash course as a strong, independent, self-satisfied entrepreneur of sexual politics, having gained more experience in one month than her fellow-travelers collect, perhaps, in a lifetime.

In a curious moment, she hesitates accepting responsibility for her actions, trying, as if by suspending the moment of making a choice, she could remove herself from any ethical decision and simply disappear, allowing events to shape her instead of vice versa. In this abnegation she resembles the woman in Sartre's "Patterns of Self Deception" who "knows very well the intentions which the man who is speaking to her cherishes regarding her [and] is profoundly aware of the desire which she inspires, but the desire cruel and naked would humiliate and horrify her" (Sartre, 309): "She let him use her hand thus, dumbly, and remained inscrutably silent as he pressed her fingertips farther down his groin" (Inge, *Good Luck*, 144–145). As when Sartre's woman, "whose aim is to postpone the moment of decision as long as possible" (310), becomes all intellect and freezes action in the present, naively trying to prevent the future from arriving, Inge describes Evelyn disowning her initial submission: "She could not allow her eyes to recognize his use of her hand" (Inge, *Good Luck*, 145). But whereas Sartre's woman is in "self-deception" (Sartre, 310), Evelyn wills herself through inertia to become a compliant sexual agent of gratification for her young black knight. She "had given in to his total possession of her" (Inge, *Good Luck*, 146), but in losing her gender-modeled self, in the dissolution of her conditioned persona, she locates her irrational self. What she achieves in the end, after her ultimate denuding—when "[p]retense was gone" (145)—is a romanticist's balance between debasement and sainthood. Having integrated abstinence and depravity, she erases the either/or fallacy—virgin or whore—and conflates categorical demarcations into a more complex subject. Wiser from her experience, she is freed from expectations. After all, by community standards, she is capable of anything. But because of her notoriety, she is empowered. Rafe is unchanged from their encounter, but Evelyn (Eve) is recreated by the events—a scapegoat, yes, but projecting her imaginative self beyond the constrictions of her present life, she is free to choose, to create herself. Significantly, the taxi driver who picks her up for the last ride to the train station does not know or recognize her. Her strength is evident in her independence, her dignity and composure, and, now coupled with her sexual confidence, analytical insight: in Inge's iconography, she rates an androgynous ideal.

The other gendermandered character in the story is that of the narrating persona, the voice of the hardly disguised Inge himself. As Voss notes, "Evelyn's reflections ... although they are ostensibly given through the mind of a woman, are easily Inge's own" (260). Too often, Inge's idiosyncrasies interfere with the narrative flow. He indulges, as he does to better effect in his early work, the male as fetishistic sex object. Of Rafe, in one example of many, he writes, "Men of physical power and beauty are rarities in the human race" (Inge, *Good Luck*, 49), and even the bus driver inspires Inge to digress about the beauty of men's legs, concluding that a "man's well-muscled leg with a slim ankle was probably more elegant than a woman's" (95). Inge's adoration of the penis is merely embarrassing, indicated by frequent lengthy descriptions along the lines of "an organ that had terrified her when she saw its full size" (149)—others are even more graphic and less effective. At times, the narrator sounds juvenile, prone to romanticizing Evelyn's sensitivity and her attempts to deal with her depressions, describing, for instance, how she is determined "to squeeze the courage out of her soul to help her enter the classroom" (56). Some passages read like notes taken by a novice psychiatrist; others resemble the sentimental scribbling of a Jacqueline Susann heroine. Some of the sex scenes are especially embarrassing, including the initial seduction scene that, according to Voss, "strains credulity" (260).

That Inge, a gay man, tells his tale through the eyes of a woman, using a limited third person that barely distances him from his subject, does not necessarily create the fatal artistic dilemma that renders the story so woefully implausible. Obviously, the gender of a skillful writer does not preclude him or her from creating convincing stories told by a narrator of the opposite sex, and Inge, of course, had frequently been critically applauded for his truthful portraits of women. More likely, the aesthetic disengagement results from Inge's inarticulate transference, the clumsy redirecting of his feelings and desires toward Evelyn. In his earlier plays, Inge's homosexuality provided him with a cleverly subversive attitude toward his male and female characters, allowing them to exchange expected, socially codified gender roles, but in this novel he overidentifies with his subject and imbues her with his own personality, so she seems more a mouthpiece—like Pinky in *Where's Daddy?*—than a character working out, from her own volition, the existential conflicts of her life, erasing the ironic distance that gave him the perspective to infuse truth into the characters that people his best plays.

5
Short Plays

The miscellaneous series of mainly unpublished plays Voss identifies as having been composed between 1966 and 1969, some produced but most remaining in manuscripts "created or revised from earlier forms" (Voss, 237), indicates a further shift in Inge's focus from creating people to harping about issues. It seems as if the more honest Inge allowed himself to be with his subject matter the less effective was his subversive attack on gender constructs. The later one-acts, most held in the Inge Collection at Independence Community College, in Inge's hometown of Independence, Kansas, suffer from the same malady that, at least partly, spoiled the dramatic integrity of Inge's last three full-length plays. Like those barely disguised autobiographical exposés in which Inge's obsession with the Oedipal conflict, rather than providing a thematic framework to ground the action in sound psychology, works instead to interrupt the natural flow of human conflict, many of the short plays from this period illustrate Inge's habit of reducing his characters to surrogate analysands mouthing amateurish psychological platitudes and connecting the dots of a plot undiluted by the true ambiguities of life.

The plays in the Inge Collection support Gerald Weales' complaint about a general tendency of writers like Inge to replace "revelation through dramatic action" (42–43) with cheap psychologizing. In much of the "talk that goes on in contemporary drama" (43), Weales detects "the remnants of a first-year course in psychology or an incompletely digested analysis" (43). He notes a deterioration in American drama of classic Aristotelian dramatic revelation, and citing Inge's work at the time of *The Dark at the Top of the Stairs*, laments how much "the casebook had triumphed over characterization" (45).

Clearly Inge was trying to find a new relevance in his work, "to generate something new, something that would 'click' with the audiences of the time" (Voss, 237), but most of the plays of this period are interesting only as they illuminate Inge's mental state when he wrote them. The purpose of the plays moves away from a focus on characters and emblematic lives to a critique of what Inge perceived to be social ills endemic of a contemporary world he neither understood nor approved of. The work becomes little more than issue-oriented devices he uses to air his laundry list of personal complaints. Instead of expressing his philosophy obliquely, through dramatic action, he states his intentions in stage directions; reduces dialog to petty arguments and trite whining; uses characters to make bitchy declarations; and employs a proxy, a personal mouthpiece, to render his tirades against popular culture. His central characters often resemble Inge himself, portrayed as depressed, once-popular writers and actors thwarted in their comebacks by an unappreciative audience, a cynical industry and hostile critics. His usual targets include television, sensational films, advertisements and pop culture. Like Professor Benoit in *The Strains of Triumph* withdrawing into passive epicureanism, Inge in these plays "quietly thumbs his nose at the angry world" (Inge, *The Love Death*, 10).

Examples of peevishness abound. In *A Corner Room*, for example, a homosexual actor has married a minor starlet to cover up his homosexuality and protect his public image as a matinee idol. In tears, he whimpers, "My life has been a God damn mess" (15). When it is her turn to cry, she tells him, "Life seems so damn sad" (18). In *The Killing*, Mac complains, "reading is just a substitute for living" (3), and in *The Love Death*, Byron aptly announces, "I'm a writer not of my time" (7). Obviously, Inge's once-clever repartee is in these plays reduced to mawkish, sentimental banter. The same is true of his use of gendermandering, which in this batch of work devolves into descriptions and declarations unsupported by the action. In *Caesarean Operations*, a culture vulture quips, "One can be queer in so many ways" (1); in *A Corner Room*, regarding the homosexual actor and his wife of convenience, Inge's note reads, "It is more as though he were the maiden, and she the husband" (1); in *The Tube Boobs*, the husband is compelled to state: "I'm the man a this house" (2); and in *Overnight*, a play that promises gender inversion, the batty wife, a sexually aggressive two-fisted drinker (who happens to be insane), claims that she "always kind of envied men" (7), complains that she is "tired of wearing these damned brassieres" (7), admits, "I hate having tits" (8) and tells her husband, "I'm not going to rape you" (9). But instead of developing the potential inherent in gendermandered drama, Inge allows the action to peter out into a series of trite insults and the play goes nowhere.

Inge's tentative attempts at absurdism, however, produced the weakest plays, creating inconsequential scenes like *A Meeting in a Room*, in which the action illustrates no more than the title implies. Others show more promise, like *Tormented Woman*, in which life is portrayed as a macabre burlesque staged in an asylum. But most never develop beyond workshop ideas, and some are blatantly derivative—*The Killing*, for instance, Inge's limp version of Albee's much more potent *The Zoo Story*.

A good example of his attempt to be "contemporary," and in doing so sacrificing his earlier aesthetic strength, is *The Call*, a feckless attempt by Inge to emulate the hip new theater of Beckett, Ionesco, Pinter and Albee. While exposing the pernicious influence of absurdism on his work, *The Call* also illustrates Inge's disregard for the virtue of his most successful plays: solid psychological grounding. The play, like many of these pieces, completely abandons any consideration of gender roles, attempting instead to create a mysterious, existential allegory fraught with angst and paranoia depicted through enigmatic situations and allusive symbols, the protagonist experiencing life as an incomprehensible conundrum. In his introduction to the published version of the play, Stanley Richards unintentionally makes the ironic point: "Unlike Mr. Inge's ealier plays with their straightforward narratives and easily grasped characterizations, *The Call* ... represents the dramatist in a new and intriguing light as an interpreter of surrealistic attitudes" (Inge, "The Call," 29–30). And while absurdism may well be a legitimate response to what Martin Esslin, in his *The Theatre of the Absurd* (1961), identifies as the "sense that the certitudes and unshakable basic assumptions of former ages have been swept way ... discredited as cheap and somewhat childish" (23), in Inge's hands the desperate moan of "metaphysical anguish at the absurdity of the human condition" (23–24) sounds more like the embittered whining of a disgruntled grouch.

The plot of the play, such as it is, involves a visit from Joe to his sister Thelma and brother-in-law Terry. Joe, who lives in Billings, has come to New York City to lead a parade of fellow conventioneers. Dressed in a colorful uniform made of "genuine Persian silk [and] hand-tooled Russian calfskin" (Inge, "The Call," 35), he has lugged a heavy trunk full of his "private things" (33) up 22 flights of stairs instead of taking the elevator because, as he explains it, "Things happen in those elevators that I don't like" (31). Terry tells Joe that Thelma, an actress who is rehearsing a new play, regrets that she could not be there to greet Joe but will join them for dinner later. Joe, however, grows progressively uncomfortable in the apartment. He dislikes the modern paintings, for instance, and his immediate discomfort provokes a litany of fears: he is afraid of elevators, heights, flying, other people, drugs, teenagers—even cold drinks. He confesses he had difficulties in accepting his mother's death, and, as the baby of the family, the one who did not, like his older siblings, abandon their mother, he reveals symptoms associated with problems stemming from Inge's patented Oedipus complex. He is also bitter that he never had the opportunity during his university years to develop what he considered his talent for doing "some very unusual things" (43). He then tries to make a long distance telephone call, and when it fails to go through he decides to find a hotel, complaining that he "just never did get used to ... other people's houses" (41). But instead of making a reservation he insists on dragging his trunk around until he finds a hotel that he knows instinctively is right for him.

The symbolism is not, perhaps, as profound (nor engaging) as Inge (and, presumably, Stanley Richards) intended it to be. The angst expressed by Joe's paranoia never achieves metaphysical or philosophical sophistication: his phobias instead betray a peevishness that undermines any sense of sympathy Inge may have expected from the most generous audience. The weight of Joe's trunk signifying the overwhelmingly heavy burden of life he carries around with him is sophomoric at best. His metatheatrical carping about modern art is equally juvenile, a thinly disguised sniping at the rival "new theatre" Inge so clumsily tried in *The Call* to replicate. His clothes, too, may indicate a sense of authenticity missing in the contemporary world of trendy advertisements and pop fashion, while the convention he plans to attend tries to assume the ominous tenor of a gaggle of prophets announcing the end of the world, but his clothes, the parade and the gathering of men "who know what's wrong with the world and intend to do something about it" (35) seem simple-minded and silly, and instead of creating a contrast between the aloofness of Terry compared to the seriousness of Joe, the effects are pretentious, not intellectually enlightening. Finally, the phone call—whether representative of Joe's attempts to connect with people, not superficially but genuinely, or his desperation to reach beyond death and commune again with his mother, lacks the metaphorical punch Inge expected to land, and the portentousness of the title, referring to the climactic inability of Joe to "get through" (45), splutters feebly, leaving the audience with nothing but a dead dial tone.

More interesting, but again without any attempt at the gendermandering that empowered his men-taming women plays, *Midwestern Manic* returns Inge to the misogyny that haunts his novel *Good Luck, Miss Wyckoff* and its prototype, his unpublished play *The Power of Silence*. For dramatic tension Inge relies on the same sort of reductive naturalism that transformed Evelyn into a craven animal driven by an uncontrollable passion into self-degradation and depravity. Though he seems to have shifted his focus from the dyad of male-female gender role functions operating in typical behavioral patterns to a more archetypal confrontation between intellect and instinct, between reason and desire, the nymphomania that debases Evelyn, that causes her to surrender her education, her cultural identity and rationality to a dehumanizing urge for sexual gratification, also afflicts Diane Dior, the self-righteous idealist in *Midwestern Manic*. Not coincidentally, Diane's "condition" mirrors other women in Inge's work whose high-minded ideals are leveled by sexual craving. The play also reinforces the image of women exuding a sort of sexual energy that causes men to risk their well-being for frantic, debilitating and crass carnal calamities. The rape fantasies that drive Evelyn Wyckoff and her prototype in *The Power of Silence* also motivate Diane Dior, and in *Midwestern Manic* the dynamic is no less severe than in both the novel and the one-act: sex becomes the equalizer, a tool to counter intellectual bullying—in this case for Harley to even the score with his ideological rival Diane, and for Diane, perversely, to liberate herself from her theoretical moralizing and cultural pretensions.

The play begins as a farce. George Krimm, a television actor, lives in "*an eastern housing complex*" (Inge, "Midwestern Manic," 41), presumably New York City. He is expecting a visit from his sister Marlene; her husband, Harley; and their preposterously named son, Wyatt Earp Ffoulkes. As a family, they represent the *nouveau riche*, as "countrified" as George is "citified." The family, however, shows up earlier than expected and catches George still with his girlfriend, "*asleep, their bodies wrapped around one another in a languorous respose*" (41). Afraid of offending his sister, assuming she will object to their premarital sex, George first tries to hide Diane, then to sneak her out of the house unnoticed. What follows is a series of classic farcical maneuvers in which the object of desire—Diane—is pornographically displayed being shuttled between the closet and the bathroom in varying stages of undress, at one point wearing only "*her bra, panties and shoes*" (49) until she is finally discovered, their ruse fooling only Marlene who believes Diane has just dropped by for a visit.

The play quickly degenerates into an ideological squabble, initiated by an obscene phone call to Marlene, between Harley and his undiluted bigotry and Diane and her progressive idealism. When Harley threatens to call the police, suggesting that the man "oughta be put in jail" (58), Diane suggests Harley try to understand the caller's motivation, explaining that his need results from a lack of "sympathy and understanding" (57). She calls him a "victim of social pressures" (59). The standoff provokes a discussion of contemporary, newsy issues, with Harley and Diane staking out predictable responses. For Harley, homosexuals are "a bunch of queers" (68) and a "disgrace to human nature" (69); Diane retorts, "Homosexuals have made some of the greatest contributions to our civilization" (58). Harley's "maniacs and perverts and killers" (60) are Diane's "unfortunate people" (60). Blacks for Harley are violent predators, "niggers [and] sonsabitches" (62); for Diane they are an underclass suffering from "centuries of deprivation" (63). Harley believes the war in Vietnam will "keep those damned Commies off our shores" (69), while Diane claims the war is an example of American imperialism and "aggression" (69). But when Diane tells the story of how she was sexually assaulted in an elevator, fending off the attacker but nevertheless sympathizing with his need "to relieve society's pressure on [his] libido" (65), Harley responds, "If *I* got caught in a elevator with a girl as pretty as you, just wearin' a ruffle around her butt, I think I might consider raping her, too" (66). The arguing continues, with Diane and Harley finally resorting to calling each other names— Harley is a hypocrite, Diane a Bolshevik—until Marlene convinces Harley to apologize as a favor to George. She and the others leave Harley and Diane alone so that Harley can make amends, but instead he "*grabs her into his arms and kisses her hungrily on the mouth*" (76). At first, Diane resists, but then she submits, shouting "that's wild!" (77), and she "*begins to unloosen his belt [as] he draws her panties down below her knees*" (77).

Through his use of naturalism, Inge reduces the ideological conflict between Harley and Diane to an extended mating dance in which the intellectual exchange of ideas becomes a seduction ritual, a prelude for the savage violent coupling at the climax of the play, as if for Inge, naked desire is the fundamental catalyst used to reconcile common sense and intellectual abstractions to produce an integrated, complete human animal. But in *Midwestern Manic*, Inge introduces a second dynamic, the tacit competition between Harley and George for the possession of their mutual love object, Diane, and the implication is not that Diane, in some form of twisted justice, gets what she deserves, but that she gets what she wants. Inge here suggests that, in the battle of the sexes, good old-fashioned animal magnetism trumps cultural affectation every time.

If Harley represents an ideal of virility for Inge—his name conjuring up the machismo image of a Harley Davidson motorcycle, that symbol of raucous masculinity (and, ironically, butch homosexuality)— George, who admits "all I got is a little M-G" (61), drips with femininity. Harley is big, American made. He owns a plant in Commerce, Oklahoma. He produces things, creates wealth and employment and drives the economy. George, on the other hand, drives a little import and stars in television shows and advertisements (the Ur taboo for Inge). Harley is loud and uncouth, boisterous, clearly a decisive man of action. George is indecisive, inactive—appropriately asleep when the play begins. Harley exemplifies the new wealth of American industry, as crass and bawdy as the post–World War II economic boom, while exhibiting neither the refinement nor the sense of entitlement that comes with privilege. His wife is a bauble, an ineffectual frigid prude, hopelessly conventional and doting, indignant about her son's language and manners, objecting to his using the word "piss" (45) and insisting that he "lifts up the toilet seat" (46) when he visits the bathroom. Six-year-old Wyatt reflects his father's brutishness and his mother's inanity, primed to carry on the family's bumpkin tradition. But they are harmless and genuine, incapable of sophistry. In contrast, George promotes subterfuge, and unfairly judges his in-laws, dismissing them as being "from Squaresville" (44). But he and Diane are the ones living in bad faith, cocooned in their inauthentic lives—they are, significantly, both actors—justifying their values with clever, abstract arguments and ripe condescension. As the obscene caller notes, even he "could do something better than George" (57), and Diane finds herself explaining how she would willingly allow a stranger to have sex with her in an elevator as long as she was satisfying some altruistic impulse or therapeutic necessity, when in truth she is just horny. Their blindness to their own situation is neatly summed up in an ironic passage when George first tries to conceal Diane from Marlene and her family.

> DIANE: Well, the only thing to do is face the music.
> GEORGE: *What* music?
> DIANE: You know what I mean.
> GEORGE: This is awful. Marlene thinks I'm a *virgin*.
> DIANE: Don't they have sex where they come from?
> GEORGE: Yes, but they pretend they don't.
> DIANE: Hypocrites! [46].

This is Inge at his satirical best, demonstrating how easily the pot calls the kettle black in the artificial, artsy world Inge viewed as filled with pretenders and dilettantes, people so consumed with petty aspirations that they lose touch with their base, honest instincts. When he managed to control his bitterness, and channel it into this sort of black humor, Inge demonstrated that he was still capable of decent dramatic writing. Of course, the bare plot line and its repercussions are read more successfully without the tiresome and long-winded social commentary that Inge could not in his later work overcome, much to his detriment as an artist.

Of the published plays, *The Disposal* (1968) structurally mirrors Inge's experience with Freudian psychology, as well as his delineation of sexuality, gender roles and essentialism. The play concerns three men on "*Death Row in a Midwestern prison*" (Inge, "Disposal," 125). The focus literally centers on Jess, a farm boy condemned for the murder of his wife and unborn child who occupies the middle of three cages on stage. Flanked by Luke on one side, a patient, paternal man's man, convicted of murder during an armed robbery, and Archie, a high-strung homosexual queen guilty of murdering his mother and grandmother, on the other, the trio form a continuum representing three degrees of virility, from the effeminate to the masculine, from the nihilistic to the stoic, with Jess straddling, as it were, the two extremes.

The action is necessarily static, as all three inmates remain confined to their cells until the guards lead Jess away to be executed. Luke must wait six months, Archie one week. Jess spends his last few hours desperate for a visit from his father. The men argue, complain, reminisce and reflect on the various circumstances that have left them on Death Row. Jess orders his last meal (which Archie plans for him in an outlandishly macabre parody of *haute cuisine*), but when it is delivered Jess cannot eat it. He shifts moods, from despondency to panic, clinging to the hope of a pardon from the governor, and when his father's visit leaves him totally disillusioned, he collapses in despair. Luke, who tries to befriend and reassure Jess, has a visit, too, from his wife, but instead of any real conversation they merely exchange platitudes. After she leaves, Luke confesses, "She talks to me ... like I was already dead" (139). Archie, who expects no one and receives no one, converses with himself, rambling in his affected manner and mocking the sincerity and emotional distress of the other two, buffered by his nihilism and self-effacing irony. A priest makes several appearances, but his presence proves as impotent as Jess's hope for a reprieve.

The premise of the play deals with the nature of guilt and man's capacity for violence, what Voss more metaphysically describes as "the undeniable presence of evil, or capacity for evil, in all of us" (246). But beneath this surface theme, the play explores how men face death, much like the characters in Sartre's "The Wall" (1939). In Sartre's story, three men caught in a sweep by Fascist soldiers in the Spanish Civil War are scheduled to be shot at sunrise. They spend the night contemplating what it means, subjectively, to experience death. The youngest, Juan, cannot accept his death, and breaks down and becomes hysterical, his emotionalism spoiling his character, so that his death is messy and, in Sartre's ethos, unbecoming. Tom, a hardened mercenary, wants to approach his death rationally, so he is doomed to frustration, futilely trying to understand what is essentially inexplicable: what it means not to exist. Only Pablo, Sartre's mouthpiece in the story, equates the senselessness of death with the meaninglessness of life, so, because he cannot project himself imaginatively into that which is perforce unknowable, he awaits his fate calmly, his resignation sparked by a keen sense of cosmic irony.

In Inge's play, as in Sartre's story, how the men face death seems inextricably linked to their essential sexuality. For Sartre, Juan's emotionalism stems from his femininity. Tom projects the masculine ideal of reason, though it fails him when he tries to comprehend the incomprehensible. Only Pablo, as a sort of Kantian ideal who enjoys a mature and fully integrated psyche, sagely acknowledges the limits of reason and accepts his death as a natural consequence of life. Ironically, however, in Inge's play, Luke, a tough, no-nonsense mechanic who appears to be the masculine ideal, is actually a simple-minded naïf who admits he was so shy as a teenager he "din lose my cherry 'till I was eighteen" (Inge, "Disposal," 131). He is a thoughtful and sensitive inmate, but as simple-minded and bigoted as any of Inge's bumpkins. He labels Archie a "morphidite and a Red" (140), as if being a homosexual and a communist were synonymous, and he cannot understand why Jess killed his pregnant wife. His life is rooted in concrete action: he murdered a man because, as he tells Jess, "I had to kill him, or he'd kill me" (136). Ambiguous about death, he nevertheless claims it is as "*ordinary* as anything else" (132), and his embracing of religion is less a testament of his faith than a method of evasion. Still, like a dedicated evangelist he insists, "I b'lieve" (134) and implores Jess to seek solace in the comforting words of the priest. He proves in the end, like so many of Inge's masquerading machismo males, to be meek and effeminate, his masculine posturing a cover for his essentially sensitive feminine self.

Archie, on the other hand, is outwardly feminine, a *bon vivant* sashaying around his cell, dropping French phrases and philosophical allusions like so many bonbons at a sorority soiree. A haughty queen dripping with sarcasm, he is a hard-edged anti-sentimentalist bent on facing his death, as he has his life, on his own terms, revising his given existence into his own version, having transformed himself from an anatomical male into a surrogated transvestite. Typically, Luke, the alpha male blind to his own femininity, abhors him. But Archie is the true tough-guy, facing death with irony and humor (the sort of qualities Sartre found so appealing in Hemingway's code, and on which he seems to have modeled Pablo in "The Wall"). Whereas Luke's murder was a result of circumstances, a crime of necessity, a form of self-defense, Archie's was strictly a crime of passion. He confesses how much he enjoyed killing his mother and grandmother, relishing the account of how their shouting they loved him while he killed them him only inspired in him greater ferocity. He brags, "*Love*. The more they used that horseshit word, the deeper I struck" (136).

A nihilist who rejects abstractions (like religion and love), Archie states matter-of-factly that he is a "realist [who] can face what's ahead of me" (129). He lectures the others like the ghost of Foucault, mocking them for succumbing to feelings that he defines as "the product of centuries of conventional thinking that society has instilled in us in order to divert us from discovering the real crimes that they perform in the name of *law*.... The world itself is the great criminal" (130). As a complement to Luke, Archie expresses himself physically as a woman while his essential character is strictly masculine.

The tripartite structure of the staging—analogous to the crucifixion at Calvary—is also emblematic of the rudimentary Freudian map of the human psyche. Luke represents the moral faculty of the superego, often expressed by father figures in Inge's work (e.g., Virgil, Dell, et al.), whereas Archie represents the id, the unbridled drive for satisfaction unfettered by regret. So it is consistent with Jess's development of his sense of self—his ego—that Inge must locate him strategically between these two ironical extremes—Luke, the masculine femme, and Archie, the feminine male.

Jess's gender identity is correspondingly conflicted. He identifies, and therefore bonds easily, with Luke. But his actions vacillate between feminine squeamishness and masculine hardiness. He defers to Luke but plays out his aggression toward Archie. He seems to have killed his wife for the same reason Tom in *Where's Daddy?* refuses to stay with Tina when she becomes pregnant: an innate inability to accept responsibility for introducing a child into a violent and difficult world. His crime categorically differs from the ones committed by Luke and Archie. No matter how repulsive their actions, they had concrete reasons for acting the way they did. Luke killed from a need for self-preservation, Archie from raw hatred and familial revenge. Jess's murder seems more poetic, as if he were protecting his wife and unborn child from the ugly truth of reality, striking them in a moment of peace and relative happiness, as if by killing them he could preserve the delicate innocence and beauty of the moment.

Jess's overwhelming need to see his father before he dies reinforces his negative view of parenthood and underscores the disappointment intrinsic to his notion of a child's expectations of love, intimacy and the indissoluble bonds of fidelity within the family structure, lending credence to his motive for killing his wife, no matter how depraved the murder seems through the objective lens of perspicacious hindsight. Jess craves his father's forgiveness, but his stubbornly self-righteous father will not accept Jess's guilt—as if his crime were proof of his failure as a parent—so he cannot logically forgive Jess for anything. He is more concerned about the $60 Jess leaves him, and he slips away after a brief encounter, giving Jess a last bit of selfishly sage advice: "as long as a person lives, a person's got to think about money" (143).

In the end, torn between hysteria and stoicism, Jess, for all his admiration of Luke and disgust for Archie, opts not to go gently—the original title was "Don't Go Gentle" (Voss, 245)—but his resistance is more pathetic than noble, not exactly what Dylan Thomas had in mind when he suggested that his father rage against the dying of the light. In a sense, Jess reverts to the coward he has always been. His very reason for killing his wife and child was to prevent them from suffering—that epicurean strain again surfacing in Inge—but Jess never considered that maybe suffering is the essence of life. And though he was ready enough to eliminate their hardships, he could not muster the courage—or perhaps more accurately, the commitment—to end his own. He lacks the backbone to confront his father, to debunk the priest, to accept his fate. In short, his cowardice at the moment of death exemplifies the cowardice by which he lived.

Curiously, when Luke asks the priest, "How'd he finally take it, Father?" (Inge, "Disposal," 145), the priest says, "Like a man" (145). But when Luke responds, "That's good" (145), the priest clarifies: "He shook and screamed and defecated. He was unconscious with terror" (146). That the priest characterizes Jess's behavior as masculine when in fact Jess exemplified the culturally expected feminine gender response to death—to break down emotionally—reinforces gender distinctions and illustrates how the priest tries to "correct" the perception by the others that feminine gender traits are not positive actions directed toward salvation. He idealizes Jess's humbling himself with sorrow and self-deprecation, and is "proud of the boy" (146), complaining that he is "sick of the world's cynics and detractors" (146). This last bit of pontificating echoes *Angels with Dirty Faces* (1938) when Father Connolly (Pat O'Brien) persuades Rocky (James Cagney) to exhibit fear and remorse while being led to his execution so that the young gang members who admire him will not revere him as a role model or martyr. Clearly Inge's sympathy lies with Jess, but in *The Disposal* he is confounded by the same problem facing Milton in *Paradise Lost*: his most engaging character, Satan, is also the most evil. In this case, Archie is one of the most vivid and entertaining of Inge's quick sketches, and the one character in the play to maintain his existential integrity throughout.

Finally, *The Disposal* creates another of Inge's unconventional family units. Luke assumes the role of father, Archie the mother, and Jess the child between them. Characteristically, too, the father and mother are respectively masculine and feminine masqueraders, the father beneath his pragmatic veneer the sappy sentimentalist and the mother under her idealistic guise the tough realist. Of their real families, to depict them as dysfunctional seems charitable. Luke never mentions his father, but describes watching his mother "screw every man that came to the house.... Any man knocked on the door, she'd have him in bed in less time than it took her to put on her lipstick" (131). Archie regrets that he could murder his mother and grandmother only once—"those hypocritical old biddies" (136)—and he and his father "never had two words to say to each other ... I was twelve years old, my old man took one look at me, with red nail polish on and mascara ... then he took off and never came back" (141). Jess's mother died early, and all he remembers of her is that she was extremely religious. Talking to Luke, he muses, "I dunno know which is worse. To have a mother that's a whore or one that's crazy religious" (131). He claims his father "liked me" (141), but admits he also "beat the shit outa me" (141). The pathetic truth is that isolated together on Death Row, the three inmates confer with more honesty than they were capable of within their individual families. It is also worth noting that their world on Death Row is composed of men, each playing, ironically, a socially determined gender role. As Archie points out, "I wouldn't mind staying in prison forever. Because it's a *man's* world, and you don't have to try and get along with women" (136). Archie may be speaking here more honestly for Inge than even Inge might have been willing to concede.

More interesting than Inge's later short pieces, the early short plays, written, according to Voss, "roughly between 1951 and 1955" (143), are much more polished and engaging than the group held at the Inge Collection. Even so, Voss suggests that the importance of these one-act plays "is not so much their quality of craft as what they reveal about the impact that analysis was having on Inge at the time they were written" (144). His indictment is hardly ambiguous, as he—one of the most benevolent of the critics writing about Inge's posthumous career—confesses that the short plays are compromised because "their composition was at least partially therapeutic" (144). Voss explains how "plays in this group reveal aspects of Inge's life as psychoanalysis may have been serving to illuminate them" (149), but he cites *The Strains of Triumph* (1962) specifically as an example of a play that illustrates "how psychotherapy might have been affecting Inge's creative life at the time" (147), pointing out that themes in the play "are all matters that almost certainly were coming into focus through Inge's psychoanalysis" (148).

The first in the series of short works published in the 1962 Random House edition of *Summer Brave and Eleven Short Plays, To Bobolink, for*

Her Spirit, is one of the few that deals only obliquely with Inge's experiences in psychoanalysis, the hint of therapy, Voss notes, evidenced by Inge's plumbing of his childhood memories, as the play "is about a collector, like young Billy Inge, of photographs and autographs of famous actors" (149). Shuman is convinced that *To Bobolink, for Her Spirit* "demonstrates the kind of warm sympathy and understanding that he has for the undramatic members of his society" (128).

But while the play, as Voss points out, certainly proves less psychologically ham-fisted than much of Inge's other work, it certainly proves less charitable than Shuman believes. For one thing, Inge's description of Bobolink's physical appearance is condescending and mean, and he presents her as being particularly unattractive. She is "*so fat that her body, in silhouette, would form a perfect circle*" (Inge, *Summer Brave,* 117). Her lips form "*a grin of guzzling contentment*" (117). Her hair is short and kinky, and "*she wears thick-lensed glasses that reduce her eyes to the size of buttonholes*" (117). Propping her up outside the 21 Club in Manhattan next to her "*stand-by*" (117) Nellie, "*a starved and eager woman*" (117), Inge creates in Bobolink a character that seems destined never to transcend her caricature. Inge seems bent on promoting the stereotype of The Fat Girl with "*the fat woman's usual disposition*" (117)—which he defines as "*stolidly complacent and happy*" (117)—and rather cold-bloodedly sums up Bobolink's friends as "*people without any personal attraction they could possibly lay claim to, and so must find in others attributes they want and lack in themselves*" (117).

Suspicions about Inge's motives, however, should be aroused early in the scene. Aside from the easy comedic moments provided by Nellie and Bobolink recalling their misadventure hunting down Tyrone Powers, and the incongruity between the awe with which the others regard her and the pedestrian pettiness of her triumphs, Inge's focus on Bobolink is perverse and subversive. He seems to have gone out of his way to pigeonhole Bobolink only to provide an excuse for releasing her from the stereotype he works to explode.

The comedy is mock heroic, the characters framing their ethical systems around trivial pursuits, elevating low behavior into episodes of epic gallantry. Bobolink turns an innocent inquiry about how certain she is that Perry Como is inside the club into a portentous existential truism: "You're never sure of anything in this world" (119). The irony too develops from the high esteem Bobolink reserves for herself in her endeavors, reflected by her sidekick Nellie playing Sancho Panza to her Don Quixote. Bobolink, the old pro, lectures the neophytes on the art of collecting autographs while also establishing herself as a paragon of self-respect and an example of how to maintain self-dignity in a self-denigrating hobby turned obsession.

More comedy is purchased in the way Bobolink and the others, who all agree she is the top dog of the autograph hounds, are so pathetically proud of her trifling achievements, evidence that the "for her spirit" of the title should be read ironically. Her spirit—her gumption and enduring faith, no matter how silly her aspirations—provides a humorous look through a fun-house mirror at a distorted ethic, and yet this allows her to expose the defects in any stratified social system based on status and ostentatious materialism, such as the one propagated by the Hollywood star system and its Manhattan incarnation within the rarified and expensive environs of the 21 Club. With her false modesty, Bobolink retains a healthy remove from the ontological implications of her quests. To her, hunting for autographs is a game like any other, the people she seeks essentially no different from her and her friends, only wealthier and more famous. She tells the others, impressed that she has secured Lana Turner's autograph, "Lana's no better'n anyone else" (118), and sagely sums up the quintessence of character: "the best ones never are stuck-up" (119), even as she is clearly stuck on herself.

Bobolink and her friends resemble the petitioners outside the chamber doors of the Wizard of Oz confronting an implacable guard who denies them entrance into the world they have idealized at the expense of their own sense of worth. But unlike Dorothy and her menagerie, which finally induce the guard to relent and let them in, the doorman outside the 21 Club remains aloof. Inge describes him as "*a man of calculated dignity [who] holds his head high and keeps it turned away from the autograph seekers as though to disclaim any association with them*" (118). What seems obvious from the doorman's affectation is his identification with Bobolink and her friends, and his determination not to recognize his own reification of status framed by the artificial value system by which the 21 Club operates. After all, the group outside the door abides by its own celebrity system, with Bobolink in the leading role. The doorman's efforts to ignore the group prove his discomfort, as he is probably more aware than anyone of the paradox underscoring how the hierarchies that orchestrate the status-sphere inside the club are replicated on the sidewalk outside.

Shuman establishes Inge's "warm sympathy" by first qualifying Bobolink as "psychologically immature" (129), then he asserts that she creates vitality out of an otherwise dismal existence by finding through her autograph collection "meaning in a life which would probably be one of utter futility were it not for her avid pursuit" (129). And while it is true that Inge "gives the protagonist a pride and, within the framework of her circumscribed life, a dignity" (130), the pride and dignity must be considered ironic, given the comical seriousness with which Bobolink addresses her "pursuit."

What prevents the play from being merely a mean-spirited portrait of unimaginative losers living empty, vicarious lives "*like patients in a rest home*" (Inge, *Summer Brave*, 118) is the way Inge subverts gender roles in the relationship between Bobolink and Nellie. A familiar couple of autograph hunters with a shared history of escapades, they differ from Inge's other masquerading types: they are lesbian. Husky, androgynous butch Bobolink, wearing "*a man's coat-style sweater, saddle shoes and bobbysocks*" (117), exudes self-confidence, sure of her instincts. Not for nothing does she dismiss Lana Turner while idolizing Tyrone Powers, preferring the tough-guy actor not as a woman desiring the hero but as a man identifying with an archetype. Nellie, the complementary bottom of the pair, calls Bobolink "Bobby" and defers to her authority. An unflinchingly trustworthy and loyal tout, Nellie fawns around Bobolink like an obedient dog. This portrait of a same-sex couple that nevertheless operates within a system of clearly defined gender distinctions marks a natural extension of the opposite-sex couples that Inge introduced in his earlier major plays—Doc and Lola, Hal and Madge, Howard and Rosemary, Cherie and Bo, Rubin and Cora—in which both the men and women in each couple exhibit expected gender behavior while essentially swapping gender roles as they pair off. But what differentiates *To Bobolink, for Her Spirit* from the other plays is that Inge in the one-act seems comfortable addressing homosexuality not obliquely, as it seems clear he was compelled to before, but directly, unwilling to shy away from same sex couples or camouflage an obviously homosexual relationship.

Whereas *To Bobolink, for Her Spirit* deals with the performance of Bobolink and Nellie and the reactions of their fans, *People in the Wind*, the prototype for *Bus Stop*, illustrates Inge's interest in the extended if unconventional family unit. The "*corner restaurant of a small country town in Kansas*" (131) represents home for Grace, the motherly proprietress; Elma, the daughter figure; and Bud the bus driver, the absent husband whose tentative presence and professional transience resemble the life pattern of a traveling salesman like Rubin Flood. Grace tries to maintain a sense of order and propriety in the café, as if to immunize Elma from the disruptive elements that file in and out with every new bus, emphasizing the operative contrast between those who remain rooted in the community and the travelers destined to move on, with Bud assuming the odd job of ferrying the intruders in and then clearing them away, the arrival and departure of his bus maintaining a natural tidal flux along the highway.

Into Grace's sanctuary this trip crash three sets of couples that Inge uses to exemplify the possibilities in various sorts of relationships. Of course, the exemplary coupling centers on the matrix of Grace, Elma and Bud. For Inge, this represents a fairly typical family, recalling household structures from not only his first four big plays but many elements of the later ones too, with the masculine woman holding down the fort while the posturing male negotiates his place within the family power vacuum. Acting as the normative value, the family unit of Grace, Elma and Bud provides at least a façade of stability, commitment and mutual concern by which the other relationships can be judged. The cowboy and the girl imply romantic possibilities, tinged with potential violence that leave the situation of the girl ambiguous: she is hopeful and hopeless. The drunk, ostensibly without a partner, nevertheless represents the disillusionment that results from betrayal, abandonment or frustrated expectations. Finally, the two old women suggest another of Inge's overtly homosexual couples that seem more satisfied in their same-sex pairing, in this stage of their lives, than the heterosexual alternatives that seem to have left Melinda, the young mother they are off to visit, in need of their help.

The cowboy, having caught the girl's cabaret act in a Kansas City club, has hounded her in the bus until at this stop she manages to escape into the restaurant. With no place to hide, she desultorily sits at the counter, pondering her limited options while complaining that the cowboy is "mean and crude" (133). But mindful of Elma, and having had plenty of experience with the kind of girl she describes as "a no-account something else" (138), Grace cuts off the girl's complaint and tells Elma to get busy, trying to quell what she considers Elma's prurient interest in the newcomers. When the cowboy enters, the girl "*cowers over her coffee*" (137). She is obviously afraid of the man, and with good reason. He is rough, heavy-handed, and physically abusive. Yet, perversely, she is intrigued enough to have "snuggled up in the back seat" (140) with him on the bus, even kissing him, and it is this action on which the cowboy bases his decision to continue pursuing her, grabbing her wrist and "*twisting until a little grimace of pain comes over her face*" (140). She threatens to call the police, but she never follows through as evidently she enjoys a bit of rough sex. When she tells the man, "You hurt me" (142), he says "I shoulda given you a beating" (143). When the cowboy tries a second time to intimidate her, Inge's note reads that she is "*[t]orn between desire and confusion*" (144). His final sadistic pitch is to tell the girl, "You don't know how *sweet* a rough, mean guy can be" (144) and prods her to "[f]inish the trip" (145). At first, she logically resists his ludicrous offer to join him on his ranch, but whether deluded by his flimsy proposal to marry her, piqued by her masochistic curiosity, or basically having decided that she has just flat run out of options, at the last moment she dashes out to catch the bus. The implication of this pairing is more tragic than romantic, as the girl's decision is based more on her desperation than any real interest in a cowboy whose best quality is his violent manner and his promise that even if "the ranch house ain't much to look at, it will be after you get there" (145).

The drunk illustrates another aspect of relationships: disillusionment. A former professor whose Harvard Ph.D. dissertation topic (he claims) involved "an analysis of the love element in Shakespeare's plays" (135), the drunk explains that his distinguished career was ruined by, classically, his hubris. He explains, "I loved her very much but I wasn't going to let her know she hurt me. If she didn't have the wisdom and the upbringing to realize my own innate superiority to other suitors, then who was I to humiliate and degrade myself by telling her how very much I cared?" (142). Because of his stubbornness and pride, he wrecked his life, losing his job and his sobriety. He now lives in a sort of self-imposed purgatory, condemned to "spend the rest of [his] life riding on buses" (146). He is Inge's ultimate narcissist, destructively self-centered. What he mistook for connubial happiness was merely self-reflection. But the issue for Inge is how the professor's ruin exemplifies another heterosexual union gone askew. In a nice twist, both heterosexual couples—the cowboy and the singer, the professor and his shrew—are presented in negative terms: in the one case of dominance and submission, and in the other self-love and misanthropy.

With Inge writing outside of the gay masquerade that bloated Kauffmann and others, he convincingly and economically renders the oddest and perhaps most significant couple in the play: the two old ladies. Inge enigmatically describes them as "*obviously sister spinsters*" (136), but given its context the word "sisters" takes on too rich an ambiguity strictly to signify kin. The spinsters are bitchy, abstinent, moralizing snipes. But they are levelheaded, and for some reason they have been forced to move in with Melinda, possibly a niece, whom they have not visited in a year. They are sensitive about intruding on Melinda's life, but their conversation also suggests that whether divorced, widowed or deserted—the husband is never mentioned—Melinda can use the help. Regardless of their mission—out of charity, necessity or a combination of both—the two old ladies represent a relationship based on reason and pragmatism, not passion and irrational desires. As if comfort was secured only in rationality and pain the only product of passion, Inge implies that pairings based on emotion and sexual attraction lead to loneliness and misfortune, whereas the two old ladies survive as productive partners—one who will "look after the house" (146) while the other will "mind the children" (146)—because their relationship is sensible, rational, and grounded in matters-of-fact.

If the rational rapport exemplified by the two old ladies in *People in the Wind* represents the key to a viable relationship, immune to the passions that destroy more volatile romantic pairings, the couple in *A Social Event* is another example of a sickeningly superficial and, in this case, heterosexual coupling based on professional jealousy, vanity, deceit and narcissism. The obvious target of this easy satire is the stereotypically artificial Hollywood couple, Randy and Carole, two actors "*whose careers are still in the promising stage*" (151). Obsessed with keeping up appearances solely in order to further their careers, they awake on the morning of the most important funeral in Hollywood, that of the famous actor Scotty Woodrow, uninvited. They feel slighted because their most tenuous contacts—a dance with, an irrelevant mention of—have not improved their status in the hagiography of the Hollywood elite, and they are left trying to console themselves for ending up on the wrong side of the bottom line dividing those who count from those who can only wish they did. After a series of rationalizations and manic covers—that they self-induce food poisoning, for instance, to explain their absence at the interment ceremony—Muriel, their maid, like a *deus ex machina*, springs the cheap coincidental irony: her mother had worked for the Woodrows when she was young, and that she herself was born "in Mr. Woodrow's beach house" (156). She has scheduled part of the day off to attend the funeral, and later, by invitation, to visit the house. This is a social coup for Carole and Randy, but their success does not come without a price, and the idea of the quintessentially neophyte Hollywood tyros riding into a funeral and reception on the back of their maid, albeit in a Cadillac, offers such poetic justice that the prejudicial implications of race, sensibility and status seem like idle carping.

Clues to Inge's disdainful, or—less flatteringly—morally superior, snobbish attitude towards his characters come early, when he describes the *mise-en-scène* by noting an "*abundant luxury in the room but a minimum of taste*" (151). Significantly, the action takes place in the couple's bedroom. Instead of a space for intimacy, it becomes an arena for social strategies, career maneuvers and industry intrigue. Myopically focused on their careers, they offer no hint of sexual attraction, and neither seems relaxed enough for sleep. Carole complains that she "hardly slept a wink all night, just thinking about it" (151). Inge portrays Randy and Carole as shallow, vain, and perfectly crass enough to exploit for their personal aggrandizement the grief of a family at the death of one of its members. Incorrigible, selfish, obsessed with their status and image, Randy and Carole project no sense of respect for the bereft. The funeral, as Carole puts it, may not be "a social *affair* exactly, but it's a social event" (155). Based solely on their emerging acting careers, they claim a social privilege, conveniently dismissing the fact that their only connection to the Woodrow family hinges on Randy's comment in an interview that "Scotty Woodrow is still the greatest" (153), a sentiment most likely inspired by Randy's being "referred to in all the columns as 'the young Scotty Woodrow'" (152). Inge subtlety implies that Carole may be responsible for their being ostracized by the Woodrows, as she once danced with Scotty, and having met his wife, admits, in a rather overt innuendo implying perhaps some calculated if inappropriate flirting, "I didn't much like her" (152).

In his vitriol, Inge creates a straw man of the couple, setting up Randy and Carole as impossibly corrupt, even though he handles the farcical material with uncharacteristic deftness. The play is laudably tight, and the satire biting. The time frame, established in the first line when Randy orders breakfast, prepares the audience for the snap ending when Muriel reveals her inside track to the funeral. And as the action drives them through a series of tactless sophistries—appealing to their agent, griping, justifying their self-serving sense of betrayal and groping for rationalizations—the couple methodically exhausts their strategic possibilities just as Muriel reveals the ineluctable anti-climax.

Inge's determination to vilify the couple—who ostensibly represents his idea of a flawed Hollywood ethos—is tempered, however, by his gendermandering of their marriage. He subverts the typical '50s couple—composed of the deferential wife deferring to the husband's authority—when he reverses the gender roles by which Randy and Carole pretend to abide. (The potential for gendermandering the couple was nicely illustrated by the Equity Library Theatre of Chicago in its 2000 production of the play in which, according to Lucia Mauro in the *Chicago Sun Times*, director Joe Falocco cast the two leads as lesbians.)

Randy is stereotypically feminine: placating, ready to capitulate, suggesting they cave immediately, telling his wife, "There's nothing to do but face the fact that we're not invited' (151). He is indecisive, almost apologetic, excusing the fact that they were not invited to the funeral by saying, "We're both pretty new in pictures" (152). Frustrated, he rhetorically—pathetically—asks, "What are we going to do?" (153) before shamelessly hawking his wife to his agent as "a great friend of Scotty's" (153) when in fact she had only met him once. Recoiling from Carole's idea that they crash the party, he is quick to suggest they poison themselves to cover their absence.

Carole, on the other hand, is scrappy and masculine. When Randy is on the verge of giving up, she insists, "there's *got* to be a way" (151). An aggressive liar, ready to take chances, she is, if possible, more cold-blooded than Randy. The closest she comes to showing respect for the dead actor is to remark, "Scotty Woodrow was practically a landmark, or something" (154). She, after all, initiates the call to their agent, suggests they crash the party, and has the gumption in the end to propose that they accompany Muriel to the funeral. More competitive than Randy, she is determined not to let the other young professional couples in their circle—Sandra and Don, Debby and Chris, Anne and Mark—beat them at their own game. Having secured her ticket into the social showground, she delivers the *coup de grace* with chilling sangfroid, summarizing her moral deficiency in her final phone call to Sandra, predicting like a bit player on a daytime soap, "it's all going to be terribly sad" (159).

Even though Inge's venture into genre satire devolves into a scathing indictment of the naked, cynical opportunism and vacuous values of the privileged few working their way up the feeding chain of the movie industry, hypocrisy in Hollywood is an easy target. The controlling irony in the play relies on gallows humor: the couple using the death of a veteran actor to promote their own fledgling careers. So, regardless of how Inge tempered his bitterness with a surprisingly urbane wit and subtlety, the comedy, no matter how crisp the writing and fun the burlesque, remains fairly pedestrian. What makes the play elastic—adaptable for a variety of production possibilities—is Inge's play on gender, his baiting and switching stereotypical male and female roles.

In *The Boy in the Basement*, Inge disinters another dysfunctional heterosexual couple whose relationship seems to have ossified from years of mutual hostility, regret and recriminations. In a bold gambit, given the scope of a one-act play, Inge actually posits three couples: Mr. and Mrs. Scranton, Spencer and his mother, and Spencer and Joker. Each pairing represents a different categorical relationship: the Scrantons, heterosexual marriage; Spencer and his mother, the Oedipal bond; Spencer and Joker, Platonic or, in Freud's terminology, aim-inhibited love.

The action of the play is static and melodramatic in shifts, just as the tenor oscillates between absurdist comedy and high dudgeon. Spencer, a mortician, lives with his invalid father who communicates only through monosyllabic grunts, and his spry, vindictive, self-righteous mother, a campaigner against what she considers community immorality. The basement of their house doubles as a mortuary where Spencer works. The play opens with Spencer coming up from the basement—signifying his closet—to meet his mother who equally significantly descends the stairs from her superior perch above the family. Spencer has just finished the difficult case of an old woman who burned to death. His mother questions him about the extent of the repairs Spencer will have to perform to make the woman presentable at the open-casket viewing, then she worries that the organ selections the family might choose for the funeral will be ones she has to practice. Immediately, however, the topic switches to Spencer's latest visit to Pittsburgh and the suspicious phone call he made from there "in the middle of the night" (164) to his mother, ostensibly asking for $200 that he attributes to car problems. His mother is not convinced, though she admits that Spencer "never took to women" (166) the way his brother did, interpreting what she perceives as Spencer's abstinence as a blessing, convinced his brother was institutionalized because of "[w]hiskey and women" (166).

Mrs. Scranton is on her way to a meeting of ladies gathering to protest what they consider inappropriate movies being shown to the area youth. Before she leaves, she upbraids Mr. Scranton for not being a decent father, but Spencer intervenes. She leaves buoyant in the zeal and faith of her crusade. But as soon as she is gone, Spencer retrieves some hidden whiskey and shares a drink with his father, with whom he seems intuitively able to communicate. Joker, Spencer's young neighbor and friend, drops by to deliver the groceries and interrupts Spencer's tête-à-tête with his father. Joker brags about his prowess with women and his college football scholarship, then he invites Spencer to chaperone a party some high school kids are planning by the river that night. Spencer declines the invitation, but as if to compensate Joker for some ineffable debt, Spencer overpays him for washing the company hearse. After Joker leaves, Spencer begins to put away the groceries, but he is again interrupted, this time by his mother returning early from her meeting. Obviously distraught, she tells Spencer that her friends found out the truth of Spencer's visits to Pittsburgh: he has been cruising gay bars, and the last time he was caught in a raid, which explains his urgent need that night for money. Embarrassed and humiliated, Spencer packs a suitcase and leaves, but he stays away less than a day. Scene two opens with his returning just in time to attend to a new body—that of Joker, drowned at the party swimming in the rain-swollen river.

Even though Mr. Scranton's on-stage presence is limited by his inability to speak, his role is significant. He sets up the ironic dialectic, shared with his son, between the masculine, Apollonian mother who attends her meetings not "to have a good time" (162) but to "keep some semblance of order in this godless little mining town" (162), and the feminized, Dionysian father and son who enjoy the intoxication of whiskey and music, and who resist the moralistic strictures of their overbearing matriarch. Mr. Scranton's physical incapacity—he has been partially paralyzed by a severe stroke—represents symbolically the breakdown of intimacy in his marriage. With his ability to communicate reduced to animal-like grunts, he relies on his wife and son to care for him. His wife, a vigorous, myopic, self-righteous teetotaler, exploits her husband's impotence, and even though his debilitation prevents him from responding, she enjoys abusing him, holding him responsible for the hardships of her life and blaming him for Spencer's and Spencer's brother's debauchery. She takes pleasure in flaunting her mobility, her control of the family, and most of all the emotional manipulation by which she rules her son. In a vicious scene, while she is all but oblivious to Spencer's distress at his friend's death, she berates her husband for drinking—having discovered the stash of whiskey he and Spencer share—and, as if the stroke was his own fault, accuses her husband of willfully frustrating her, telling him, "You don't *want* to hear me. You never did want to hear me" (184). Spencer, on the other hand, readily conspires with his father against his mother. When he and his father are alone, drinking whiskey and listening to a waltz, "*the atmosphere is quite merry*" (174). Spencer proves unusually faithful and sympathetic to his father, as if they share the same paralytic malady. In a cathartic paroxysm of guilt, Spencer apologizes to his father three times in one quick speech (169), ostensibly because Mrs. Scranton will not allow any alcohol in the house, but the ambiguity implies a more universal, existential regret that transcends the immediate situation.

Spencer's inarticulate remorse stems more from his inability to counter his mother's influence than from his frustration with having to sneak whiskey into the house or the powerlessness he feels in easing his father's suffering. A victim of his Oedipal fixation, Spencer's apologies to his father indicate an acute self-loathing. Unable to leave his family but miserable living there, Spencer typifies the Freudian homosexual born from a dominating mother and weak father, whose guilt associated with not being able to overcome the infantile cathectic bond with his mother drives him to promiscuous sex and retards his capacity to live on his own terms. While Spencer resents her moralizing authority, referring to her sarcastically as "Her Royal Highness" (169, 174, 175), his mother casts herself as a corrective force in the household, the Apollonian countering the messiness in a world of passion, death, and madness. She demands order and sobriety, and prefers to mask the horrors of life. She upholds appearances, allows no alcohol in the house, protests what she considers immoral films, and focuses more on Spencer's cosmetic talents with the cadavers than the feelings of the families' grief. Regarding Mrs. Herndon, disfigured when she was burned to death, she asks Spencer, "Did you fix her up to look all right?" (164). And she tells the men who bring in Joker's body that Spencer will "have the boy looking like he could sit up and speak to you" (182). When her fellow prudes publicly "out" Spencer at the meeting over which she presides, her concern is that she will not be able to "ever keep my head high again, when I walk down the streets of this town" (176). In her longest and most revealing speech, delivered, according to Inge's note, with "*the bearing of a tragic victor ... leaning on the table in anguished prayer*" (177), she confesses her Oedipal guilt, claiming to have loved Spencer "more than I loved my husband" (177). She accuses Spencer of "degeneracy" (177) and in a fit of self-aggrandizement asks God why he would punish her, as she has dedicated her life to keeping her "mind and heart and body pure and free from all physical craving" (177). Her equating sex with impurity and "lewd depravity" (177) underscores Spencer's psychological impediments.

Contrasting her Apollonian posturing, Spencer represents the daemonic Dionysian force of chthonian madness. He works in a subterranean world (the basement) where he deals with death and decay and from which he emerges threatening the heavenly domain his mother maintains upstairs. On weekends he slips off to prowl the underground world of illegal gay bars "where men meet other men and join together in ... in some form of unnatural vice" (177). But in accordance with their psychologically determined behavior, Spencer and his mother exist in a kind of arrested dialectic, complementing each other as opposite impulses in a mutually destructive bond. Spencer, confronting his *mauvais foi*, tries to leave, but too dependent to break from his mother, he returns, an existential failure. His mother, who before he left had accused him of humiliating her, causing God to abandon her, and basically ruining her life, welcomes him back, resuming her role as his serial enabler. Spencer's return marks his defeat, her victory, and the restoration of a semblance of balance in the house. Her vindication and his acquiescence, however, are muted in platitudes, as when Spencer tells her his life has been reduced to "[o]ne dead body after another" (181) and she responds, "Now, Son, let's not complain" (181).

The third couple, Spencer and Joker, seems at first the most atypical, but actually their relationship is modeled on the same idealized man/boy Greek ideal of pederasty as Tom and Pinky's in *Where's Daddy?* Spencer's obvious attraction is to Joker's youthful vitality, his optimism and potential. Joker, vibrantly heterosexual, claims girls like him because he is "real independent with 'em" (170), presenting himself as the exact opposite of the dependent, guilt-ridden, Oedipally obsessed Spencer.

Joker delivers the ironical punch line in Spencer's life, telling him, "I bet in some ways you never grew up, Spencer ... you're like a kid, too" (173). The brief scene between Spencer and Joker allows Spencer his only honest moment of pleasure in the play, which makes Joker's death even more egregious, symbolic and grotesque, underscoring the impossibility of Spencer's ever finding happiness in such a relationship. Inge compounds the tragedy by suggesting that it was Spencer's declining Joker's invitation to chaperone the riverside party that possibly contributed to his drowning. Thus Joker's lifeless body, being carried into the house as if in the wake of Spencer's return, becomes the most striking image of Spencer's self-abnegation, of his death-in-life existence. In an eerie final tableau, Spencer realizes his most intimate moment with Joker when the boy's naked body lies on his embalming table, and having to endure his mother's sordid insinuations and thoughtless braying—"You can eat your breakfast while he's draining, can't you?" (184)—he opens Joker's main arteries as if committing suicide himself.

One of Inge's most intricate plays, *The Boy in the Basement* displays an absurdist humor missing in Inge's other work, while the cynicism underscores the hopelessness of Spencer's existential dilemma. For these reasons, among others, many critics, including Shuman, consider *The Tiny Closet* a sister to *The Boy in the Basement*. Both titles echo innuendos: the basement and the closet, synonymous images of gay masquerading. Like Mrs. Scranton, who lives in an *"old Victorian house of fussy dignity"* (163), Mrs. Crosby's house offers a *"big living room ... Victorian in design"* (189). By emphasizing Victorian architecture—and by extension, sensibility—Inge exploits the common misconception that the Victorians were prudish killjoys—though the duplicitous self-righteous hypocrites who inhabit his dystopias emphatically do suffer from a rare strain of moral degeneration. Finally, both plays share an unsettling Pinteresque humor built around Mrs. Scranton's and Mrs. Crosby's exaggerated hypocrisy, their inflated self-righteousness, and their outrageous one-liners. In a bizarre exchange pungent with grotesque comedy, Mrs. Scranton demonstrates her insensitivity:

> MRS. SCRANTON: You're a regular artist in your work. Imagine— burned to death, a poor critter like her, when her henhouse caught fire.... Her family wants the most expensive funeral.
> SPENCER: Well, they'll get it.
> MRS. SCRANTON: Is the organ tuned? [165].

The oedipal/sexual double entendre is as jolting as Mrs. Scranton's callousness. In the same manner, Mrs. Crosby tells her confidant, Mrs.

Hergesheimer: "I'd rather he was a Communist. At least you know what a Communist is up to. But a man that makes hats? What can you tell about such a creature?" (198).

Aside from these formal considerations, similarities end. Spencer and Mr. Newbold share little but their Freudian pathologies. Spencer may be pathetic, but his humanity toward his father and Joker—to some degree his mother too—creates a sympathetic identification that Mr. Newbold never elicits. Mr. Newbold is pestiferous: unpleasant, anal and arrogant, a whining queen. Whereas Spencer's generosity seems genuine and humanistic, onanistic Mr. Newbold cares only for his hats. Spencer opens the veins of his dead love-object. Mr. Newbold has a tantrum on the couch. He exudes all the charm of one of Molière's oleaginous flaneurs. Officious and condescending, he treats Mrs. Crosby as if he is master of the house, whimpering that he needs "*some* place, just some little place, that's completely private" (191).

Though inexcusably petty, and garrulous to a fault, Mrs. Crosby is too comical to pose as serious a threat to Mr. Newbold as Inge implies, and Mr. Newbold's inanity mitigates any sense of injustice Mrs. Crosby exemplifies. A dandy who works the floor of a pretentious shop "*somewhere in a Midwestern city*" (189), Mr. Newbold rents a room from Mrs. Crosby, a shameless hypocrite and inveterate snoop. The action begins with Mr. Newbold descending the stairs (à la Mrs. Scranton), "*impeccably dressed in the most conservative clothes*" (189), complaining to Mrs. Crosby that "someone has been monkeying with the lock on the door" (191) of the closet in his room. But by padlocking the door, Mr. Newbold, perhaps not so inadvertently, has provoked Mrs. Crosby. His secrecy is enough to pique her curiosity, his arrogance enough (for her) to justify invading his privacy. Regarding his closet, he "gave strict instructions" (191). When he rented the room, "no one was to go near the closet" (191). As soon as he leaves, of course, Mrs. Crosby is on the phone to her crony Mrs. Hergesheimer, ridiculing Mr. Newbold. Speculating on what Mr. Newbold could be hiding in his closet that could cause him to be so apoplectically sensitive, she tells her friend, in an uncharacteristically comical understatement, "I don't think he's the type of man that has love letters" (193). Bizarrely, she speculates that he "may be harboring a *spy*, or a criminal, or a lunatic" (194). Her suspicions, manifest by her use of patriotism to cover her perversions, reflect the irrational Cold War paranoia rampant during the Eisenhower years, ripe with the persecution of "strangers" epitomized by United States Senator Joseph McCarthy's tactics as a member of the House Committee on Un-American Activities (HUAC). (Mrs. Crosby's otherwise outrageous and unbelievable behavior seems less so after the political maneuvering following the September 11, 2001, attacks on the United States, including the passage of the Patriot Act and the irrational fear of dissent fanned by craven politicians.)

In farcical comedy, Mr. Newbold would be found out, but then he would also be asked to design hats for the two ladies, become the toast of the town, land a job with a major firm, move to New York and score a walkup in the West Village. As it is, in Inge's attempt to guide the play away from its farcical core into a more absurdist enigma, Mrs. Crosby discovers Mr. Newbold's fetish — hats — and when Mrs. Hergesheimer asks "why would he stay up in his room making hats?" (197), Mrs. Crosby exclaims, "he's just peculiar" (197). She concludes, "I'd rather be harboring a Communist than a man who makes hats" (198). But Mr. Newbold shares Mrs. Crosby's paranoia. Instead of going to work, he sneaks back to the house, and lacking "the courage to confront the women" (196) he "finds a closet to hide in" (196) from where he overhears Mrs. Crosby shaming him. Once Mrs. Crosby finishes her diatribe — "he won't act so superior then" (199) — Mrs. Hergesheimer "flutters out of the house" (199). When Mr. Newbold exits the closet, he first seductively tries a few poses in one of his hats before he *falls to the sofa and cries like a hopeless child* (200).

The theme of the play is shame. Mr. Newbold, Mrs. Crosby, and Mrs. Hergesheimer all pretend virtue under cover of propriety. Mr. Newbold, playing the fastidious male-at-work during the day, prefers to dress in women's clothes at night. Mrs. Crosby feigns allegiance to Mr. Newbold's rights to privacy while rifling the space he asked her specifically not to invade. Mrs. Hergesheimer encourages Mrs. Crosby in her intrigue, then retreats, claiming "there's nothing wrong with making hats" (198) and tries to discourage Mrs. Crosby from asking him to leave, insisting Mr. Newbold "hasn't done anything really wrong" (198).

In the end, *The Tiny Closet* is a classic revenge play: Mr. Newbold slights Mrs. Crosby, who then exacts vengeance. Mrs. Hergesheimer, the necessary witness to the fact of revenge, acts (oddly enough) as the agent of a normative-value (qualified only by her romanticizing Mrs. Crosby's truly destructive, spiteful action) against which Inge posits his pseudosadomasochistic couple: Mr. Newbold and Mrs. Crosby. While playing the passive, supportive female of the house, and allowing Mr. Newbold to act as if he were the landlord and she the obedient maid, Mrs. Crosby accentuates her complicity in the gender role she self-presents, but she undercuts it in action, just as Mr. Newbold exaggerates his masculinity to snatch a few minutes of cross-dressing. In a perverse way, Mrs. Crosby personifies Mr. Newbold's conscience, exemplifying his guilt and self-loathing. The real mirror into which he gazes, posing in one of his hats before collapsing in tears, only feeds his masturbatory fantasy, but Mrs. Crosby, his reality check, reflects the undeniable, accurate image of the way he sees himself through the eyes of society.

With *Memory of Summer*, Inge continues to explore the forms externally enforced conscience can take. The trite motif governing the play—the seasons of aging—is assigned (in this case) to Viola, "*a slim woman in her forties, with a delicate prettiness*" (203). Viola is not necessarily too far gone into the fall of her life, but she is aware of her fading bloom, as it were, enough to have constructed a world of never-ending summer—or perpetual youth—in which she can forever "hurry to the beach, where all the young people are laughing and playing" (204). Presumably a woman of means, she prefers the edge of the continent, the vitality of the sea, to her "husband and a fine home" (204) back in St. Louis. She is impulsive, dramatic, a victim of excess—Inge's version of Edie Sedgwick. Cared for by Alice, her long-serving nanny, Viola has come to the bleak seaside of "*a now-desolate resort*" (203), convinced she is still on holiday, the beach is crowded with "young people" (204), and she will "dine at the inn" (205). Alice tries to persuade her that, in fact, her holiday is over, "there aren't any young people here now" (204) and "there's no one at the inn" (205). Viola insists on going for a swim, though the sea is rough and the water cool. In frustration, Alice goes for a doctor, leaving the Coast Guard to deal with Viola.

The action is sandwiched between Alice's leaving Viola with the Coast Guard and Alice's return. By the time she reenters, Viola is lewdly (if obliquely) propositioning the young man. She invites him to drop by her cottage for a drink, remarking how handsome she thinks he is and coyly telling him, "you probably are thinking I'm one of those horrid old women who go around flirting with handsome young men" (208). Alice's return has the effect of her relieving the Coast Guardsman from babysitting Viola, and after he rebuffs Viola's overtures he eagerly frees himself from her desperate flirting and escapes down the beach. Alice, like the Coast Guardsman, acts as a check on Viola's enchanting reality, though Alice's control is more benevolent and humanistic than the robotic correctness of the Coast Guardsman. When Viola recalls parties littered with flirting and dancing, nights she would "come home long after midnight" (205), Alice argues matter-of-factly, "the summer's over" (204), "the shops are all boarded up" (205), and "the orchestra played its last dance on Labor Day" (205). She confesses to Viola, "I wish I could reason with you" (205). In response, Viola plunges into the sea. Later, Alice implores her to "be reasonable" (211), but Viola is beyond reason. With her vision of an everlasting "lovely day at the beach" (212) fixed in her mind, she submissively allows Alice to guide her back to her doctors.

The odd thing is how Inge freezes Viola and the Coast Guardsman in formal stereotypes. Because his focus is elsewhere, on the conflict between fantasy and reality, of imagination and logic, Inge exploits the culturally conditioned gender roles of the pair without subversion, shaping the play around that strict dialectic: the pure passion of Viola contrasted by the sheer good sense of the Coast Guardsman. Viola, the Dionysian, loves wine, music and dance. When she tells him, "I had a lovely swim" (207), he responds, "We can't let you go in any more" (207). She tries to romanticize their encounter, calling the Coast Guardsman "gallant" (208) and comparing him to "an angry sea god" (210), herself to a vulnerable "disobedient naiad" (210). The Coast Guardsman, physically typical of Inge's buff young bucks (Turk, Bus, Hal, Bo, et al.), is unusual in this play as he presents the Apollonian ideal of sanity and reason, sobriety and order, coolness, distance and duty—so unlike many of Inge's other pin-up studs parading their machismo to cover their femininity. Viscerally unable to understand Viola's passion for the post–Labor Day violence of the sea, he asks Alice, without a trace of irony or self-consciousness, if Viola is "*loco*" (206). He literally calls her to her senses, the authoritarian No to her contrarious Yes. He declines her offer for both a drink and a sexual liaison, stolid as Joe Friday.

In a naturalistic context, Viola is a fairly banal character. Supercilious, though clearly psychotic, she exhibits an enviable zest for the froth of life, desperately trying to preserve the exciting spontaneity of a beach resort during high season, preferring the gaiety of the transients at the inn and the potential savagery of the ocean to the sterility implied by her dull inland existence. She lives her life on her own terms, and not inconsequentially she has the means to do so, maintaining her romantic sensibility with no concern for the expense. In this context, *Memory of Summer* could be read as a Marxist morality play critical of the idle rich, exposing a class of decadents with enough time on their hands to cultivate pernicious habits and delicate neuroses.

On a metaphorical level, however, Viola represents a childlike resistance to corruption, signifying a sentimental identification with innocence recoiling from the harsh demands of adulthood, as she shuns responsibility for the carefree idyllic pleasure of an unending seaside holiday. And just as the setting and the time of the play contradict Viola's luxurious nostalgia—the drabness of the boarded-up resort a sore reminder of the passing of summer, the chill in the fall air promising the coming of winter—Alice and the Coast Guardsman denote the conflict between

Viola the imaginative naïf and her minders, the superego forces designed to curb her desire.

Viola's brief dip into imaginative fulfillment echoes Eliot's ending of *The Love Song of J. Alfred Prufrock*: "We have lingered in the chambers of the sea / By sea-girls wreathed with seaweed red and brown / Till human voices wake us, and we drown" (Eliot, 1,159). The play concludes with no resolution because the two extremes—her personal will confronted by external social restraints—are never reconciled, and Viola's brief interlude of madness remains just that: a temporary excursion into unfiltered desire before she is returned to the drugs and therapy through which the realists in her life assert their control.

The absence of gendermandering in the play prevents Viola from rising above her metaphorical status, mitigating the impact of the action and anchoring the characters deeply in the socially conditioned, anthropologically determined gender expectations that disallow them even the dramatic illusion of free will so necessary in creating any cathartic sympathy for Viola. Inge's dip into symbolism is a tidy exercise, but Viola never falls from her reification back into humanity, and so she emerges from her swim without having experienced the least bit of sea change and remains, as a character, little more than a vulnerable dreamer.

In *Bus Riley's Back in Town*, Bernice performs the same function as Alice and the Coast Guardsman in *Memory of Summer*, acting as a rational Apollonian counter to the Dionysian urges distressing Jackie. Inge sets up the same dialectic as in *Memory of Summer*, opposing the moral strictures of Bernice and her erstwhile husband, Ralph, with the combustive, haphazard magnetism affecting Jackie and Bus. Bernice and Ralph, the only gendermandered characters in the play, form a responsible, conventional couple settled with their child into a predictable routine. Jackie, on the other hand, is irresolute, often stoned on tranquilizers, and prey to her emotions. Impulsive, desperate for passion, she is another one of Inge's damaged misfits. Yet, for all her traumas, she still has hope, at least until the end of the play when she finally gives up any expectations of reviving Bus's love for her. Bus is raw, wild, and alive with wanderlust, but he is even more damaged than Jackie, incapable of ever reclaiming the fresh, spontaneous vitality of unconditional love they once shared.

The action opens with only the bartender Howard and a Salesman haunting the Fiesta Room of the Hotel Boomerang, a pathetic joint "*in a small town in the middle of Texas*" (*Summer Brave*, 215). Surrounded by faux Mexican décor, they reinforce the sterility and stagnation choking the community in its decline, complaining about the loss of business in a town where "one of the finest houses ... [is now] a funeral parlor" (235) and reminiscing about the glory days when Del Loomis, a powerful developer, ran a prosperous "one-man town" (218). One thing Del could not control, however, was his daughter, Jackie, and her fervid attraction to Bus Riley, a local "half-breed" (222) with whom, while still a minor, she became pregnant. Howie blames Del's downfall on Jackie's affair with Bus, claiming that Del was "in love with her himself" (219). Incestuously obsessed with his daughter—an archetype not unlike Noah Cross in *Chinatown* (1974)—Del had Bus sent to prison for a year and forced his daughter into an abortion.

Now a worthless drunk, Del and his town are ruined. Bus disappeared as soon as he was paroled and seems to have taken the spirit of the town with him. Jackie stayed, but she is so sapped of innocence that any romantic notions of love she ever entertained have long since been dispelled. While Bus traveled the world with the United States Navy, Jackie, still unmarried, stagnated at home, caring for her miserable father and spending time with Bernice and Ralph. But on the night of the play, Jackie manages to ditch Bernice and Ralph and enter the bar alone, asking Howard if Bus is back in town. Howard tells her that Bus has been around for a few days to visit his father, hospitalized after being seriously cut in a knife fight. She obviously has not lost interest in her former lover, asking Howard, "Is he still a *god*?" (217). Determined to see him, she tries to call him from the bar's pay phone. Meanwhile, Bernice and Ralph show up looking for Jackie, Bernice suspecting that she might try to contact Bus and hoping to prevent her from doing so. Submissive to the point of calling his wife "Mama" (220) and "Mother" (224), Ralph resists the role of "protecting angel" (226), insisting "We're not Jackie's guardians" (220). Bernice, however, has other ideas, and has assigned herself the role of Jackie's governor. A stark realist who admits enjoying only movies with "a story that's *real*, that shows just how nasty people really are" (221), she fusses over Jackie, worrying about her taking sleeping pills and now attempting to see Bus again. Bernice claims that because of "all that she's been through" (222) she is determined "to spare her from going through anything more" (222). Bernice complements the other side of Inge's dialectic: the common-sense spoilsport opposing Jackie's instinctive, self-destructive desire.

Significantly, Bus has returned to give his father a critical blood transfusion. His coming home does the same thing for the town, itself on life-support, hemorrhaging both spiritually and economically. As soon as he enters the bar, the air crackles with action. He is vivacious, spirited and raucous, a stark contrast to the others: the bleary, burned-out Salesman; dreary Howard, fazed by habit; the potted palms of Bernice and Ralph, bound in a mundane marriage, their lives dulled by habit. Bus, handsome in his Navy whites, remains a transient whirlwind of sexual prowess. Fearful of this force, Bernice slips Jackie out of the bar without Bus seeing her, and Ralph, after paying the bill and speaking briefly with Bus, leaves too without a word about Jackie. But when Howard hints that Bus has just missed "an old friend" (226), Bus immediately makes the connection, saying "maybe it's a good thing I din see her" (226). He brags about his adventures traveling the world with the Navy, inquires about some of his old girlfriends, but he never asks about Jackie. Even when he realizes all of the other girls he knew have married, died or moved away, he decides to "go down to the Mexican quarter [to] pick up a chick there" (228).

But like a wayward child, Jackie, at her first opportunity, escapes again from Bernice and Ralph and returns to the bar. When Bus tries to slip out the back, Howard convinces him to stay. In an awkward exchange, the two former lovers make it clear that they have different perspectives regarding their relationship. Jackie tells Bus that she "was praying you'd call me" (230), but Bus explains that he "ran into trouble with your old man once, Jackie. I din want that again" (230). She tells him how her father, and her life, has changed, but Bus consciously keeps their reunion superficial. She confesses, "I'm still in love with you" (234), yet when she recalls romantic moments from their past, Bus cuts her off, saying, "I don't fall in love anymore" (233). In spite of his aloofness, Jackie tries to rekindle their past relationship, but Bus treats her like any other pick-up, rudely reserving a room at a nearby hotel. Crushed, Jackie at first leaves, trying to maintain what dignity she has left, but in a few minutes she returns, convinced that empty abstractions like love are worthless compared to the materialistic satisfaction Bus offers her, even if she has to play the part of "an ordinary girl ... you happen to pick up" (239). Jackie gives up her romantic illusions and now accepts what the doctors told her when her father institutionalized her, that she is "too sentimental about things" (239). Likewise, Bus has graduated from any romantic affectations of love to a rough-hewn nihilism, claiming, "Love, to me, is something they put you in jail for [and now he is] in this business strictly for kicks" (239).

Bus and Jackie represent new types Inge introduces into his oeuvre: young people burned by youthful passion whose spirit is destroyed by love. This cynicism can be traced back to Epicurus, who warned against intense emotional states, especially a desire for sex—which he considered long before Freud the most intense pleasure drive—because sexual stimulation inevitably leads people into relationships that put them at risk for even more painful experiences. Of course, the alternative suggests the sort of relationship Bernice and Ralph exemplify. Inge offers no middle ground: the moth always embraces the flame, just as those infused with overabundant passion are irreparably burned by it. Inge implies that characters like Bus and Jackie are living essentialist nightmares in which their essences work against them and their free will is diminished in the throes of biological drives they can neither explain nor control. His apparent hard-core naturalism is tempered, however, by his unyielding sympathy for the human predicament: how people, acutely aware of inexplicable suffering, suffer all the more by their inability to do anything about it.

Punishment and control are again featured in *The Rainy Afternoon*, a frightening indictment of adult brutality and its effect on children. What appears on the surface to be a game of children playing grown-ups develops through crass materialism into a sadistic masquerade that ends in sexual exploitation and senseless humiliation. Inge extends his gendermandering in this piece to adolescents, implying that gender role-playing and reversals acquired through emulation are often chosen or swapped even by children to gain advantages in relationships. The children then perversely become youthful embodiments of Inge's adults.

Wilma appropriates a masculine role through which she dictates the behavior of the others in the game, noting wryly, "Girls have as much fun as boys do" (245), then she ironically assigns Vic the role of father while expecting him to adopt a passive role in the family hierarchy. Billie Mae assumes the safe subservient roles of, first, the pliant friend, then the naughty baby, and finally the abused maid. Vic reluctantly plays the husband, but submissively, dependent on Wilma not only for instructions in real life, as she directs him in the skit, but equally reliant on her in their make-believe family. Their understanding of relationships depends on their experiences with their parents at home, and by acting out their family drama they mirror their parents' behavior. The results, Inge implies, are not particularly encouraging.

The action takes place in "*the interior of an old barn in a small Midwestern town*" (243). It is a dreary day, "*raining a slow, constant drizzle*" (243). The setting and the weather create a depressing reality the children seem bent on imaginatively transforming. In other circumstances, their playing could be seen as a creative defense against the harsh reality outside the barn. But the situation as Inge presents it resembles a loge in hell more than a haven for innocence.

The two girls, Wilma, "*the older and more aggressive*" (243) and Billie Mae, who "*plays the game with some uncertainty*" (243), play "house" (245), pretending to be adults and "*treating the dolls like children*" (243).

Wilma's aggression seems to stem from the abuse she suffers from her parents. Her first command to Billie Mae is "spank your baby and make her behave" (243). When Billie Mae responds that her baby is behaving, Wilma is adamant, demanding that Billie Mae spank "and scold her" (243). In her make-believe world, adults are social vampires, concerned with "society people" (244) and prone to hypocritical comments regarding their social circle. When Wilma plays Vic's wife, she parrots talk of money envy and rank consumerism. Vic follows suit, but is less convincing, his idea of wealth extending not to finery and manners but to cars.

Billie Mae's home-life seems healthier, more conducive to a loving parent-child relationship. She is gentle and considerate, as if her parents treat her with respect. But because she so easily complies, wilting under Wilma's dominating personality, her decency is portrayed as a weakness, a character deficiency in the Malthusian world of adults. She is trusting and honest, but until those qualities are scraped away like so much cancer, she too will be abused. In the end, of course, Billie Mae learns to hate, a graduate under Wilma's tutelage.

In this brief snippet of pornography, mixing sex and violence, Wilma subjugates Billie Mae. She urges Vic to "spank her hard" (247) then to kiss her. Yet Billie Mae reacts as if someone told her there is no Santa Claus. If the excuse is that she is *"only seven or eight"* (243), therefore incognizant, then her change at the end is untenable. She merely resorts to having a tantrum, like Mr. Newbold. But in the existential crunch, Mr. Newbold regresses to a fetal retreat while Billie Mae hardens through the encounter, shouting before she leaves, "I hate you" (254), her new cynicism Wilma's gift.

Wilma gains control over Vic when she switches gender roles on him, challenging him by appropriating a masculine subject that he is ill prepared to deal with. After skirmishing over whose father has the best car, she traps him by asking a question he cannot answer: "Wanta play house?" (245). From within her masculine persona, she hit him with a feminine essential, the baseball equivalent of an impossible knuckle ball, and back on his heels Vic is soon asking, "What do you want me to do?" (246). After leading the other two through a series of socialite banter—Wilma, softening them up—she systematically corrupts them both. She teaches Billie Mae to threaten and hate. She feminizes Vic, punctuating the lesson with sexual abuse. Wilma spreads cruelty like a virus.

Disillusionment, a theme echoed throughout Inge's short plays, frames *The Rainy Afternoon*. Wilma's parents have ruined her innocence, and she, in the short span of the play, manages to spoil Billie Mae's too. Inge's equating growing up with corruption, depicting a child's emergence into adulthood as a lesson in violence and hypocrisy, indicates a move for Inge from naturalism into a finer strain of romanticism. Billie Mae is transformed from a caring, honest child, into an angry, vindictive sniveler, while Vic, supposedly initiated into carnal knowledge but provided no context for intimacy or expressions of love, experiences only manipulation and *"several moments of absolute and mysterious silence"* (254). Billie Mae learns what to expect from her friend: abuse, exploitation and humiliation. Vic learns what to expect from women: easy emasculation and sex-as-control. Wilma embodies Inge's ideal *femme fatale*, the cunning beast endowed with masculine strategies: a gendermandered bitch.

The children in *The Rainy Afternoon* pervert intimacy. Inge revisits the theme in *The Mall*. In his introductory notes, he writes that his intent in the play is "to contrast certain kinds of love and dramatize people in their pursuit of love" (256). He sets up his coupling geometrically, introducing pairs of characters in dialectical relationships. This structural symmetry provides Inge a moral framework within which to position his characters. The crones, for instance, paired with the matrons, separate two value systems: the carefree but precarious life of the alcoholic bums, scrawny old winos scratching for food, with the safe, predictable humdrum life of the matrons, women so well-fed they have to exercise to lose weight. Other pairings follow: the sailor with the young girl, Barney with Clara, Dell with Barney, Clara with her Man. Innocent. Degrading. Platonic. Promiscuous.

As in *Memory of Summer*, the time is fall and the setting a deserted *"mall of an amusement park in a seaside resort town"* (257). Inge notes a *"feeling of rejection in the atmosphere"* (257). The line of action follows the several sets of lovers, with the matrons and the crones providing a type of Greek chorus, amplifying the action beyond its immediate effect. The matrons rest on one bench *"after one of their daily walks"* (258), unwilling to live in the moment—afraid, in fact, of their immediate present, despairing of their past, and living toward a never-never future where they will be slimmer, spry and svelte. They complain (like Viola), "September's a sad month" (258), acutely tuned to the clocks of their lives quietly running down. Their pretentious conversation drips with superficiality. They are vain, dull, stodgy and afraid of "the people one sees here after sunset" (259). Matron 2 concludes the play with the ironic line, "This is no place for us" (274). Their dour sterility is markedly out of place among the rich, painfully passionate lives of the people who end up on the boardwalk.

Those people include the crones, beggars jaded from years on the street but who still delight in *"the ironies they look for"* (258). They mock the matrons, picturing their middle class mania: "Junior needs all his strength 'cause he's layin' the new maid, and little Geraldine is always hungry when she returns from the opium den" (260). But they respect love, true, innocent love (à la Inge), framed in all the trappings of gauche romance. They appreciate the good looks of the young sailor, and one reminisces about "putting a few feathers in my hair and jewels on my fingers and goin' off somewhere to dance" (261). Crone 2 recoils from Barney and Dell, repelled (like Bernie in *Natural Affection*) by the smell of disinfectant she recognizes from "them loony bins" (262). They remain cynical and free from conventional constraints, as if not to would constitute a major existential crisis. Only the romantic interlude of the young girl rejoining the sailor—a fit of sentimental excess—brings the crones to tears, but the effect of the action seems more like a Victorian prompt to the audience than an attempt at genuine pathos.

Barney, an unstable "*large man*" (261) just released from a mental hospital, returns to the mall seeking Clara, a streetwalker with whom he is infatuated. Dell, accompanying him, assumes the role Alice performed in *Memory of Summer*, and he too, like Alice, is more of a nurse than a friend, though again like Alice, he seems not to mind. Barney, his ego reduced to childish demands for affection, is not quite as detached from reality as Viola, but he is disconnected from the collective context of the scene at the mall. Lacking discretion or restraint, he represents another one of Inge's characters in need of external checks, doomed by a passion beyond reason. He warns Dell, "I gotta have me a woman" (263), and because "Clara loved me once" (263) he fixes on her as the object-cathexis of his desire. When Dell, his acting superego, tries to assert control, Barney calls him "Mother Dell" (263), rejecting his "advice and warnings and protections" (263). Like Viola, Barney represents a type of neurotic Freud identifies as being unable "to maintain clear and sharp lines of demarcation" (Freud, *Civilization*, 13) between the outside world and his own desires. Freud notes, "At the height of being in love the boundary between ego and object threatens to melt away. Against all the evidence of his senses, a man who is in love declares that 'I' and 'you' are one, and is prepared to behave as if it were a fact" (13). As a result of his pathology, Barney's desire is misplaced, a common malady for a man suffering in love, producing an emotional state in which "he ascribes to the external world things that clearly originate in his own ego" (13). In Freudian terms, Barney has been institutionalized because his ego has failed "to achieve a progressive conquest of the id" (Freud, "Dependent Relationships," 656). His aggressiveness boomerangs, provoking Clara. She tells him bluntly, "it's all over 'tween you and I" (Inge, *Summer Brave*, 268). When he tries persuasion, declaring, "I got real love in my heart" (269), she responds,

"Crap!" (269). She then tells him she is meeting another man and that Barney should leave her alone. She is scornfully, even violently unreceptive, and the more Barney persists, the more she resists. When Barney grabs her, she kicks him in the groin and slaps him viciously. As she leaves with her new boyfriend, all Barney can manage to do is shout insults, pathetically calling her a "two-timin' bitch!" (274).

Dell's attention to Barney is altruistic and nonsexual, but he is more of a handler than a companion. There are obvious parallels between Dell and Virgil, Bo's sidekick in *Bus Stop*. Virgil deals with Bo's demands that the external world conform to his desire, even as Cherie resists his projections, by reasoning with him, playing the role of a gentle mentor. Of course, Bo is not clinically neurotic, and Cherie is neither violent nor uninterested. With Barney, Dell is faced with a more serious challenge because Barney's irrationality is pathological. Dell, another dedicated epicurean, prescribes quietude, suggesting Barney visit a farm, and cautions him that he should quit his pattern of "chasin' gals again and ... gettin' mad and excited and worked up" (263). His reasoning cannot penetrate the blind drive of Barney's overheated will. He points out that women like Clara "love *everybody* once" (263), but Barney will not compromise and answers with an imperative: "Clara's gonna love me again" (263). Dell's inefficacy is evident when Clara attacks Barney and all Dell does is exhort Barney to "[f]ight back" (271). He never intercedes, and as Barney lies whining on the mall, Dell, "*hovering over him protectively*" (271), can only mutter a limp I-told-you-so. Dell exemplifies love as samaritan benevolence, but his development as a person with any psychological depth is minimized, reduced as he is to representing Barney's anemic superego.

The sailor, at the mall to meet a young girl from the night before, is spellbound by love. He confesses, "when I came ashore this time, I didn't realize anything like this was gonna happen" (265). He and the girl met on a blind date and now feel as if they cannot live without each other. As often in Inge, the conflict exhibited by the girl involves instinct and guilt, desire and authority. She has lied to her parents to get out of the house for a chance to meet the sailor. Anxious to follow her instincts, she fears her father will "give her an awful beating" (266) if she stays out late. The sailor, scheduled to ship out that evening, sums up their dilemma: "You fall in love. And it makes your whole life up until then seem kinda pointless" (266). The girl promises to meet him when he returns, but when he tells her he will not be back for "a year or so" (266), she runs off in tears. But her passion overrides her reason, and she returns, making plans with the sailor to "do something crazy ... like getting' married" (272). She agrees to stay with him until he sails, even though her decision will certainly invite her father's wrath. The two young lovers represent an idealized romantic encounter that leaves them "*in a fast embrace*" (273, 274). Their happiness, however, is tinged by their impending separation and the violence the girl must endure from her father (he himself another hostile, punitive agent of the superego). Inge implies that even the most quixotic romantic engagements inevitably lead to suffering, but suffering is passion, and the alternative is to become as life-denying and dull as the matrons who feel so out of place among the tortured souls littering the boardwalk, afraid to bite into the fruit of life, preferring instead "to go on a severe diet" (259).

Inge returns to this theme of suffering as a by-product of desire in *An Incident at the Standish Arms*, in which a woman's spontaneous surrender to passion is spoiled by her subsequent overwhelming sense of guilt. Ostensibly about "upper middle-class hypocrisy" (Shuman, 160), the play works with an ambiguity that undercuts the strict moral opprobrium the woman's behavior might otherwise incur. The woman is as much a victim as perpetrator as she struggles to maintain her superficial mask of human dignity while succumbing to the animal urges of her instinctual life. This Manichean schism in her psyche—pitting forces of goodness and evil—again reflects Freud's theories of the psychical duel between the id and the superego, and in this context the woman suffers from a "punishing conscience" (Freud, "Dependent Relationships," 655). Freud observes that "[t]he reproaches of conscience in certain forms of obsessional neurosis are ... distressing and tormenting" (654), and that "[f]rom the point of view of instinctual control, of morality, it may be said of the id that it is totally non-moral, of the ego that it strives to be moral, and of the super-ego that it can be super-moral and then become as cruel as only the id can be" (655). This need to be good in order to satisfy the nature of the ego, and yet to be driven by the necessities of the id, creates the "punishing conscience" of the superego as the source of the woman's suffering.

The action takes place in a "*pretentiously stylish living room of a luxurious apartment*" (Inge, *Summer Brave*, 277) where the woman, a divorcée, lives with her 12-year-old daughter. She has spent the afternoon in a sexual liaison with a taxi driver she picked up (the pun unavoidable). The contrast in their social standing is immediately evident. She is a delicate, "*attractive woman in her mid-thirties, dressed now in a filmy negligee, her bare feet in satin sandals*" (277). She thinks in euphemisms, recoiling from the cabby's graphic jabs, as if she can hide from the truth of her situation in palliative, oblique language. She cringes when he recalls how she was "givin' ... the works" (279) and appreciates her being "a sexy broad"

(280). She pleads with him to leave, first telling him that she "must be alone now" (278), then that her daughter will be "home from school any minute" (278), and finally that she would be embarrassed if the management "suspected anything" (278). Desperate for him to leave, she tries to explain that she was attracted to him because he "looked like someone I … once knew" (279) and that she only invited him up because she misses her husband "in these ways" (280). She can neither hide nor understand her guilty feelings, confessing, "It was wrong of me. I … I don't know what made me do it" (280).

The cabby is coarse, "*a big dark man of rough good looks*" (277) who claims to have had lots of affairs but is completely baffled by the woman's sudden change in attitude, from initiating the engagement and being sexually solicitous to expressing such overwhelming trepidation and remorse. The play begins with the woman "*running into the room as if fleeing someone*" (277). When the cabby follows, he is "*amused and mystified*" (277), feeling as if he has "done dirty on her somehow" (281). He complains, "I never saw a dame turn like you do" (279). He first attempts to identify with her, explaining that he has a family too and "don't want trouble no worse'n you do" (278), then he tries to help her accept her sexual need as a normal human desire. When she insists, "it isn't right" (280), he counters, "I don't argue with myself about things like that" (280). To him, satisfying animal urges is natural and healthy, something to enjoy, not fear. But as insensitive as he is inarticulate, as self-centered as he is tetchy, he feels insulted by her excuses and precautions. After she implores him to leave by the service elevator so that no one in her apartment complex will be suspicious, and then refuses to kiss him goodbye, "to leave off friendly" (281), he explodes with indignation. He is resentful, his value system skewed by materialism and class envy. He screams after breaking a vase, "You've made me feel cheap!" (281). The cabby, not the woman, obsesses about petty vanity and appearances, then damns the woman "and all your kind" (281) before storming out, leaving the woman to pick up the pieces, an image of her shattered life. Overcome with guilt she "*lies prostrate on the divan, shaking and sobbing*" (281).

When her daughter arrives home from school, however, the woman pulls herself together, "*assuming her normal respectable posture*" (281). The arrival of the daughter punctuates, in a nod to O'Neill, the injurious effects of adult hypocrisy: the sins of the parents are indeed visited upon the child. But the sin may not, in fact, be the mother's to give. Ironically, the daughter resembles the cabby more than she does her mother. Already she is "*indignant*" (281), hard, and quick to take offense. Unlike the fragile and deeply conflicted woman, the daughter is superficial and mean. Inge, through the mother, iterates Nietzsche's note that the "refinement of morality increases together with the refinement of fear" (Nietzsche, 75). In her one truly loving gesture, she allows her daughter safety in schadenfreude, and refuses to show her or share the terrible crack in her life where the pain flows in.

To avoid Shelley's thorns of life, Inge opted for the writer's perspective: voyeuristic, curious from a distance, playing it safe as a recluse removed from engagement, an anchorite immune from emotional threats. This philosophy of detachment embodies the epicurean cure: no expectations, no disappointments. According to Epicurus, the absence of pain rather than the presence of pleasure was the true path to human happiness. He counseled his disciples to "'flee from every form of culture'" (quoted in Russell, 244), and "advised abstinence from public life ... to live unnoticed" (144–245). Epicurus warned against sexual gratification and love affairs, promoting friendship as the most desirable form of social intercourse. "It was a valetudinarian's philosophy, designed to suit a world in which adventurous happiness had become scarcely possible" (245).

Epicureanism can also be characterized as a pathological withdrawal from society, akin to paranoia or agoraphobia. In this context, Inge more closely resembles Lucretius, whom Bertrand Russell cites as the "only eminent disciple of Epicurus" (248). Like Inge, Lucretius "committed suicide, and appears to have suffered from periodic insanity" (248), and he "feels towards Epicurus as towards a saviour" (248). Given his often-desperate disillusionment, Inge approaches Epicurus in a similar manner. And, as if to proselytize this philosophy, this strategy, Inge ends his collection of short plays with perhaps his most metatheatrical statement, *The Strains of Triumph*, a primer of epicurean philosophy as well as a comment on the paradoxical dilemma of a writer who must remove himself from life in order to render it persuasively.

Two types of competition frame the action: a college track meet and a triangular love affair. The track meet involves Tom, a genuine team player, who waits with Ann for his event; Ben, displaced from Iowa, who realizes he is no longer Ann's favorite; and Professor Benoit, who occupies the center of the play while paradoxically haunting the periphery of the action. Inge considers the track meet a metaphor for life: one either plays the game or spectates. Within this metaphorical context, Ben's refusing to compete in the relay competition mirrors his withdrawal from the dating game after Ann jilts him. He confesses, "I never knew before ... what it is to lose" (Inge, *Summer Brave*, 293). But his decision lets down his teammates who immediately brand him "a lousy sport" (294). They appeal to his loyalty, but Ben, in a quiet epiphany, chooses instead to become an apprentice to Benoit and his epicureanism.

The love triangle involves Ben, a stereotypical naïf, and Ann, who claims that she and Ben "grew up together" (286), bragging, "I know how deeply he feels things, much more than he shows" (286). Ann intends to break up with Ben because she thinks she has found a man who completes her, who, with her, creates "one person" (288). Cruelly, Tom and Ann have both experienced what they are about to inflict on Ben—rejection, the destructive power of love—echoing a theme from *The Rainy Afternoon*: they, as Wilma does to Billie Mae, visit the violence done to them onto another, their happiness purchased at Ben's expense. They trade smarmy lines that pass, in their love-struck eyes, as a depiction of ideal love, then they act out their own ideal. Tom tells her, "they meet and fall in love, and they become like one," (288), and she concedes, with an unfortunate absence of irony, "I never realized, before we met, that I was incomplete in any way" (288).

When these two egoists return to break the news to Ben—that she and Tom are infatuated with each other, and have already decided to get married—Ann fatuously tries to reassure Ben: "I really like you an awful lot" (295). Insults come easily to Tom as well. He tells Ben, "If you don't have a date, you can dance with Ann all you want" (295). But suddenly when the newest campus couple is called back for Tom's race, all three face an existential dilemma: to abandon their safe vantage on the hill, or skip the fray. Tom and Ann choose engagement. Tom returns to the track to run his race, and Ann promises to meet him "at the gate" (296). Ben chooses detachment, but the separation is so painful he is reduced to behaving like a blathering child. Tom fends off Ben's residual anger by pleading with him: "I don't want you to hate me" (296). Ann scolds Ben too: "you can't hate Tom" (296). This sloganeering—of not hating being redemptive, of teaching people to hate being a form of corruption—resonates from *The Rainy Afternoon*, with Wilma's teaching Billie Mae to hate crowning the episode. Ironically, when Ben loses the ability to hate, a loss supposedly considered a virtue, he will have succeeded only in removing himself from a commitment to life.

Such is the stuff of Professor Benoit's lectures to his acolyte Ben: a pastiche of epicurean ethics and self-pity. From his vantage on a "*small hillock behind which lies an open field*" (285), Benoit assumes his safely detached role of a "solitary spectator" (291). As if to help Ben protect himself emotionally, Benoit, like a missionary seeking converts for his cult, seduces Ben into the charms of self-disenfranchisement. He confesses that he too had a bad experience with a woman: "The reality of her seemed too much for me to bear, and I fled" (291). Benoit draws Ben out of an emotionally painful but actual heterosexual relationship into a coolly Platonic homosexual one, even as the action favors a straightforward gay pick-up. Benoit first identifies with his victim: "*Every*one loves the games. Although not everyone cares to contend in them" (291). Then he redirects his pathos back onto himself: "I wonder if I have lived my life at all, if my life has not been, rather, a period of observation on earth, watching others live" (291). Ben, old beyond his years, sighs, "I've always played in the games" (298). Recognizing Ben's resignation as an opening, Benoit seals his seduction: "One doesn't have to run in the races to enjoy them" (298). By allowing Benoit the point of view of the audience—of an observer of a game played on stage—then exposing Benoit as a watcher being watched, to whom life is "beautiful and exciting ... from a distance" (298)—Inge creates a pornographic tableau, baroque with desire and repression, sealed with a sly *double entendre* by Benoit: "come up on my hillock and watch" (298).

Unlike Joker in *The Boy in the Basement*, Ben is feminized. And because he cannot maintain his masculine gender role, it is no wonder that Ann prefers Tom, the masculine standard bearer in the play, the tougher of the two suitors who brags that he "learned to take it" (287) after his earlier romantic disappointment. Tom not only races, he wins. But instead of accepting rejection as "a part of growing up" (287) the way Tom does, Ben sulks, sobs and throws tantrums, unwilling to separate himself from his object-cathexis. But Ann has no real choice. A persistent good sport, she is also conceited, insensitive and pragmatically self-centered, a perfect match for Tom who is, after all, equally unctuous, condescending and bleating.

The coupling of Tom with Ann reinforces the accepted stereotypical gender roles their family and peers expect from them. But Ben's anxiety about his relationship with Tom and Ann, which stretches probability, exposes more complex issues he is reluctant to confront about his sexual identity. He is also a victim of his own skewed expectations, as ill prepared to manage a crush on a 19-year-old coed as he is to deal with the existential issues in his life. Whereas his initial loss involved Ann, his second is categorical: desire itself. But his sniveling self-pity disqualifies him as a representative of the melancholic type of Everyman dear to reclusive romantics from Rousseau to Thoreau. Ben, finally, is merely pathetic, even as he emerges as a tenable candidate to share Benoit's prescription for happiness: to live a vicarious life, following the epicurean dictate that "recommended a temperate withdrawal from public life" (Quinton, 307).

Although Inge's use of role reversal for dramatic effect is diminished by his focus on Freudian psychotherapeutic theories, the gendermandering that helped make his major plays so subversive and, possibly, successful, pervades the short plays too. Each features characters struggling with gender assignments, a thematic consideration that not only illustrates Inge's struggle with his own sexuality but also questions the very foundations of cultural definitions regarding gender identities. Voss warns that "many of these plays exhibit dimensions of aberrant sexuality" (144), citing as especially egregious *The Rainy Afternoon*, *The Boy in the Basement* and *The Tiny Closet*, and he concludes that "they are all valuable for what they reveal from a very important time in [Inge's] life, a time when, even in the midst of depression and psychoanalysis, he continued to write with intense imagination and soul-searching creativity" (149). Actions that Voss deems "aberrant," however—childhood sexual hazing, homosexuality and transvestism—are not necessarily themselves perversions as much as markers setting limits to acceptable cultural habits, outside of which many of Inge's characters are abandoned, left in a no-man's land of androgynous duplicity without any clear demarcations by which they can define themselves. Shuman also emphasizes that the one-act plays address "a large variety of classical psychological disorders" (124). Along with homosexuality, transvestism and "the Oedipus problem" (125) he lists sadism, "nymphomaniacal tendencies" (125) and pathological daydreaming. But to treat these inclinations as maladies, as both critics tend to—with Voss, perhaps, less judgmental—underscores the plight with which Inge and his characters struggle: forced into an ontological either/or fallacy, they live in a shadow world of repression, frustrated by arrested desire, unable to reconcile their natures with the social prohibitions that undermine and yet determine their gender roles in the culture.

Bibliography

Atkinson, Brooks. "Inge's *Picnic.*" *New York Times*, sec. 2.1, March 1, 1953.
Badinter, Elisabeth. *The Unopposite Sex: The End of the Gender Battle*. Translated by Barbara Wright. New York: Harper and Row, 1989.
Bentley, Eric. "Pity the Dumb Ox." *New Republic*, March 16, 1953: 22–23.
Ben-Zvi, Linda. "Review of *A Life of William Inge: The Strains of Triumph.*" *American Literature*, June 1990, 62.2: 356–357.
Berger, Maurice, Brian Wallis, Simon Watson, eds. "Introduction." *Constructing Masculinity*. New York: Routledge, 1995. 1–7.
Brooks, David. "The Power of Marriage." *New York Times*, national edition: A29, November 22, 2003.
Brustein, Robert. "The Men-taming Women of William Inge." *Harper's*, November 1958: 52–57.
Byars, Jackie. *All That Hollywood Allows: Re-Reading Gender in 1950s Melodrama*. Chapel Hill: University of North Carolina, 1991.
Centola, Steven R. "Compromise as Bad Faith: Arthur Miller's *A View from the Bridge* and William Inge's *Come Back, Little Sheba.*" *The Midwest Quarterly*, Autumn 1986, 28.1: 100–113.
Clurman, Harold. "Theatre." *The Nation*, August 3, 1974: 91–93.
_____. "Theatre: A Good Play." *New Republic*, March 13, 1950: 22–23.
Coleman, Barbara J. "Maidenform(ed): Images of American Women in the 1950s." *Forming and Reforming Identity*. Edited by Carol Siegel and Ann Kibbey. New York: New York University Press, 1995. 3–29.
Dennis, Patrick. "A Literate Soap Opera." *New Republic*, December 30, 1957: 21.
Dowd, Maureen. "Is Condi Gaslighting Rummy?" *New York Times*, national edition: A35, October 9, 2003.
Driver, Tom. "Hearts and Heads." *The Christian Century*, January 1, 1958: 17–18.
Eliot, T.S. "The Love Song of J. Alfred Prufrock." *American Poetry and Prose*. Edited by Norman Foerster, et al. Boston: Houghton Mifflin, 1970. 1,157–1,159.
_____. "Tradition and the Individual Talent." *Criticism: The Major Texts*. Edited by W.J. Bate. New York: Harcourt Brace Jovanovich, 1970. 525–529.
_____. *The Wasteland*. Foerster, et al. 1,161–1,169.
Esslin, Martin. *The Theatre of the Absurd*. 3rd edition. New York: Penguin, 1991.
Feldman, Shosana. *What Does a Woman Want?* Baltimore: Johns Hopkins University Press, 1993.
Fisher, James. "The Angels of Fructification: Tennessee Williams, Tony Kush-

ner, and Images of Homosexuality on the American Stage." *Mississippi Quarterly*, Winter 49.1 (1995–96): 13–53. August 24, 2003 http://persweb.wabash.edu/facstaff/ fisherj/new/angeloffructification.html.

Freud, Sigmund. *Civilization and Its Discontents*. Translated by James Strachey. New York: W.W. Norton, 1961.

_____. "The Dependent Relationships of the Ego." Gay. 651–658.

_____. "Leonardo da Vinci and a Memory of His Childhood." Gay. 443–481.

_____. "A Special Type of Choice of Object Made by Men." *The Freud Reader*. Edited by Peter Gay. New York: W.W. Norton, 1989. 387–394.

_____. "Three Essays on the Theory of Sexuality." Gay. 239–293.

Govan, Michael. "Note on the Series." *Constructing Masculinity*. New York: Routledge, 1995. viii.

Handy, Bruce. "Roll Over, Ward Cleaver." *Time*, April 14, 1997: 78–85.

Hayes, Richard. "The Stage." *Commonweal*, 57 (1953): 603.

Heller, Dana. "Introduction: Plotting the Family." *Family Plots: The De-Oedipalization of Popular Culture*. Philadelphia: University of Pennsylvania Press, 1995.

Inge, William. *Bad Breath*. William Inge Collection, Independence Community College, Independence, KS.

_____. *Caesarean Operations*. William Inge Collection, Independence Community College, Independence, KS.

_____. "The Call." *The Best Short Plays of 1968*. Edited by Stanley Richards. Philadelphia: Chilton, 1968. 27–46.

_____. *A Corner Room*. William Inge Collection, Independence Community College, Independence, KS.

_____. "The Disposal." *Best Short Plays of World Theatre*. Edited by Stanley Richards. New York: Crown, 1968.

_____. Foreword. *Four Plays by William Inge*. New York: Random House, 1958.

_____. Foreword. *A Loss of Roses*. New York: Random House, 1960.

_____. *Four Plays by William Inge*. New York: Random House, 1958.

_____. *Good Luck, Miss Wyckoff*. Boston: Little, Brown, 1970.

_____. *The Killing*. William Inge Collection, Independence Community College, Independence, KS.

_____. *Loss of Roses, A*. New York: Random House, 1960.

_____. *The Love Death*. William Inge Collection, Independence Community College, Independence, KS.

_____. *A Meeting in a Room*. William Inge Collection, Independence Community College, Independence, KS.

_____. "Midwestern Manic." *The Best Short Plays 1969*. Edited by Stanley Richards. Philadelphia: Chilton, 1969. 39–77.

_____. *Natural Affection*. New York: Random House, 1963.

_____. *Overnight*. William Inge Collection, Independence Community College, Independence, KS.

_____. Preface. *Natural Affection*. New York: Random House, 1963.

_____. Preface. *Summer Brave and Eleven Short Plays*. New York: Random House. 1962.

_____. *Splendor in the Grass*. New York: Bantam, 1961.

_____. *Summer Brave and Eleven Short Plays*. New York: Random House. 1962.

_____. *Tormented Woman*. William Inge Collection, Independence Community College, Independence, KS.

_____. *The Tube Boobs*. William Inge Collection, Independence Community College, Independence, KS.
_____. *Where's Daddy?*. New York: Random House. 1966.
Juhnke, Janet. "Inge's Women: Robert Brustein and the Feminine Mystique." *Kansas Quarterly*, Fall 1986, 18.4: 103–112.
Kauffmann, Stanley. "Homosexual Drama and Its Disguises," *New York Times*, national edition: sec. 2: 1, January 23, 1966.
Koprince, Susan. "Childless Women in the Plays of William Inge." *Midwest Quarterly*, Spring 2000, 41.3: 251–263.
Linscott, Mrs. Herbert B. "Suffragette Evening." *Bright Ideas for Entertaining*. Jacobs. 1905. quoted in *Harper's*, June 1997: 29–30.
Mauro, Lucia. "Short Plays by William Inge." *Chicago Sun Times* February 17, 2000 http:// www.eltchicago.org/williaminge.html.
McClure, Arthur F. *Memories of Splendor: The Midwestern World of William Inge*. Topeka: Kansas State Historical Society, 1989.
McIlrath, Patricia. "William Inge, Great Voices of the Heart of America." *Kansas Quarterly*, Fall 1986, 18.4: 45–53.
Meyerowitz, Joanne. "Introduction." *Not June Cleaver: Women and Gender in Postwar America, 1945–1960*. Edited by Joanne Meyerowitz. Philadelphia: Temple University Press, 1994.
Mordden, Ethan. *The Fireside Companion to the Theatre*. New York: Fireside, 1988.
"New Play." *Newsweek*, February 27, 1950: 81.
"New Play in Manhattan." *Time*, February 27, 1950: 74.
"New Play in Manhattan." *Time*, December 16, 1957: 42, 45.
Nietzsche, Friedrich. "Notes (1880–81)." Translated by Walter Kaufmann. *The Portable Nietzsche*. Edited by Walter Kaufmann. New York: Penguin, 1976. 73–75.
O'Neill, Eugene. "Beyond the Horizon." *The Plays of Eugene O'Neill*. New York: Random House, 1964.
Paglia, Camille. *Sexual Personae*. New Haven: Yale University Press, 1990.
Quinton, Anthony. "Political Philosophy." *The Oxford History of Western Philosophy*. Edited by Anthony Kenny. New York: Oxford University Press, 2000. 293–390.
Rapf, Joanna E. "The Fear of Loving: Daniel Taradash on His Adaptation of *Picnic*." *Literature Film Quarterly*, 1991, 19.1: 2–6.
"Realism and Naturalism." *American Poetry and Prose*. Edited by Norman Foerster, et al. Boston: Houghton Mifflin, 1970. 823–831.
"Reviews." *Newsweek*, March 2, 1953: 83.
Russell, Bertrand. *A History of Western Philosophy*. New York: Simon and Schuster, 1972.
Sartre, Jean-Paul. "Patterns of Self-Deception." *Existentialism from Dostoevsky to Sartre*. Edited by Walter Kaufmann. New York: Meridian, 1989. 309–324.
Shakespeare, William. "The Tragedy of Macbeth." *The Complete Works of Shakespeare*. Edited by David Bevington. 4th ed. New York: HarperCollins, 1992. 1223–1255.
Shapiro, Judith. Inaugural Address at Barnard College. October 27, 1994.
Showalter, Elaine. *Sexual Anarchy: Gender and Culture at the Fin de Siècle*. New York: Penguin, 1990.
Shuman, R. Baird. *William Inge*. New Haven: College & University Press, 1965.

Tannahill, Reay. *Sex in History*. 1980. Lanham, MD: Scarborough House, 1992.
Vorlicky, Robert. *Act Like a Man: Challenging Masculinities in American Drama*. Ann Arbor: University of Michigan Press, 1995.
Voss, Ralph F. *A Life of William Inge: The Strains of Triumph*. Lawrence: University Press of Kansas, 1989.
Weales, Gerald. "The New Pineros." *American Drama Since World War II*. New York: Harcourt Brace Jovanovich, 1962. 40–56.
Wertheim, Albert. "Dorothy's Friends in Kansas: The Gay Inflections of William Inge." *Staging Desire: Queer Readings of American Theater History*. Ann Arbor: University of Michigan Press, 2002. 194–217.
West, David. *An Introduction to Continental Philosophy*. Cambridge: Polity Press, 1996.
Williams, Tennessee. "Cat on a Hot Tin Roof." *Plays 1937–1955*. New York: The Library of America, 2000.
Yeats, William Butler. *Selected Poems and Two Plays*. Edited by M.L. Rosenthal. New York: Macmillan, 1962.

Index

absurdism 40, 143–145, 161, 165, 167
Albee, Edward 8, 43, 46, 47, 110, 114, 115, 144
All My Sons 1
Angels with Dirty Faces 152
Apollo (Apollonian)/Dionysus (Dionysian) 16, 17, 24–25, 53, 55, 63, 64, 69, 79, 87, 98, 100, 110, 121, 162, 163, 164, 169, 170
Aristophanes 17, 21
Aristotle 9, 36, 142
Arnold, Matthew 129
Atkinson, Brooks 38
Ave Maria 52

Badinter, Elisabeth 13
Baxley, Barbara 69, 78
The Beatles 18
Beatty, Warren 97, 109
Beckett, Samuel 43, 144
Bentley, Eric 36, 37
Ben-Zvi, Linda 47
Bergen, Candice 18
Berger, Maurice 18
Berry, Chuck 18
Bewitched 19
Beyond the Horizon 22
Bloom, Harold 36
Bly, Robert 17
Booth, Shirley 104
Booth Theatre 45
The Boy in the Basement 32, 33, 161–165, 182, 183
Brooks, David 132–133
Brustein, Robert 29, 37, 38, 39–44, 46–48, 56, 87, 90–92
Bus Riley's Back in Town 35, 170–173

Bus Stop (film version) 74
Bus Stop (play) 1, 2, 5, 8, 24–25, 31, 33, 38, 40, 66–76, 156, 177
Butler, Judith 18
Byars, Jackie 18, 19
Byron, George Gordon 26

Caesarean Operations 143
Cagney, James 152
The Call 144
Camino Real 1
Cat on a Hot Tin Roof 1, 23
Centola, Steven R. 28
Chaucer 66
Chinatown 171
Clurman, Harold 37–38, 40, 104
Coleman, Barbara J. 14
Columbia Pictures 19
Come Back, Little Sheba 1, 5, 19, 28, 29, 31, 34, 37, 38, 40, 45, 49–56, 57
Como, Perry 154
A Corner Room 143
The Cosby Show 19
Crane, Stephen 115
Crothers, Rachel 21
The Crucible 1

Dante 67
The Dark at the Top of the Stairs 1, 2, 5, 28, 31, 34, 35, 36, 39, 40, 76–87, 103, 142
Davis, Sandra 11
Death of a Salesman 1
DeGeneres, Ellen 18
Dennis, Patrick 38
Dennis the Menace 19
The Dick Van Dyke Show 19

The Disposal 148–153
Dowd, Maureen 13
Dreiser, Theodore 115
Driver, Tom 38, 76–77
Dworkin, Andrea 137

Eisenhower, Dwight D. 166
Eliot, T.S. 51, 105, 170
Ellenstein, Peter 3
Epicurus (and epicureanism) 172, 177, 180, 181
Equity Library Theatre of Chicago 160
Esslin, Martin 144
Eugene O'Neill Theatre 109

Falocco, Joe 160
Father Knows Best 18–19
Fausto-Sterling, Anne 18
Fellig, Arthur (Weegee) 115
Felman, Shoshana 13, 16
Fichte, Johann Gottlieb 76
Fisher, James 46
Flaubert, Gustave 114
Foerster, Norman 114
Ford, Wallace 45
Foucault, Michel 151
Freud (and Freudian) 14, 34–37, 40, 49–50, 56, 76, 92, 96–97, 99, 103, 105, 106–107, 108, 110, 113, 114, 115, 121–122, 123, 148, 151, 161, 163, 166, 172, 176, 178, 182; Electra complex 35, 77, 79, 82–85, 100; family romance 14, 77, 110; Oedipus complex 34–36, 77, 78, 79, 82–85, 86, 98, 100, 103, 107, 108, 109, 111, 112, 120, 123, 124, 133, 142, 145, 148, 161, 163–164, 165, 183
Friedan, Betty 15
Front Porch 2

Garner, Peggy Ann 71
gendermandering 4, 7, 8, 20–21, 22, 23, 24, 25, 29, 31, 32, 33, 41, 42, 45, 47, 48, 51, 55, 56, 58, 62, 64, 65, 66, 74, 76, 78, 79, 81, 86, 90, 99, 103, 106–107, 115, 118, 120, 122, 123, 125, 132, 134, 137, 139, 140, 143, 145, 160, 170, 173, 175, 182; and gerrymandering 20–21, 25
Gibson, William 44

Gill, Brendan 39
Gillette, Anita 72
The Glass Menagerie 1
Gledhill, Christine 19
Goheen, Margaret 2, 3
Goncourts, Edmond and Jules 114
Good Luck, Miss Wyckoff 7, 61, 66, 134–140, 145
Govan, Michael 17
Grace, Nancy McCampbell 11
Guanier, Lani 20

Handy, Bruce 21
Haney, Carol 109
Haskell, Molly 18
Hayes, Richard 38
He and She 21
Heckart, Eileen 1
Hegel, Georg 49–50, 56
Heller, Dana 14, 15
Hingle, Pat 1, 38
Holden, William 2
homosexuality (in Inge's work) 29–36, 41, 44–48, 78, 79, 85–86, 87, 103, 110, 115, 116, 118, 122, 125–126, 129, 133–134, 140, 142, 143, 149, 150, 156, 157, 162–164, 165, 182, 183
Horace 105
HUAC 166

I Love Lucy 19
An Incident at the Standish Arms 178–180
Independence Community College 3, 7; and Junior College 2, 3
Inge Collection 2, 7, 142, 153
Ionesco, Eugène 43, 144
Irigaray, Luce 13

Jim Crow laws 20
Juhnke, Janet 40, 56
Jung, Carl 70

Kant, Immanuel 20, 76, 101, 112, 150
Kauffmann, Stanley 29, 30, 30, 44–48, 87, 110, 124, 158
Kazan, Elia 95, 104
Keats, John 26, 37
Kerr, Walter 124
Kierkegaard, Søren 70
The Killing 143, 144

Koprince, Susan 4, 47–48, 60, 80–81, 91
Kriseva, Julia 13
Kushner, Tony 46

Lawrence, Jerome 3
Leave It to Beaver 14
Lewis, Theophilus 39
A Life of William Inge: The Strains of Triumph 7
Life with Father 18
Linscott, Mrs. Herbert B. 17
Loden, Barbara 97
Logan, Joshua 12, 41, 64, 104
A Loss of Roses 28, 33, 34, 36, 38, 103, 104–114, 115, 120, 126
The Love Death 26, 143
The Love Song of J. Alfred Prufrock 170
Lucretius 180

Macbeth 21
The Mall 33, 175–178
Malthusian 174
Mann, Daniel 45, 109
Marxism 169
Mauro, Lucia 160
McCarthy, Joseph 135, 166; and McCarthyism 30
McClure, Arthur F. 4, 26–29
McCullers, Carson 62
McIlrath, Patricia 4, 27
Meeker, Ralph 1, 12, 58
A Meeting in a Room 143
Memory of Summer 168–170, 176
Merton, Robert
metrosexual 118
Meyerowitz, Joanne 5, 14, 15
Midwestern Manic 145–148
Miller, Arthur 1, 8, 43
Milton, John 152
Missouri Repertory Theatre 27
Molière 166
Monroe, Marilyn 74
Moonglow 2
Moore, Mary Tyler 14
Mordden, Ethan 37
Mulvey, Laura 19
Murphy Brown 18
Murray, John 26
Music Box Theatre 12, 78
The Music Man 39

My Son Is a Splendid Driver 7, 32
My Three Sons 19

Nadel, Norman 38, 124
National Endowment for the Humanities vii, 2, 8
Natural Affection 33, 34, 38, 39, 103, 114–124, 130, 176
Naturalism 112, 114–115, 120, 138, 145, 147, 173, 175
Neewollah 2, 57
Nelson, Peggy 45
"New Voices" award 3
Nietzsche, Friedrich 16, 20, 114, 180
Norris, Frank 115
Novak, Kim 2

O'Brien, Pat 152
Ode: Intimations of Immortality 101
Oklahoma! 39
O'Neill, Eugene 8, 22–23, 179
Orton, Joe 125
Osborne, John 43
Othello 130
Overnight 143

Paglia, Camille 5, 16, 98, 99, 100
Paradise Lost 152
Parker, Mary Louise 75
Patriot Act 167
People in the Wind 156–159
Perkins, Tessa 18
Picnic 1, 2, 5, 8, 19, 30, 34, 38, 40, 41, 56–66, 104, 105, 107, 130
Pine, Larry 75
Pinter, Harold 43, 144, 165
The Power of Silence 145, 146
Powers, Tyrone 154, 156
Promise Keepers 17

Quayle, Dan 18
Quinton, Anthony 182

The Rainy Afternoon 33, 173–175, 181, 183
rape fantasies 136, 146
Rapf, Joanna 60, 62, 91–92
regionalism (in Inge's work) 26–28, 37–38, 40, 44
Richards, Stanley 144, 145
Rockwell, Norman 83

Romeo and Juliet 73
The Rose Tattoo 1
Rousseau, Jean Jacques 182
Rule, Janice 1
Russell, Bertrand 180

Saari, Charles 78
Salmi, Albert 71
Sartre, Jean Paul (and *mauvais foi*, or "bad faith") 28, 60, 85, 109, 112, 114, 139, 148, 149–150, 164
Schopenhauer, Arthur 63, 76
Schubert, Franz 52, 53, 55
Sedgwick, Edie 168
sentimentality (in Inges's work) 4, 26–28, 29, 39, 41–43
Shakespeare, William 21, 73, 130, 158
Shapiro, Judith 11
Shelley, Percy Bysshe 26, 180
Showalter, Elaine 5, 11, 14, 61, 137
Shuman, R. Baird 32–37, 38, 39, 40, 47, 76, 80–81, 103, 120, 154, 155–156, 165, 178, 183
Snyder, Tom 2
social Darwinism 115
A Social Event 159–161
Spivak, Gayatri 13, 16
Splendor in the Grass 7, 28, 34, 39, 46, 92–102
Sports Illustrated 30
Stanley, Kim 1, 12, 68
Stein, Howard vii, 8
The Strains of Triumph 34, 143, 153, 180–182
A Streetcar Named Desire 1
Suddenly Last Summer 1
Summer Brave 28, 41, 64–66, 90, 105
Supreme Court of Massachusetts 133
Susann, Jacqueline 140
Sweet Bird of Youth 121

Tammany Hall 20
Tannahill, Reay 16
Taradash, Daniel 60
Taubman, Howard 38
That Old Black Magic 73
Theatre Guild 12, 45

Thomas, Dylan 152
Thoreau, Henry David 182
The Tiny Closet 33, 165–168, 183
To Bobolink, for Her Spirit 154–156
Tormented Woman 144
Travolta, John 71
The Tube Boobs 143
Turner, Lana 155, 156

Vance, Carole 18
A View from the Bridge 1–2
Vorlicky, Robert 5, 19
Voss, Ralph 4, 7, 31–32, 34, 39–44, 47–48, 64–65, 76, 92, 103, 104, 113, 114, 124–125, 126, 133, 134, 140, 142, 149, 152, 153, 154, 183

"The Wall" 149–150
Warford, Jill 3
The Wasteland 51
Watts, Richard 39
Weales, Gerald 41, 142
Wertheim, Albert 4, 29–31
West, David 13
Where's Daddy? 32, 46, 103, 124–134, 141, 151, 164
William Inge Award for Distinguished Achievement in American Theatre 3
William Inge Award for Lifetime Achievement 3
William Inge Conference 3
William Inge Theatre Festival 1, 3, 4, 8
Williams, Linda 19
Williams, Tennessee 1, 8, 23, 39, 43, 46, 110, 114, 115, 121
Wizard of Oz 155
Wood, Michael 19
Wood, Natalie 95
Wordsworth, William 101
Wright, Teresa 1

Yeats, W.B. 126

Zola, Émile 114
The Zoo Story 144

www.ingramcontent.com/pod-product-compliance
Lightning Source LLC
Chambersburg PA
CBHW032102300426
44116CB00007B/849